Penguin Education

Marxian and Po
An Introduction
Arun Bose

Penguin Modern Economics
General Editor: B. J. McCormick

Political Economy
Editor: K. J. W. Alexander

Arun Bose

Marxian and Post-Marxian Political Economy

An Introduction

Penguin Books

Penguin Books Ltd,
Harmondsworth, Middlesex, England
Penguin Books Inc, 7110 Ambassador Road,
Baltimore, Md 21207, USA
Penguin Books Australia Ltd,
Ringwood, Victoria, Australia
Penguin Books Canada Ltd,
41 Steelcase Road West,
Markham, Ontario, Canada
Penguin Books (N.Z.) Ltd,
182–190 Wairau Road, Auckland 10, New Zealand

First published 1975
Copyright © Arun Bose, 1975

Made and printed in Great Britain by
Richard Clay (The Chaucer Press) Ltd
Bungay, Suffolk
Set in Monotype Times

Penguin Modern Economics Texts

This volume is one in a series of unit texts designed to reduce the price of knowledge for students of economics in universities and colleges of higher education. The units may be used singly or in combination with other units to form attractive and unusual teaching programmes. The volumes will cover the major teaching areas but they will differ from conventional books in their attempt to chart and explore new directions in economic thinking. The traditional divisions of theory and applied, of positive and normative and of micro and macro will tend to be blurred as authors impose new and arresting ideas on the traditional corpus of economics. Some units will fall into conventional patterns of thought but many will transgress established beliefs.

Penguin Modern Economics Texts are published in units in order to achieve certain objectives. First, a large range of short texts at inexpensive prices gives the teacher flexibility in planning his course and recommending texts for it. Secondly, the pace at which important new work is published requires the project to be adaptable. Our plan allows a unit to be revised or a fresh unit to be added with maximum speed and minimal cost to the reader.

The international range of authorship will, it is hoped, bring out the richness and diversity in economic analysis and thinking.

B. J. MCC.

Contents

Part Two
**Problems of Contemporary Capitalist and
Socialist Economies:
A Post-Marxian Analysis**

Part Three
**Marxian and Post-Marxian Theories about
Economic Theories**

Editorial Foreword

A notable weakness of contemporary economics is the extent to which much of economic theory is developed 'in a vacuum', and without any serious intention that it should ever be applied to any particular real economic problem. It is possible to offer many excuses for this of which the inadequacy of data has possibly been the most credible. Whereas at one time the disinterestedness of policy makers was also a credible – though not adequate – explanation of this gap between theory and applied, nowadays there is an almost embarrassing anxiety on the part of policy-makers to have guidance from applied economics. There are signs that the economics profession is slowly responding to provide this guidance, but the gap between theory and application remains very wide.

Marxists make an article of faith of 'the unity of theory and practice', but Marxist economists have not established this unity in their work to any great extent. A few Marxist economists have explored the characteristics of modern capitalism and added to our understanding of it and in doing this have usually leant as much upon non-Marxist theoretical concepts as upon Marxist ones. Again the explanations lie in part on the side of those who might be expected to use the results of applied Marxism. In the socialist countries too much Marxist energy is devoted to socialist apologetics and to theological warfare, not only between the socialist and capitalist world but also between different socialist schools or countries. The skills of too many socialist economists are harnessed to political polemics. In the capitalist countries labour movements and their leaders do not, on the whole, expect much help from economists, Marxist or otherwise – although, again, there are notable and praiseworthy exceptions. Much of what passes for Marxist economics is pedagogical and at a fairly low level, aimed at instilling into activists in the labour movement a particular view of capitalism, the world and the future.

This book is of quite a different order from such political polemics or education. It is a difficult book, partly because it integrates much that has already been written about Marxist economics by professional economists and also because it is, in parts, highly original and path-breaking. Students in the final year of an honours course will encounter only the usual difficulty; economics is not an easy subject. Readers who have not taken a formal course will find it very hard going in places, but the author makes suggestions about preparatory reading on page 38, to which could be added *Marx on Economics* edited by Robert Freedman (Penguin, 1971); and several of the readings in E. K. Hunt and J. G. Schwartz, *A Critique of Economic Theory* (Penguin, 1972). The rate of return to the effort expended in reading this text book is very high. First, the reader is introduced to Marx's own theory of value and of exploitation, this and later Marxist approaches are criticized and a post-Marxian theory of value is developed. The reader is led away from a simple-minded adherence to the view that labour is the only source of value to an appreciation of a theory of capital which is firmly rooted in the Marxist tradition. This post-Marxian theory is then used to explain the features of modern economies, both capitalist and socialist, as well as to discuss the transition from one system to the other. Here we get applied Marxist economics of a high order, full of insights and stimulation. The book concludes with an important contribution to the history of economic thought, a discussion about the origin and nature of economic theories.

Mr Bose's book has too great a depth to make it possible to do it justice in a few lines of introduction. Of its many virtues the greatest is its combinations of vigorous open-mindedness with a clear commitment to social progress.

K.J.W.A.

Preface

I started work on this book when I spent a year (1960–61) at Trinity College, Cambridge, under the Commonwealth Universities Interchange. My interest in the theory of Marxian political economy dates back to 1937–40, when I was an under-graduate studying economics at Cambridge, with my work being largely in the hands of Maurice Dobb and Piero Sraffa. (Dissatisfaction with the social philosophy of the rationalist Bertrand Russell, the anarchist Peter Kropotkin, of Gandhian *satyagraha* and Bengali terrorism, sampled during my last years at high school in Calcutta, had already made me curious about Marxian political economy.)

During extra-curricular sessions, both Maurice Dobb and Piero Sraffa discussed economic theory and Marxian political economy, leaving an indelible impression on my mind. The former left me with the thought that Marxian political economy could, and should, survive (in a period in which it was taboo academically) and develop as a science, through a constant clash of ideas with those who disagreed with it – e.g. Dennis Robertson, who also supervised my studies for a while. Piero Sraffa impressed me with his conviction that it was perfectly possible, though difficult, to develop a theory of political economy into an *exact* science, based on absolute precision of concept – however much we may approximate in empirical work – which could be wielded as effectively as a surgeon's or a welder's tools, to dissect or dismantle, and then reassemble the 'unseen' interconnections of the economic process, whose cognition is essential for revolutionary political action. In this undertaking, he thought that the literature of Marxian political economy – the main corpus, *Theories of Surplus Value* and *Grundrisse*, was still almost completely 'hidden' to those who could not read German (or French) – was available as a treasure-trove to those who were not put off by Marx's repetitive, and somewhat dated, style of writing.

These early impressions and interests survived, and were somewhat enriched, when I participated in the British Communist movement as a student, and later spent ten years as a full-time Marxist Communist 'activist' in the Indian Communist movement (1940–50), when there were dress rehearsals of almost all that has happened in the Indian Communist movement in recent years. On the one hand, I realized again and again how much strongly-held theoretical beliefs (about economics, almost as much as about politics) motivated even the most 'spontaneous' political actions by Marxists, non-Marxists and anti-Marxists. On the other hand, whenever I tried to use Marxian political economy – as was the current fashion among Communists – as a sacrosanct, dogmatic theology, the contrast between its easy but ephemeral success in winning recruits at political conferences or in the streets and its limitations as a potent instrument for revolutionary political action was brought home to me very sharply.

Around 1957, when I decided to resume the study of current literature in advanced theoretical economics, I discovered that work based on the use of scientific, mathematical methods in economics had advanced, wearing seven-league boots, but, or so it seemed to me, very little fresh, creative work was being done on Marxian political economy. After my return for a year to Cambridge, and after reading Sraffa's recently published *Production of Commodities by Means of Commodities*, I decided to try my hand at it (though the author of the book may feel that I have misunderstood his intentions, or, having understood them, have chosen to give his theory a different interpretation, which must be judged on merits). An onrush of modern contributions by mathematical economists to the study of Marxian political economy, specially in the 1970s, has made my task easier. But they also explain why the book could not be completed earlier.

Some of the material of this book has been published in the form of notes and an article in the *Economic Journal* (September 1964, December 1965), a communication in *Science and Society* (Summer 1972), as well as in the form of a major article, 'Marx on value, capital and exploitation', in *History of Political Economy* (Fall, 1971). When working on this, I had the benefit of useful discussions with Sukhamoy Chakravarty, who very kindly went through an early draft, and helped to familiarize me with some results of modern linear economic theory. He also let me read his privately circulated monograph on Marxian political economy.

In the course of writing that article, I realized that it was possible to extend its main findings to construct a post-Marxian political economy, which could throw light on some neglected and opaque aspects of the (institutional) mutation of capitalist and socialist societies. At a later stage, it occurred to me that a modern post-Marxian political economy could also draw sustenance from establishing a connection with the modern theory of collective choice. Discussions with Amartya Sen and Prasanta Pattanaik over the Appendix to chapter 6 as well as chapters 12, 14 and 15, have more or less given me confidence that this is worth investigating.

In writing this book in its final form, between March and December 1973, I have benefited from the writings and suggestions made by those who have been named above.

I am specially thankful to Amartya Sen who very kindly went through the entire manuscript, including several drafts of the Appendix to chapter 6 and of chapter 14, and made mostly constructive suggestions (almost all of which I have tried to incorporate). Prasanta Pattanaik also went very carefully through the Appendix to chapter 6, and helped me, as did Amartya Sen, to eliminate some inaccuracies. Both of them helped with thought-provoking comments on chapters 13, 14 and 15, which have been taken into account in a final re-write of these sections.

Before I started writing out the chapters of the book in an integrated form, I had the benefit of an initial discussion with Mrinal Datta Chaudhuri. In response to his queries, I thought it worth stating the 'rules of theorizing' to be invoked in later chapters (though I do not know how successful the attempt is).

Comments by him and Amartya Sen, about the problem of defining the precise relationship between neo-classical general equilibrium theory, the modern literature, in the neo-classical tradition on 'market failure', and Marxian and post-Marxian 'general interdependence models', have helped clarify some of my ideas on these matters.

I must also thank Maurice Dobb, Edward Nell and Ronald Meek for helping me with constructive comments (positive and negative) on the *History of Political Economy* monograph, or on particular points which were referred to them. Victor Kiernan's general encouragement was also most helpful at the start of the present project.

However, none of those whose published work has been freely used by me (with due acknowledgement at the appropriate places), or who have given me general encouragement or advice on specific points, must be blamed for any errors and obscure passages that might remain, despite my best efforts to eliminate them.

Finally, the staff of the Kirori Mal College Library at Delhi University must be thanked for their unfailing kindness and patience in meeting my constant requests for books and periodicals, over a number of years.

Note: I take this opportunity to refer to Selections from Antonio Gramsci's *Prison Notebooks*, which I was only able to read after completing the main manuscript. I was delighted to find in these remarkable notes several ideas which resemble those used in my work. The more general among these ideas are his criticism of the vulgarization of Marxism as a 'mechanistic economic determinism' (Gramsci, 1971, pp. 164–5), and his elucidation of the Marxian concept of a 'market equilibrium' or a 'determined market' as being 'equivalent to a determined relation of social forces in a determined structure of the productive apparatus . . . guaranteed . . . by a determined political, moral and juridical superstructure' (p. 410). Gramsci's discussion of the role of the 'elite' in *any* society, including a socialist one (pp. 334–5), and his notion of 'implicit parliamentarism', of 'black-marketing' in votes, not only under a fascist, but also under a proletarian dictatorship (pp. 255–6), fit in quite well with what has been said in chapters 14 and 15 of this book.

Above all, there is expressed in these notes a convincing argument (pp. 255–6) in support of a principle of theoretical controversy which I have tried to uphold. This is the argument that in an ideological, unlike a military struggle, it seldom pays to demolish an opponent's weakest positions first in order to assemble the maximum forces to demolish his strongest positions. A hundred weak arguments against still weaker ones may be ineffective against a few strong arguments. In the ideological struggle to achieve lasting results, each strong argument must be matched by a stronger one.

1 General Introduction

1 Vision and theory

The recently revived interest in the 1970s in Marxian political economy is expressed in the form of an ardent desire for a revolutionary break with standard, academic economic theory, as it is taught in both the non-Communist and the Communist world (i.e. as non-Marxist, or explicitly anti-Marxist in the non-Communist world, and as meticulously 'orthodox Marxist' in the Communist world).

There is much stress, especially in the non-Communist world, on the radically new vision (or 'paradigm') of the economic process represented by Marxian political economy, once it is freed from the shackles of orthodox interpretations (for example, Hunt and Schwartz, 1972, pp. 7–33; Nell, 1972, pp. 32–52). Indeed, the search for a new vision of the economic process, as an integral part of a new *weltanschauung*, is probably the single biggest factor in the current revival of interest in Marxian political economy.

The present study, like a few other recent contributions (e.g. Nell, 1970, pp. 477–9), is an attempt to lend precision to this new vision by bringing its *theoretical* structure into focus. For Marxian political economy, and its modern extension, *post*-Marxian political economy (on which more will be said in a moment), represent a theoretical discipline (in a sense to be defined in section 3 of this chapter), albeit one whose aim is not only to 'explain' the world, but to do so in order to 'change' it (Marx, 1949b).

Anyone who wants the vision of Marxian political economy *minus* the theory, will be stopped, not only by the professed anti-Marxian economist Keynes (1936, p. 355), who asserted that there was an economic theory behind every vision (pp. 383–4), but also by Marx, who asserted that the 'material transformation of the economic conditions of production . . . can be determined with the precision of natural science' (Marx, 1904, p. 12; 1970, p. 21). He will find little in this book to hold his attention.

On the other hand, the pure economic technician distrusts all visions of the economic process as 'visionary', except in purely mathematical terms, such as is represented by the von Neumann growth model (to which there will be many references in this book). But he may still find the present work, which emphasizes the social implications of such mathematical 'visions', at least as interesting as others which compare, from a purely analytical point of view, the Marxian model of competitive equilibrium with the von Neumann model (Morishima, 1964, section 5; 1973, sections 1 and 14).

If the present work brings some submerged, neglected or suppressed parts of the Marxian theoretical structure into focus, or itself neglects some parts of it on which some other writers concentrate, this is mostly because it complements, rather than contradicts, some other modern studies on Marxian political economy.

2 Marxian and post-Marxian political economy

The method of exposition adopted in writing this book is to unearth and decipher some Marxian concepts and doctrines which have hitherto suffered from neglect, in the light of a selective survey of the major landmarks in the century-old controversies on Marxian political economy. The aim is to identify the major building-blocks of what can accurately be called *post-Marxian* political economy.

It is recognized that until some modern advances in mathematics and in economic theory were joined together, the significance of these neglected Marxian concepts could not be grasped (see chapter 3 and chapter 5 of this book for detailed references). The most important tools of analysis and theorems pressed into service are borrowed from the modern work of Sraffa (1960, 1962; Lutz and Hague, 1963, pp. 305–6, 325), whose influence on controversies in Marxian political economy has been indirect, but strong (Meek, 1961; Dobb, 1970; Nuti, 1970; Bose, 1971, 1972; Hunt and Sherman, 1972; Medio, 1972). The constructive criticism of von Bortkiewicz (1907), and, somewhat paradoxically, the destructive criticism of Samuelson (1957) also yielded notable insights which are used in constructing a post-Marxian political economy. Credit is also taken for clarification of some relevant issues in parallel developments in economic theory which had, formally and in origin, very little to do with Marxian political economy, viz. the modern (Cambridge) critique of neo-classical capital and distribution theory (Pasinetti, 1966; Garegnani, 1970), the modern interest in alienation as an economic problem (West, 1969, traces the concept back to Adam Smith), modern developments in a mathematical–political–economic theory of collective choice over the past two decades (Arrow, 1963; Inada, 1964; Sen, 1971; Pattanaik, 1970).

The coinage of the term post-Marxian political economy for the end-product of the developments noted in the previous paragraph seems justified. The end-product *is* an *extension* of Marx's political economy because (a) it uses concepts and theorems which Marx used, and in the use of some of which Marx pioneered (see chapter 6, section 1 for details), and (b) it fits into the overall multidisciplinary framework of Marx's materialistic interpretation of history, or the specific Marxian (as distinct from the Hegelian) version of a 'relational' theory of the world (Ollman, 1971, Part 1, ch. 2). On the other hand, it is, strictly speaking, a *post*-Marxian theory, because it validates some propositions of Marxian political economy, extends others and discards a few (see chapter 4, section 3 and chapter 8, section 5 of this book for a summary account).

3 Criteria for assessing alternative theories

To begin with a critical survey and end with a reconstruction, has two obvious disadvantages. First, it seeks to draw the threads together from widely separated areas of theoretical economics and related disciplines, each of which is highly specialized, using esoteric concepts, terminology and chains of reasoning, which few are familiar with. This disadvantage is inherent in the subject-matter, but may be offset currently by:

1 The all-pervasive scepticism about every kind of economic theory (so that no one version is sacrosanct),

2 The readiness to consider new ideas (especially those which have been suppressed or ignored),

3 The desire to break the shackles imposed by over-specialization (*within* economics, *between* economics and politics, etc.),

4 The use of mathematical tools in the analysis of a variety of subjects (which, among other things, makes inter-disciplinary communication easier).

(If the reader shares these attitudes, he may find the detailed references given in most cases in later chapters, when findings of related disciplines are quoted, useful as a first introduction to unfamiliar areas.)

The second, more serious disadvantage of the procedure adopted in writing this book has to do with the philosophical habits or preconceptions of the reader.

Most modern intellectuals (economists as a tribe not excepted) are under some kind of positivist influence, of which, however, most modern Marxists are suspicious. This creates a problem as to what 'rules of theorizing' should be invoked when surveying the controversies about Marxian political economy, or in constructing a post-Marxian political economy. Fortunately, the mutual interaction of these two modern philosophical traditions, each of which, for good or ill, is now fragmented into more than one well-articulated trend, might make it easier for all concerned to agree on a set of rules of theorizing which could serve as a working basis for the investigations carried out in this book.

On the other hand, working out a *full set* of such rules of economic theorizing (or, in Part Three of this book, theorizing *about* alternative economic theories), would involve trying to write a treatise on a self-contained economic philosophy, whatever that might mean. Alternatively, it would involve trying to write a treatise on the philosophical aspects of economic theory, which is roughly how Robinson (1964) seems to have interpreted the meaning of the words 'economic philosophy' in her Josiah Mason lectures.

Both of these procedures would offend Marxian canons. Marx had *no* theory of 'economic determinism' (which *could* supply a *self-contained* economic philosophy). Indeed, a trace of a 'pluralistic' approach to the interpretation of historical events, i.e. a preference for an explanation 'from politics' rather than 'from economics', can be found in the Marxian literature, albeit for the explanation of the less important aspects of historical development. Moreover, as has been rightly clarified recently (Ollman, 1971, pp. 17–18), remarks by Marx and Engels on the relative importance of 'economic' and 'noneconomic' factors in historical events can be best interpreted in terms of a notion of 'mutual determination' (in much the same way as, in a set of simultaneous equations, unknowns are mutually determined). On the other hand, there *was* no Marxian philosophy (nor *could* there be), *before* Marxian political economy was worked out, or *independently* of it. (Incidentally, it is worth noting in this context a point stressed recently: 'historical materialism' and 'dialectical materialism' as popular labels for Marx's views did *not* originate with Marx himself (Ollman, 1971, pp. 9–10).)

In any case, the writer of the present study does not feel any useful purpose will be served by violating the Marxian canons on this particular point. At the same time, to spare the philosophically-minded unnecessary discomfort, the following definitions and 'general rules of theorizing' followed in this book are being written down straightaway. (Possible objections to them will be discussed in sections 4–6 of this chapter, as well as in later chapters where these rules are invoked to discuss specific problems.)

Definitions

1 An economic theory consists of a mutually compatible set of propositions about economic phenomena (including economic institutions) in terms of precisely defined concepts, assumptions and deductions (predictions).

2 A parable or fable in economic theory is a model in which artificial assumptions about unobservable, mythical objects (entities) are introduced to predict a result that survives the dropping of these assumptions.[1]

Rules

1 An economic theory should admit 'ought' or 'ought not' type of propositions deduced from a set of premises containing both 'ought' and 'is' type of propositions. (This is a straight-forward application of what is often referred to as Hume's Law, which says that it is impossible to deduce an 'ought' proposition from a series of 'is' propositions, or from a set of self-evident principles; that to deduce an 'ought' proposition, we need at least one 'ought' proposition in the set of premises (Hare, 1961, pp. 29, 44; Sen, 1970, chapter 5; Pattanaik, 1971, p. 29). Of course, 'universalizability' (viz. in exactly similar circumstances exactly similar judgements will be made) which would produce an exception to Hume's Law (Sen, 1970, pp. 132–4, Pattanaik, 1971, p. 29) is *not* being assumed. (The first premise of Marxian political economy, which is our concern in this book, being class conflict in a capitalist society, 'universalizability' should obviously be ruled out.) This rule also ignores the Robbinsian dictum, which is in reality a very arbitrary value-judgement, that if

1. It should be noted that a truncated, only partially 'true-to-life' economic model which suppresses some essential aspects of reality is ultimately *indistinguishable* from an economic 'parable' which deliberately incorporates mythical entities. There is nothing to choose, on grounds of 'realism', between a simplified purely 'circulating capital' model of capitalism (with no fixed capital and scarce land), and a 'parable' of capitalism in which indirect labour 'embodied' in commodities – coal or shovels – is supposed to be known from direct observation, as explained in chapter 8.

there is disagreement about ends, it is a case of 'thy blood or mine – or live and let live' (Robbins, 1932, p. 132), which would banish the rule altogether.

2 *Some* assumptions of an economic theory and *all* its results (predictions) should be empirically testable, i.e. be observable in fact or in principle. This rule is *called for* by rule 1, and complements, and is itself complemented by, rule 3.

3 The 'is' propositions admitted as assumptions or results (predictions) in the *final*, 'realistic' form of an economic theory, i.e. when it is free from simplifying assumptions, must *exclude* a reference to mythical or artificial ('fictional') objects, i.e. objects which are not empirically observable, in fact or in principle. In other words, in an economic theory in its final form, we cannot have an 'is' proposition which refers to something which isn't. Assumptions that refer to such artificially conceived objects will be referred to in this book as a class of '*artificial*' assumptions. (Another class of 'artificial' assumptions, which do *not* refer to mythical objects of the type considered here, is referred to in connection with rule 6 below.)

4 An economic theory should consist of both strictly existential propositions which predict *all* possibilities (e.g. it is not necessary for the long-run profit rate under capitalism to fall), and are only *verifiable*, as well as *falsifiable* propositions which do *not* predict all possible outcomes – the long-run profit rate and the wage rate *cannot both decline*, for, if one goes down, the other must rise, *though both may rise*. The application of this is discussed in chapter 7.

5 Subject to rules 1–4, the principles of Occam's razor should be adhered to, i.e. 'entities should not be multiplied unnecessarily' (Hicks, 1948, p. 18; Kolakowski, 1972, pp. 22–4). This implies, among other things, that a theory which predicts the same results with fewer assumptions or 'primitive terms'[2]

2. These refer to undefined notions in a particular branch of knowledge, e.g. notions of point and line in Euclid's geometry, though they may also refer to notions borrowed from other branches

compared to others, should be preferred. In other words, *ceteris paribus*, an axiomatic approach should be preferred.

6 The method of *abstraction* involves the construction of alternative, simplified, 'truncated' models of the economic process, each one of which suppresses some *essential* aspects of reality, and hence involves the use of 'artificial' assumptions, even though none of the objects which *are* taken into account involve 'mythical' entities referred to in connection with rule 3 above. The method of simplifying abstraction is *unavoidable* (because, in theoretical analysis, we can follow only one line of argument at a time (Sraffa, 1960, p. 34). It is also *justifiable*, as is the construction of 'parables' (definition 2) *provided* the predictions of the simplified models are confirmed by the 'final' or 'complete' model.

7 The use of 'parables' or 'fables' (definition 2) in economic theory is legitimate.

8 Alternative economic theories which predict the same quantitative results are not to be dismissed as otiose if they point to alternative behaviour-patterns of men and classes in society, or to alternative economic institutions through which they function (e.g. a method of solving simultaneous equations which is seldom used suggests an alternative to Walrasian *tatonnement* for identifying equilibrium values in a competitive capitalist model, as indicated in chapter 6, section 4. It should not be dismissed as otiose simply because the concept of *tatonnement* is already available).

4 Comment on possible Marxist and positivist objections

Possible Marxist (or neo-Marxist) objections to the theorizing rules listed in the previous section are likely to be concentrated on definition 1 for an economic theory and on rule 6, which recommends the use of the method of abstraction and the implication which legitimizes the use of simplified models on the same footing as 'economic parables' (definition 2).

---

of knowledge, in which case, they are not to be regarded as primitive notions (Suppes, 1969, pp. 246–8).

In recent writings on Marxian theory, much attention is paid to what both defenders and critics recognize as *deliberate* imprecision in Marx's use of technical terms, including the key word 'capital', which are invested with *multiple*, sometimes *inconsistent* meanings.[3] As will be made clear in chapter 2, section 1, the key term capital has a *triple* meaning in Marxian political economy, viz., as a collection of *things*, as saleable products (commodities) which includes non-material labour-power, and as a (coercive) *social relation*. Acceptance of this usage as being *necessary* for investigating the main propositions of Marxian political economy would, of course, invalidate definition 1 adopted in the present study. However, there is no convincing proof that economic phenomena defy analysis, or even that it is impossible to validate the main results of Marxian political economy, by a theory which fulfils the requirements of 'precision' in concepts and terms imposed by our definition 1. So we will stick to precise definitions and let the results spread over this book be judged on merits.

Possible neo-Marxist objections to the method of abstraction, sanctioned by rule 6, may be backed by the argument that (a) ideological differences must inevitably arise in theorizing about economic phenomena (if only because they reflect the class standpoint of the theorists) that (b) they cannot be resolved because, in the social sciences, in contrast to the physical sciences, 'controlled experiments' cannot be conducted to settle disputes and that (c) we should admire Marx for the 'arsenic' of class hatred he administered, but reject his theories as mere 'incantations' (Robinson, 1966, pp. xi, 22).

3. See Ollman, 1971, Part I, chapter 1: 'With words that appear like bats' – the chapter title being a quotation from Pareto, who likened Marx's words to bats, which resemble both mice and birds. As far as the *facts* about Marxian texts go, Pareto's comment is certainly correct, though the implied ridicule is somewhat misplaced. It will be argued in chapter 2, for instance, that *one* of several meanings Marx assigned to the word 'capital' stands out as the most important, and makes Marxian economics qualitatively different from non-Marxian economics.

Marx flatly rejected such an argument, when, in his preface to the first edition of *Capital*, volume one in 1867, he advocated the use of the 'force of abstraction' in economic theory as an adequate substitute for controlled experiments under laboratory conditions in the physical sciences (Marx, 1954, p. 8). Marx also declared in his *Theories of Surplus Value*, volume four, that abstract analysis 'is the necessary prerequisite of genetical presentation, and of the understanding of the real, formative process [in economic life] in its different phases' (Marx, 1971, p. 500).

On this particular point, Marx was evidently on the right track. Partisan ideological predilections originating in ethical beliefs, or in the self-interest of classes and individuals probably do give rise to differences in economic theory which cannot be *obliterated*. But rigorous abstract analysis can make explicit the value judgements which might be involved, and this, *by itself*, may make some people change their minds. Furthermore, rigorous analysis can also *reduce* the range of ideological differences, in so far as value judgements are made with varying degrees of intensity, some being 'basic' and others being 'non-basic' (which are subject to revision on the basis of an argument about the facts) (Sen, 1971, ch. 5, section 3, pp. 59–61). (A possible case of what might be treated by some readers at least as a 'non-basic value judgement' is the proposition 'labour is the only source of wealth and value', discussed in chapter 3.) Possible Marxist objections to the rule 7 above, which legitimizes the use of 'parables' in economic theory, are discussed at some length in chapter 8, where the 'labour values' model of competitive capitalism of Marx (*Capital*, volume one) is defended as a valid parable in economic theory, and need not be discussed here.

On the other hand, possible positivist objections to our 'theorizing rules' may start with criticisms of rule 1 – which sanctions the derivation of 'ought' propositions from a mixture of 'ought' and 'is' propositions – on the grounds that (a) 'ought' ('normative') propositions (like 'capitalist exploitation', for instance, which is the central preoccupation of Part One of this book) *ought* to be kept out of economic theory, and (b), if they *must* be admitted, they should not be mixed up with the facts or 'is' propositions, but be tolerated as pure, normative propositions which are above all argument. This is the Robbinsian amendment to Hume's Law, referred to in section 3, and is very close to the neo-Marxian objection to rule 6 discussed by Robinson, referred to above. The objection will be disregarded, for the reasons already stated in rejecting the neo-Marxian argument.

Rule 4 – which admits 'existential propositions' along with falsifiable ones – may also be suspect in the eyes of strict, Popperian neo-positivists (logical empiricists). Their objections will be disregarded in the present study for two rather different reasons. First, as will be shown in chapter 7, section 3, a comparison, by employing rigorous methods of analysis, of the alternative 'doctrines' of the falling profit-rate ends with the conclusion that the profit-rate over the long-run may not fall. This is an 'existential' statement, which, however, is not *meaningless*, as strict Popperians would like to make out all existential statements to be (Kolakowski, 1972, p. 216). Second, predictions regarding institutional change (a central preoccupation of Marxian political economy, as also of this book, as seen in chapters 10 and 11) are more likely to be in the form of existential statements, rather than refutable ones, but that is no reason for agreeing with the Popperian view that such predictions should not be attempted. All that is necessary is to take the precaution of not judging falsifiable statements as (existential) verifiable ones. There is no confusion in rule 4 on this point.

A final positivist objection to the whole set of 'theorizing rules' listed in section 3 is in terms of recent expressions of hard-headed scepticism about *new* attempts at mathematization of economic theory in the absence of an adequate empirical background such as existed when the mathematization of physics was achieved in the seventeenth century (Phelps Brown, 1972, p. 10, quoting Oskar Morgenstern). Such practical scepticism has been reinforced by misadventures with new economic theories in recent years which are based on supposed 'statistical constants' in economics, such as the Phillips curves which sought to establish a correlation between a 2 per cent annual increase in real productivity, a little under a 2·5 per cent level of unemployment and a stable level of product prices (Worswick, 1972, p. 82). On this view, there should be a further rule imposing a general moratorium on new economic theories and models (including the 'post-Marxian' one presented in the present study), at least until the existing ones have been subjected to more reliable empirical testing.

No such rule, which would knock out most of the chapters in Part Two of this book, has been incorporated in the collection presented in section 3 for two reasons. First, the inadequacy of the empirical background available for a science of *political economy* is by no means so obvious once 'qualitative' (non-measurable) empirical data of a 'general historical–descriptive kind' in supplying assumptions or for confirming predictions are admitted (as they have been for economic theory in general by Morgenstern (1950, pp. 3, 33) in a standard work). Second, there has admittedly been a 'relative overproduction' of non-Marxian economic models in relation to data obtained by deliberately designed observations (Morgenstern, 1950, p. 32), on which most such models depend. But there has been relative under-production of Marxian economic models, both with reference to *qualitative* empirical data (of the kind referred to above), as well as to *quantitative* empirical data now available, on the basis of utilization of modern scientific methods of observation, *some* of which can be adapted for the purpose while others may mislead, being *designed* to conceal or distort what Marxian political economy wants to reveal.

Objections to the approach adopted in writing this book, which are more formidable than those discussed in this section, are discussed in the next two sections.

The first of these, discussed in the next section, is a wide-ranging critique of *all* theories of general economic equilibrium (Marxian economic theory being included as one such theory), from what could be identified as a strictly 'phenomenalist' standpoint. This is the standpoint according to which economic theories are judged *only* from the viewpoint of descriptive efficiency, and no distinction is permitted between 'essence' and 'phenomenon' (Kolakowski, 1972, p. 11).

The second objection is based on the tenet that 'economics is not (cannot be) a theoretical science', which is deduced from the recognition of the 'dialectical' nature of some economic phenomena. (As will be made clear in section 6, the sense in which the term 'dialectic' is used in the context of this critique is neither Hegelian nor Marxian, or rather that it overlaps, but does not coincide with, the Hegelian or Marxian sense of the term.)

These two critiques, represented by the recent writings of two prominent mathematical economists, Kornai and Georgescu-Roegen, are singled out in the present study for a good reason. They tar with the same brush, as it were, *both* the critics and the defenders of Marxian political economy (some of whom are taken seriously in the present study), and seem to pull the rug from under the feet of both. The next two sections might reassure the reader that the present study cannot easily be faulted from the standpoint of these critiques, i.e. that the book might still be worth reading.

5 The concept of general economic equilibrium and Walrasian, Marxian and post-Marxian theories

The conclusions of Kornai's critique (Kornai, 1971, Parts 1 and 4), which are essential from the standpoint of the present study, may be summarized as follows.

Statements

1 A theory is (a) in the *logical–mathematical* sciences: a theorem or a body of theorems logically deducible from a set of mutually consistent axioms (Kornai, 1971, p. 9), and (b) in the *real* sciences: a systematic *description* of the essential interrelations between the variables of reality. *Economic theory* is *not* a logical–mathematical discipline but rather a real science (p. 10).

2 Walrasian general equilibrium theory is the only economic theory which *looks like* a 'finished' or 'mature' real-science theory (p. 5). But it is unrealistic, highly restrictive and analytically *inconvenient*, because its axiomatization complicates instead of simplifying (pp. 16–17, 27–31), which makes it only an (unsuccessful) 'intellectual experiment' (p. 17).

3 Marxian value theory – in *all* its versions – is essentially Walrasian (pp. 356–7).

4 The as yet non-existent 'mature' economic theory of the 'real-science' type can only be provided by an 'economic systems theory', whose building stones have been contributed by various modern critics, ranging from Robinson as author of *The Economics of Imperfect Competition*, to Hurwicz as builder of the 'greed process' model, Simon, the formulator of non-maximizing behaviourist models of the firm and Galbraith as theorist of 'countervailing power' and the 'new industrial state'. This list of modern critics *excludes*, however, the 'ultra-axiomatizers' whose axiomatization complicates, instead of simplifying, the analysis. It also excludes the modern Marxian innovators (Kornai, 1971, pp. 356–7, pp. 367–72).

Now, it is at once obvious that Kornai's conclusion (statement 1) is a total repudiation of the definition of a theory (definition 1, section 3), and of the rule, section 3, adopted in the present study. It shuts out all 'ought'-type propositions from economic theory, and seeks to convert economic theory into a purely descriptive science. It is not surprising, therefore, that in a book of 376 pages, *no* interest is shown in Marxian (or modern) discussions of the nature of capital or in the question of capitalist exploitation although chapter 7 *is* devoted to an analysis by 'economic systems theory' of what is *not* the same thing, viz. of the conflict and compromise within economic institutions.

What *is* surprising is that modern philosophical doubts about the *possibility*, in any branch of knowledge, of *both* types of theory defined by Kornai are completely ignored by him. There is no discussion of the famous theorem of Godel's, which has the implication that any proof of the formal system *L* must use methods and notions not contained within *L* itself (for elaboration see Newman, 1965, pp. 523–4; Nagel and Newman, 1971, chapter 7). It has already been noted in the literature that this theorem implies that consistency, from within the system, of economic theories of the 'axiomatic' type (i.e. of Kornai's 'logical–mathematical' type) cannot be proved (Massey, 1965, p. 1158). But it is hard to see why a generalized Godel's theorem should not also undermine economic theories of the 'real-science' type, which are supposed to embody 'systematic' description of inter-relations between variables of reality.[4] On the other hand, once notions (e.g. 'ought'-type propositions) borrowed from 'outside' the system are admitted (as permitted by rule 1, section 3), mutually consistent propositions about economic phenomena (as in definition 1, section 3 of economic theory) seem to be possible, strictly in terms of the implications of Godel's theorem.

On the other hand, Kornai is on much stronger ground with his conclusion in statement 2. Specifically, there are few defenders at present of the Walrasian *tatonnement* procedure, whose well-known defects have produced the recent verdict that 'what looked like being one of the basic theorems of economic knowledge', based on such a procedure, 'is no more than an example' (Bliss, 1972, p. 100). Walrasian *tatonnement* plays no role in the post-Marxian political–economic analysis presented in chapter 6 (and its Appendix), and used in Parts Two and Three.

However, the baby is thrown out with the bath-water, when Kornai interprets his conclusions (statements 2 and 4) to purge economic theory of every vestige of a general-equilibrium notion, and to construct an 'economic systems theory' which does without it altogether.

4. Although too little work seems to have been done about the generalized implications of Godel's proof, Samuelson has asserted that economists or physicists do not (which is a fact), and need not (which is yet to be proved) worry too much about Godel's proof (Samuelson, 1965, p. 1166, n. 2).

As argued in chapter 2, section 1, a general equilibrium (or general interdependence) theory to demonstrate the *workability* of the capitalist market-mechanism, guided by the 'invisible hand', is needed by different writers for different (even diametrically opposite) reasons. Adam Smith needed it, because he wanted to argue that it works *ideally* (or at any rate better than feudalism). It was also needed by Ricardo, who thought that he had found a proof that it worked *badly*, though he saw no alternative to it. It was needed *no less* by Marx, who wanted to prove that the capitalist market-mechanism is comparable, as a *workable* system of *exploitation* of one class by another, to feudalism, or to ancient (European) labour slavery, neither of which are ruled by the market's 'invisible hand'.

Thus, only if we are *not* interested in the problem of capitalist exploitation, can we dispense with proofs of general interdependence. If we *are* interested, we must have a 'general interdependence' theory involving proofs of long-run equilibrium values in some form.

The label 'general interdependence' could perhaps be adopted, and be contra-posed to the label 'general equilibrium', which is under fire from Kornai (and others). A 'general interdependence' theory to handle the problem of capitalist exploitation could serve the purpose, in so far as it could dispense with the Walrasian *tatonnement*, and remain uncommitted to a 'Pareto–optimal' outcome, which is a hallmark of Walrasian general equilibrium theory (see discussion in the Appendix to chapter 6).

However, in this book, the label 'general equilibrium' is retained to refer to Marxian or post-Marxian political–economic models of competitive capitalism, because there is one 'Walrasian' property which every theory of 'general interdependence' under competitive capitalism must have. This is the insight which made Walras cast the problem of general interdependence and long-run values in a competitive-capitalist market system in the form of the equilibrium values derived from a system of simultaneous equations. As will be argued (chapter 3, section 7 and chapter 5, section 2) the

Marxian theory of value, capital and exploitation suffered much more from the *lack* of this insight, than from a rough sketch of a *tatonnement*-like demand–supply adjustment procedure in the Marxian theory of market price and market value, which is overemphasized by Kornai (1971, pp. 356–7), providing the basis of his conclusion that Marxian value theory is Walrasian (see statement 3).

6 Can economics be a theoretical science?

Georgescu-Roegen's olympian survey (1966) of the scientific approach in the natural sciences culminates in challenging propositions.

Statements

1 The economic process cannot be fully understood without the use of 'dialectical concepts', which are esoterically defined below.

2 The necessity of using such dialectical concepts makes it impossible for economics to be a quantitative theoretical science modelled on mechanics, as attempted by the Walrasians (1966, pp. 103–8). Analyses of the economic process of all societies in terms of their common, immutable, elementary components could take care of qualitative novelty, but produce uninteresting results (1966, pp. 111–13).

3 However, 'analytical similes' – as distinct from analytical *theories* – are useful for detecting errors of reasoning and making clearer chains of correct 'dialectical reasoning' in economics (1966, p. 121).

Definition

1 Dialectical concepts are concepts which defy the fundamental law of logic, the Principle of Contradiction: 'B cannot be both A and non-A', which is only a part of Hegelian dialectics (1966, p. 23).

Why, in this study, it has *not* been found necessary to use 'dialectical' concepts as defined by Georgescu-Roegen, has already been explained in section 4. Actually, Georgescu-Roegen's examples illustrating his position on this point are not very convincing (except when he is discussing neo-classical consumer-demand theory, with which we are very little concerned in this book). 'Feudalism' is cited as an example of a 'dialectical concept' because it refers to a constantly evolving phenomenon (1966, p. 31). But he himself defines 'feudalism', as well as 'capitalism', in very precise, non-dialectical terms and compares them with the aid of an 'analytical simile' which is illustrated by a marginal-productivity diagram borrowed from neo-classical economic theory.

These doubts apart, running through Georgescu-Roegen's list of three propositions is like skidding past a dangerous corner (i.e. statement 2) and then breathing freely once statement 3 is reached in the end. It turns out that though economics can *never* be a 'theoretical science', it *must* use 'analytical similes', *not* excluding Marxian ones (1966, p. 361). Over a (possibly important) semantic issue that remains to be settled, no bones need be broken!

7 What is 'new' in this book

This section is devoted to a quick preview of the main contents of this book, with the focus on some new ground broken.

Part One contains a critical assessment of Marx's own, and later Marxian attempts to construct an integrated theory of value, capital and exploitation under the ideal conditions of competitive capitalism. The upshot is a post-Marxian theory, which, as already indicated in section 2, fulfils Marx's original purpose. The novel features of the approach adopted, or the results presented, are given below.

Statements

1 The rejection of the dogma of the Ricardian socialists that labour is the only source of wealth and value, as the basis of a theory of capitalist exploitation. The dogma is untenable in any realistic model of capitalist production, is inconsistent with a major Marxian tenet and was denounced by him at one place as a 'bourgeois idea' (see chapter 3, section 3).

2 The separation, for purposes of solution, of the three *distinct* problems of the existence, the identification and the stability of the competitive equilibrium, which Walrasian theory tries to solve as a *single* problem by the *tatonnement* process. Marx tried, unsuccessfully, to separate the three problems, but could not solve any (chapter 6, section 1). The three problems are successfully separated in a post-Marxian theory of political economy (chapter 6, section 2). The identification problem is solved by the method of 'reduction to dated labour', which is based on a method of solving simultaneous equations systems seldom used (chapter 6, section 4). The solution of the stability problem, as well as the *nature* of the problem as it arises, depends on institutional changes in different phases of capitalism (chapter 6, section 5).

3 A Torrens–Marx method of valuation of used fixed capital employed in production is found preferable to alternatives such as a Torrens–von Neumann or a Torrens–Sraffa method, or the Morishima 'rentals' method (chapter 6, section 3).

4 The impossibility of grading lands of different qualities *before* prices are determined makes Ricardian differential rent theory unusable (as pointed out by Samuelson and Sraffa). The impossibility of validating the proposition that the organic capital composition in agriculture is lower than in non-agriculture makes Marxian absolute rent theory unusable. The solution adopted is to use the Marxian theory of 'monopoly rent' as a normal feature even in the context of a model of competitive capitalism, with a competitive land market (chapter 6, section 3).

5 A long-run positive rate of profit and of exploitation under competitive capitalism is postulated on the basis of a Marxian 'accumulation' hypothesis instead of the much-criticized 'profit-maximization' hypothesis (chapter 6, section 6).

6 Certain formal theorems of the modern mathematical–political theory of collective choice are interpreted to validate Marxian alienation and exploitation in a competitive capitalist

model, which has the advantage of incorporating an explicitly stated political dimension (see Appendix to chapter 6).

In Part Two of the book, an attempt is made to show that a wide range of types of institutional change in advanced and backward capitalist and socialist societies can be analysed with the help of a few formal properties and results of post-Marxian competitive capitalist models of Part One. These formal properties or results are given below.

7 The isolation of the 'stability' problem of a competitive capitalist equilibrium, and the identification of its institutional nature (already referred to in statement 2).

8 The property of what is definable as the 'partial decomposability' of realistic models of capitalist production under competitive conditions (which is, incidentally, also the formal basis of the destruction of the dogma that 'labour is the only source of value', referred to in statement 1).

9 The Marxian 'capital accumulation' hypothesis which makes it possible to reconcile a post-Marxian theory of competitive capitalist equilibrium with a theory of capitalist exploitation (referred to in statement 5).

10 The insight, incorporated in the modern mathematica political–economic theory of collective choice, that political voting and the economic market mechanism are special cases of the more general category of collective social choice. (This is *not* to be confused with an untenable neo-classical proposition which says that the capitalist market-mechanism is a system of consumer-voting through which consumers exercise 'sovereignty'.)

These formal properties or results of Part One are summarized and discussed together in chapter 9, with which Part Two begins. The application of statements 7–9 to explain the geneses of capitalist colonialism, imperialism and neo-imperialism, and patterns of foreign-aided and self-reliant development of backward contemporary capitalist or socialist economies will be found in chapters 10 and 11. Statement 8 is used in chapter 12 to explain, analytically, the observed historical 'irreversibility' of transitions to socialism in a number of countries. The only application of statement 10 discussed is with reference to alternative Marxian economic models of socialism (chapter 12), although it probably has applications to contemporary backward capitalist economies subjected to economic controls.

Part Three is made up of a few chapters written in lieu of a conclusion to the present study. It contains a systematic, though inconclusive, discussion of the Marxian *taxonomy* of alternative economic theories, after taking into account the post-Marxian political economy presented in Part One, and its 'practical' applications discussed in Part Two. The new material contained in Part Three is given below.

11 A post-Marxian classification of alternative systems of theoretical economics which makes a distinction between:

Politically neutral 'existential' or 'superficial' economic theories analysing 'surface phenomena';
Politically pro-labour 'vulgar economy' proper;
Capitalist (bourgeois) apologetics;
Socialist apologetics (chapter 18).

12 An investigation of the hypothesis that a principle akin to Niels Bohr's 'Principle of Complementarity' in physics can be invoked to justify the coexistence and complementarity, or 'convergence' of alternative (non-apologetic) systems of theoretical economics, specially of Marxian and post-Marxian political economy on the one side, and 'existential' (Marshallian) *economic* theory on the other (chapter 17).

It must be emphasized that what is new about the present study is simply that its novel features, listed in this section, are not to be found, in whole or in part, in other available books on Marxian political economy. Some of them have, however, been incorporated in published articles, unpublished (mimeographed) papers or mentioned in correspondence with the present writer. Furthermore, the formal results, which are interpreted in a Marxian context to produce these novel features, have almost all been published; only their interpretation in the Marxian context is rare. (Necessary acknowledgements have been made in the pages that follow.)

However, it is *not* claimed that *all* cases of absorption of some of the insights and results of modern economics into Marxian theoretical systems, or vice versa, have been taken into account in the present study. The important work on Marxian macroeconomics by such writers as Fan-Hung, Tsuru and Sherman (see Horowitz, 1968; Sherman, 1971; for detailed references) is ignored, chiefly because the implications of their work from the viewpoint of the present study is not yet clear to the present writer.[5] (The much-admired work of Michal Kalecki, which is also on macroeconomics, is ignored for somewhat different reasons. Its Marxian properties are hard to identify.)

8 A reader's guide

The present work is sub-titled 'An Introduction' – and so it is – since Marxian political economy is a vast subject, and so would post-Marxian political economy be, if its theoretical core (which is mainly what the present writer has tried to identify in this book) is accepted. But it is an *advanced* introduction, mainly addressed to economists who are well versed in modern economic theory, except for Marxian political economy, to which they might perhaps need an introduction. Modern economists who are familiar with some version of modern linear theory (and also, preferably, Sraffa's commodity-production theory) will have little difficulty if they have read at least *one* of the following: Sweezy's *Theory of Capitalist Development* (1949), Lange's *Marxian Economics and Modern Economic Theory* (1935–6), Robinson's *An Essay on Marxian Economics* (1942), or Samuelson's *Wages and Interest: A Modern Dissection of Marxian Economic Models* (1957).

5. However, chapters 8–12, 16–18, of Schwartz's important work (1961), in which analytical tools similar to those used in this book are employed, do seem to establish a connection with macroeconomics. (The book contains no references to Marx or Marxian political economy.)

Readers who are *not* economists, but are interested in a *non*-obsolete introduction to Marxian theoretical economics, as distinct from empirical (descriptive) literature which uses Marxian categories, will get the best out of the book if they have read (or are willing to read) at least Marx's short pamphlets *Wage Labour and Capital* (1950a), or *Value, Price and Profit* (also called *Wage, Price and Profit*) (1950b), and Dobb's *Classical Political Economy* (1937).

However, neither Marxian political economy, nor its proposed extension, post-Marxian political economy, can be understood without at least an elementary knowledge of algebra, more specifically, of simultaneous equations systems (though nothing more, not even a knowledge of the calculus, is required). Well-known results of modern mathematical economics are quoted, discussed, but *not* reproduced. At some risk of repelling the mathematically inclined, even algebraic notations for representing simultaneous equations are dispensed with in Part Two, where numerical examples are given instead. This is chiefly because, since the simultaneous equations systems used are *not* supposed to represent economic models with scale-free properties, the algebraic notations would have to be unusually cumbersome.

However, to judge the rights and wrongs of the argument, a knowledge of the theory of equations is required, and, for the Appendix to chapter 6 and chapter 14, section 6, familiarity with the notation employed in symbolic logic will be necessary. But it is unlikely that mistakes will be found in the mathematical results which the reader will be asked to take on trust.

Part One
Alternative Theories of Capitalist Exploitation:
A Critical Survey and a Post-Marxian Reconstruction

2 Essential Ingredients of a Theory of Capitalist Exploitation

1 Introduction

As already noted (chapter 1, section 5) Marx, and his prominent predecessors and successors, worked out theories of general economic equilibrium, partly for the same reasons, partly for different reasons.

Thus, Adam Smith wanted to prove what earlier, mercantilist writers denied, viz. that the capitalist market system 'works' on the basis of an 'invisible hand' which identifies the private self-interest of each with the interest of all, and promotes the growth of the wealth of nations better than any mercantilist interference with market forces would.

Ricardo grappled, unsuccessfully, with an alternative to Smith's 'proof' of the 'workability' of the capitalist market mechanism, because he thought Smith had side-stepped important problems and failed to give a proper proof. Ricardo was also less interested than Smith in 'idealizing' the capitalist market system. But he had *no* theory of exploitation of workers by capitalists (in his theoretical system, only landlords who appropriated a 'pure economic surplus' earned on intra-marginal land could be identified as exploiters).

Marx recognized, no less than the writers just named, that the workability of the capitalist market-mechanism had first to be proved, if only to remove neo-mercantilist doubts, shared at least by some German socialists (about whom more will be said in chapter 3). Only then, he felt, could the 'weapons of criticism' be turned against it, as a prelude to 'criticism with weapons' for the revolutionary overthrow of the capitalist system.

However, the declared aim of Marx's theory of value (general economic equilibrium) was to clarify the nature of capital (as very accurately indicated by the title of his main work)[1] even in the 'ideal' conditions of a free, competitive capitalism. These 'ideal' conditions were very precisely defined in terms of the absence of pre-capitalist, statutory, monopoly restrictions in early capitalism, or of non-statutory restrictions imposed by private monopolies (or trade unions) in late capitalism, on the free sale and purchase of consumer goods, produced means of production, of scarce land, or of labour (or more strictly, of 'labour-power' or 'capacity for labour').

So Marx tried to establish that in such a model of free, competitive capitalism, there exists a long-run equilibrium where (a) capital represents a *coercive* social power, acting through (and in spite of) the competitive market structure, and (b) workers are exploited by capitalists, who appropriate '*surplus value*' (which is the product of 'surplus labour' performed by workers) in the form of capitalist profit, interest and rent.

Thus, like Smith, Ricardo or Walras, Marx had a theory of long-run equilibrium values (though, as we shall note in later chapters, none of them were able to work out a strict proof of the existence of such values in mathematical terms). But, unlike them, Marx's theory of long-run values was integrated with a theory of capital and exploitation under competitive conditions.

Marx held that the theories of value and distribution in classical political economy contained *fragments* of a theory of *surplus value* originating in capitalist *production* under competitive conditions. Thus, the phenomenon of capitalist exploitation even under ideal, competitive conditions, was theoretically recognized. But a consistently worked-out, convincing theory of exploitation was missing – chiefly, Marx felt, because the nature of capital as a social, coercive power was not understood. To the authors of these theories, capital

1. *Capital*, volumes 1–3, and *Theories of Surplus Value*, sub-titled volume 4 of *Capital* (Marx 1954; 1957; 1959; 1964; 1968; 1971).

was *only* 'stored up' or 'accumulated' labour, embodied in money or commodities which were used as means of production or were consumed as wage-goods (against 'wage-advances' by capitalists to labourers). What they could not grasp was the fact that capital is *also* a social relation between men, the embodiment of the coercive power of the capitalist acting on labourers, compelling them to perform 'surplus labour', for the population of 'surplus value'.

Marx makes this criticism of Adam Smith, accepting Lauderdale's charge that Smith's exposition of surplus value, based on the Lockean notion that capital is *not* an original source of wealth, is inconsistent with his assertion that profit is an original source of revenue (Marx, ch. 3, section 6, pp. 90–91). He makes more or less the same criticism of Ricardo on this point (Marx, 1968, ch. 15, section 2, pp. 400–401).

According to Marx, only von Thünen (1863; Marx, 1954, ch. 25, p. 621) recognized exploitation of workers by capitalists in unambiguous terms. However, Marx conceded that Simonde de Sismondi, too, had recognized the problem of capitalist exploitation (Marx, 1954, ch. 32, p. 762), and also that Ricardo, in a passage in his *Principles of Political Economy*, had referred to the true nature of capital, viz. that it is not accumulated labour which is employed by the labouring class, but accumulated labour which employs this class (Marx, 1968, ch. 15, section 4, p. 421).

The references just noted serve as the first of several reminders in the present study that Marx judged each contribution to theoretical controversy mostly on merit, without prejudice. Thus, Lauderdale is backed as against Smith, even though he argued that profits are necessary payments to capital for its function in substituting labour, or doing what men, unaided, cannot do (Marx, 1964, ch. 4, section 12, p. 257). Sismondi's contribution on this point is acknowledged, even though he is named in the *Communist Manifesto* as the 'head' of the 'school of (reactionary and utopian) petty-bourgeois socialism' (Marx and Engels, 1950, p. 54). Von Thünen is singled out as the only one who unambiguously recognized capitalist exploitation – even though he was the first to have a marginal productivity theory of distribution, which is the *bête noire* of modern Marxist (and neo-Marxist) economists.

2 Mystification of the capitalist mode of production

Why did the contributions of Lauderdale, Sismondi, Ricardo and von Thünen not go beyond insights into the 'problem of surplus value'? Marx was not the first economist to ask *this kind* of question, nor was he the last. But it is generally acknowledged, on the authority of Joseph Schumpeter (1949, p. 354; 1955, pp. 35–8), that the role of 'ideology' in economic theorizing, 'discovered' by Marx, has something to do with the answer. However, as we shall see in chapter 17, in Marxian literature, 'ideology' in economic theorizing has multiple expressions, each of which *could* be invested, as will be argued in chapter 18, with precise meaning.

One Marxian meaning of the word 'ideology' is 'false consciousness' (Lange, 1963, pp. 328–9). This can refer to an 'epistemological problem' of the relation of the knower to what he knows (Northrop, 1958, p. 13). It can originate in deliberate (intentional, motivated) falsification in the service of a special social class, which is the main example of 'apologetics' (Marx's term) or 'special pleading' (Schumpeter's term). Another, milder, form of apologetics could be 'unconscious' falsification which is the outcome of 'class limitations' of 'bourgeois economists'. According to an interpretation given by the anonymous writers representing the Institute of Marxism–Leninism of the Central Committee of the Communist Party of the Soviet Union (Preface to Marx, 1964, pp. 20–21) an 'internally consistent and scientifically grounded' solution of the problem of surplus value could not be found by bourgeois economists because of their 'class limitations' (connected, presumably, with their sociological origin).

Actually, Marx employed the term 'ideology' understood as 'false consciousness' also as a problem of 'ontology', which refers to the *object* of scientific knowledge, rather than merely to the 'epistemological' relation of the knower to the object known (Northrop 1959, p. 23), which, as we have noted, is the basis of 'apologetic' falsification.

Marx had a major hypothesis – which has not been systematically investigated by economists who specialize in doctrinal history – that the capitalist 'mode of production' created a peculiar (if not unique)[2] ontological problem of 'mystification'. It is this problem of 'mystification' which could not be removed unless one had first of all a theory recognizing its existence, which, according to Marx, was responsible for the failure of the political economists to work out a theory of surplus value or capitalist exploitation. Under capitalism, he argued, there is a 'transformation of social conditions into things': the 'best spokesmen of classical political economy' cannot separate these two aspects (analytically) and 'fall into more or less inconsistencies, halfway statements and unsolved contradictions' (Marx, 1959, ch. 48, pp. 809–10). Indeed, according to Marx, the basic function of economic theory, its *raison d'être*, was to 'de-mystify' capitalist economic relationships, especially the nature of capital, and integrate the theories of value, capital and distribution with a consistent theory of capitalist exploitation (Marx, 1959, *idem*; 1938a, p. 246).

This Marxian hypothesis will be discussed intermittently in later chapters of this book (mainly in Parts One and Three). But two points should be noted at this stage.

First, according to Marx, the phenomenon of 'mystification' under capitalism was similar to the more general phenomenon of 'commodity fetishism' (Marx, 1954, ch. 1, section 4, pp. 71–85), which made market relations between producers in *any* form of commodity production (pre-capitalist, capitalist or post-capitalist) appear *only* as an impersonal relation between things, so that producers are subordinated to 'what they produce' (or the 'rule of the market'), through a process of 'alienation'. (As we shall note in chapter 14 Marx thought

2. It did *not* exist in European feudalism (Marx, 1954, Part 1, ch. 1, section 4, pp. 76–7), nor would it exist in a hypothetical Robinson Crusoe economy. But it *did* exist under ancient slavery (Marx 1950b, section 9, p. 389).

the proper function of economic theory was to 'lay bare' both the 'exploitation' and 'alienation' of producers under capitalism, and a socialist society had to eradicate both.)

Second, Marx's doctrine of 'mystification' proves that Marx did *not*, contrary to Schumpeter's belief (1955, p. 36), 'reduce' his analysis of ideologies to 'emulsions of class interests', i.e. to apologetics proper, conscious or unconscious. Marx identified capitalist 'mystification' as an 'objective', *ontological* problem, as distinct from 'apologetics' which arises as an *epistemological* problem. Mystification under capitalism (though it could also arise, as we have seen earlier in this section Marx had noted, in a slave society) transgresses all class bias: all could be its victims; a pro-labour, anti-bourgeois bias is no insurance against its influence. It distorted the vision of all; both the capitalists and the victims of their exploitation. (As we shall see in the next chapter, section 3, the Ricardian socialists failed, according to Marx, to develop a scientific theory of capitalist exploitation because their vision was distorted by capitalist mystification.)

3 Ingredients of a capitalist exploitation theory

As we shall note in chapter 6, section 1, major progress at the technical level in 'de-mystifying' the notion of capital was in suspense for nearly a century after Marx made a start in this direction. At the same time, unlike Marx's predecessors – none of whom had worked out a complete and consistent theory of capitalist exploitation – some of his contemporaries and successors *did* work out such theories.

There is no trace of any impact of the Marxian programme of 'de-mystification' of capitalist relationships on these theories, except (indirectly) on one point. None of them try to make capitalist exploitation a question of *facts* alone in the form of a strictly positive statement. (This is, of course, *excluded* by Marx's 'mystification' doctrine, which says that under capitalism many things are *not* what they seem to be.)

However, these theories, like Marx's theory of capitalist exploitation, have the merit of logical consistency. The form or 'structure' of these theories – in terms of their 'essential ingredients' – is also similar. So the remaining sections of this chapter are devoted to a discussion of the basic structure of all these theories.

A survey of the literature, both affirmative and critical, about Marx's theory and various post-Marxian theories of capitalist exploitation suggests that they contain, or are expected to contain, *four* essential ingredients.

Ingredients

1 A set of propositions *defining* exploitation, usually containing (a) empirically verifiable descriptive ('positive') statements about the structure of the economy or about the institutional framework), and (b) statements which are of the 'ought to be' or what 'could be' variety.

2 The successful incorporation of the notion of exploitation, as defined, in a theory of long-run equilibrium values (or prices) under capitalism (competitive or monopolistic, or both) – complete with proofs of the existence (and, preferably, of uniqueness) of equilibrium.

3 A statement of the reason (or reasons) as to *why* there must be exploitation in long-run equilibrium, i.e. why the '*rate* of exploitation' must be *positive*.

4 A set of empirically verifiable theoretical predictions about long-run tendencies under capitalism.

Ingredient 3 does not need explaining: rather than have a theory of a zero rate of capitalist exploitation it is always better to do without the concept of capitalist exploitation! A theory of capitalist exploitation which contains ingredient 4 is obviously more interesting than one without it, since a theory of capitalist exploitation is hardly needed for its own sake. (Actually, although only Marx's and Marxian theories spell out 4, the others also carry definite implications regarding 4.) But ingredients 1 and 2 as essential features of any theory of capitalist exploitation do need explaining at some length. This is attempted in the next two sections.

4 Positive and prescriptive statements in a theory of capitalist exploitation

There is, in every economic theory of exploitation under capitalism, ingredient 1a, e.g. in the modern Pigovian theory of exploitation under capitalism (see chapter 3, section 5 for details), imperfections in 'factor' and/or product markets are assumed; in Marx's, and other socialist theories of exploitation (see chapter 3, sections 2–4), there is the institutional datum that workers own no means of production, which are exclusively owned by a separate class of people, the capitalists.

But is ingredient 1b essential? The answer is yes, because there seems to be no way of constructing a theory of exploitation under capitalism which makes such exploitation *entirely* a question of 'fact', i.e. of what 'is' as against what 'ought to be' or 'could be'.

Thus, the modern Pigovian theory of exploitation under capitalism (which is *not* socialist or anti-capitalist except on special assumptions) rests on a definition which says there is exploitation whenever the factor price is less than the value of the marginal product. It is implied (but *only* by a value judgement) that this is *not* as it *should* be, and various remedies are discussed as to how it *could* be removed.

The definitions underlying the socialist theories of capitalist exploitation (discussed in chapters 3–6) also contain more broadly-defined 'prescriptive' statements.[3] Of course, they not only postulate what ought to exist, but what could be proved (analytically)[4] to exist, viz. a society where all the means of production are owned by labourers, so that there is no exploitation by capitalist owners of private property in the means of production. As we shall see in chapter 3, section 3, the Ricardian-socialist theories of capitalist exploitation also

3. The term 'prescriptive' is used here to refer to commendatory statements of every kind, which, if they are sincere (as they are in a socialist theory of capitalist exploitation) involve a 'pro-attitude' (Pattanaik, 1971, p. 19; Nowell–Smith, 1954).
4. Not only by using a Marxian analytical apparatus, but also by using the apparatus of neo-classical general equilibrium theory, at least since 1938 (Lange, 1936–7), but strictly since 1908 (Barone, 1908).

contain definite 'normative' elements, although these are somewhat naively passed off as strictly positive ('factual') propositions.

Thus, all available theories of capitalist exploitation conform to our 'theorizing rule' (rule 1, chapter 1, section 3) which says that an economic theory should admit 'ought' propositions deduced from a set of premises containing both 'ought' and 'is' propositions. (Objections to this rule are discussed and rejected in chapter 1, section 4.)

5 Why a theory of long-run equilibrium must go along with a theory of capitalist exploitation

Why Marx needed ingredient 2 in his theory of capitalist exploitation, i.e. a reconciliation of the notion of exploitation with a theory of relative price-determination, has already been discussed in section 1 of this chapter.

But, more generally, *any* theory of capitalist exploitation must achieve, or be capable of achieving, such a reconciliation, simply because in a pure capitalist model, everything has a price.

Relative product-prices cannot be explained in terms of *non*-exploitation, while property-incomes (which are circularly or unidirectionally interdependent with product prices in *any* complete model of general economic equilibrium) are explained in terms of *exploitation* – without running into a contradiction.

So it is hard to make sense of Robinson's oft-repeated dictum, which *generalizes* her criticism of Marx, that 'it was merely an aberration to mix up the analysis of relative prices with the problem of exploitation. . . . The important question is what determines distribution between wages and profits in the economy as a whole' (Robinson, 1965, p. 176).

Actually, as we shall see in chapter 3, section 4, doubts about the possibility of reconciling a notion of a general rate of return on capital with a theory of relative price-determination has been largely responsible for a modern 'opening' towards neo-Marxian theories of the class struggle and exploitation in a competitive capitalist system.

6 The impact of changing capitalist realities on theories of capital and exploitation

The list of ingredients of a theory of capitalist exploitation given in section 3 is not necessarily complete. Marx evidently included in the list the additional requirement of a rational explanation, on the basis of historical evidence, of the precise way in which capitalist 'mystification' of economic (and political) realities led to the elevation of shallow pseudo-theoretical concepts into a bourgeois 'religion of everyday life', which suits the interests of the ruling classes (Marx, 1954, pp. 14–16; 1959, ch. 48, p. 809).

This has to do with an as yet extremely underdeveloped branch of specialized knowledge, viz. a systematic study of the inter-relations between economic realities and economic ideas. However, beyond a few *obiter dicta* in *Theories of Surplus Value*, and a still untested hypothesis in his 'Afterword' to the second German edition of *Capital*, volume one (Marx, 1954, pp. 13–16), Marx hardly left any clues. No more than some fragments and impressionistic or anecdotal statements have been added by Marxists and others over the past seven decades. Some of this evidence will be referred to in chapters 17 and 18. Beyond that, this particular Marxian hypothesis will not be discussed further in the present study.

3 Non-Marxian Theories of Capitalist Exploitation

1 Introduction

In this chapter, it is proposed to discuss some post-Marxian theories of capitalist exploitation which actually *do*, or at least *seem* to, resemble Marx's, but are different in essentials. The purpose is two-fold. First, to distinguish them from Marx's theory, with the help of some results of modern mathematical economics, so that we are better prepared to discuss Marx's own theory in chapters 4 and 5. Second, to use the criteria for judging economic theories discussed in chapter 1, section 3, for making an assessment of these theories (as Marx's and later Marxian theories will be assessed in chapters 4 and 5). We shall then be ready to discuss a post-Marxian theory of capitalist exploitation in chapter 6.

2 The Walras–Lange–Lerner theory of capitalist exploitation

In 1935, Lange published a theory of workers' exploitation under competitive or monopolistic capitalism (Lange, 1935), which is astonishing in its simplicity. It was partially endorsed by Lerner in 1939–40 (1939; 1940), and more categorically re-endorsed by him recently (Lerner, 1972). It has also received basic support from Samuelson recently (1971, pp. 407–8, 422; 1972, pp. 52–3).

Lange's original version starts with the 'institutional datum' (also specified by Marx) that workers do not own capital or the means of production, which are exclusively owned by a separate class of people, the capitalists. To this is added the definitional assumption, made from an explicitly stated socialist viewpoint (Lange, 1935, p. 77) that this is not as it *should* be ('normatively') or *could* be ('factually'). It follows, directly, that *if* profit (interest) incomes are positive in long-run equilibrium, workers are exploited *because* they own no capital, by those who do. Lange argued that profit (interest) incomes *will* be positive because:

Technical progress is necessary to maintain the capitalist system;
Technological progress takes the form of a 'constant increase in the organic composition of capital';
Rising organic composition of capital takes the form of replacement of workers by machines.

Thus the 'industrial reserve army' is constantly replenished, and wages are prevented from swallowing up profits (Lange, 1935, pp. 83–5).

Now, Lange was emphatic that this theory of capitalist exploitation does *not* rest on a definition of exploitation in terms of a 'surplus' produced by workers, which is appropriated by capitalists. It is compatible with *any* notion of capital (e.g. as a supply of a quantity of 'waiting') and of profit (interest) as a *quid pro quo* or a 'reward for waiting' received by capitalists, and can be integrated with any otherwise satisfactory theory of relative prices and of distribution (Lange, 1935, p. 77).[1] In this theory, capitalists coerce and exploit the workers *not* by appropriating a 'surplus' produced by workers, but by denying workers the right to undertake 'waiting', and to own the means of production they work with.

Lange's 1935 theory is a *tour de force* which shows how easy it is to take over the neo-classical theory of value, capital and distribution wholesale, and to turn it against capitalist apologetics. It is of a piece with, and as ingenious as, Lange's

1. Actually, in his 1935 article, Lange ultimately expressed his definite preference for a Walrasian general equilibrium theory of prices, and rejected Marx's 'prices of production' theory (pp. 77–9). However, in his later work, he seems to have changed his mind (1963, pp. 113, 298–9). Reasons for the change are not stated in this volume, nor is there any reference to his earlier article in it.

neo-classical economic models of socialism (which will be discussed in chapter 13).

However, in the 1970s, few would share Lange's confidence in the 1930s in Walrasian general equilibrium theory as an *impeccable, unshakeable* foundation for a theory of capitalist exploitation under competitive conditions. Thus, there are doubts about proofs of the 'existence' of equilibrium, or of 'convergence' towards an equilibrium in Walrasian general equilibrium models. To assume *tatonnement* (groping) as Walras did is to imagine exchanges take place only at market clearing-prices; but most markets are not organized where possible because auctioneers cry out prices (Bliss, 1972, pp. 94–7). If 'recognized dealers' are assumed to operate instead, each setting his own price for his commodity (other than money) and waiting for others to come and transact business with him (up to the extent of his demand or supply for that commodity), then we are still left with professedly 'unrealistic' models (Fisher, 1972, sections 1 and 2). There are also difficulties with proofs of existence of equilibrium in a monetary economy, since it is not easy to rely on fixed point theorems which play a crucial role in non-monetary general equilibrium models (Hahn and Brechling 1965, p. 130).

Of course, too much should not be made of the 'unrealism' of alternative (institutional) assumptions that are required to validate Walrasian general equilibrium models. For 'who is to say which assumption is realistic?' (Hahn and Brechling, 1965, p. 311).

But before the Walrasian model is accepted as the basis of a theory of capitalist exploitation, one must make sure that it has no serious consistency problems. The modern critique of neo-classical capital theory has posed the question as to whether without treating capital as a single, perfectly malleable object, a Walrasian system can be in full equilibrium, with (a) equality of the net rates of return on all kinds of capital goods, with the price of capital goods being equal to their cost of production, as well as (b) the equality of the net rates of return on capital goods and the quantities of new capital goods currently produced (Nuti, 1970, p. 223). Since the unrealism of the malleable capital assumption is beyond all dispute, this reduces to a consistency problem of some magnitude.

So we turn, in the next two sections, to *non* neo-classical theories of capitalist exploitation, before we return again, briefly, to consider an alternative neo-classical theory of exploitation under capitalism (but not necessarily of exploitation *by* capitalists, viz. the Pigovian theory).

3 The Ricardian socialists and capitalist exploitation
Who were the Ricardian socialists?

Marx described Ricardo as 'the head of the school which determines value by labour time' in his early work, *Poverty of Philosophy* (Marx, 1956, p. 107). He also declared that '... the English socialists turned the Ricardian formula of exchange against political economy' (1956, p. 11). In this early work, a polemic against Proudhon, Marx also mentioned by name William Thompson (1824), Thomas Hodgskin (1827) and John Bray (1839) as representatives of this group of writers. He also made detailed assessments of the writings of Hodgskin and Bray, as well as Piercy Ravenstone (another writer usually identified with this trend) in his *Theories of Surplus Value*, Part 3 (Marx, 1971, ch. 21, pp. 238–325).

Schumpeter paid some attention to the Ricardian socialists (1954, p. 121; 1955, p. 479), though he expressed a very poor opinion of Bray (Schumpeter, 1955, p. 460, n. 24), whom Marx took rather seriously (Marx, 1956, pp. 77–84; 1971, pp. 319–25).

The Ricardian-socialist doctrines of capitalist exploitation

In a sense, the Ricardian-socialist doctrines of capitalist exploitation represent the polar opposite of Lange's 1935 theory discussed in the previous section.

Where Lange makes *no* attempt to 'de-mystify' capitalist relationships, and takes over the neo-classical concept of capital intact, the Ricardian socialists *over-do* their 'de-mystification', so to speak, by trying to do away with the categories of circulating and fixed capital altogether, and by defining labour as the 'only source of wealth' (Thompson, 1824, chapter 1, section 1, p. 6). Schumpeter has suggested (1955, p. 649) that this 'Ricardian-socialist dogma' was inspired by a passage in the famous chapter 'On Machinery', in Ricardo's *Principles*, which says '. . . the capitalist begins his operations by having food and necessaries in his possession of the value of £13 000 . . . at the end of the year the workmen replace in his possession food and necessaries of the value of £15 000 . . .' (Ricardo, 1951, pp. 388–9). Marx, who also thought Ricardo's value theory was the basis of Ricardian-socialist doctrines, nevertheless criticized them for 'underestimating the importance of materialized past labour' (Marx, 1971, pp. 266–80).

To the doctrine 'labour is the only source of wealth', the Ricardian socialists added the institutional datum that, in a capitalist society, labourers do not own subsistence funds, which are advanced by capitalists. It is then asserted that 'unequal exchanges' between capitalists and labourers in the labour market favour the capitalists, to 'prove' that profit-incomes are positive, and capitalists exploit labourers (see, for instance, passages from Bray's writings quoted extensively by Marx, 1956, pp. 77–87).

Why under capitalism labour is not *the only source of wealth*

The Ricardian-socialist proposition 'labour is the only source of wealth' has been interpreted (e.g. Veblen, 1906, pp. 577–8; Schumpeter, 1955, p. 479) and *is* interpretable (see pp. 63–9) to say 'labour is the only source of wealth or (exchange) value'. It can also be interpreted to say 'labour is the only (ultimate) factor'. This proposition, in all its interpretations, is open to unanswerable objections as a basis for a theory of capitalist exploitation.

The proposition is *not* 'self-evident' *either* as a pure 'normative' proposition, *or* as a 'positive' (factual) proposition. Veblen's attempt to disarm objections on the ground that it is 'self-evident' in terms of neo-Hegelian *weltanschaung* is unacceptable, unless one is willing to agree that *any* statement in Hegelian dialectics is self-evident or self-validating (Veblen, 1906, pp. 585–7).

The proposition *cannot* be accepted as a 'socialist' value-judgement pure and simple, because it clearly *has* to do with *facts* about the structure of production and exchange (and distribution) in a capitalist society.

Propositions

1 Labour is the only *ultimate* source of wealth (value) – it is a verifiable statement about observable facts, but *only on a special assumption*.

2 The assumption in question is 'all products can be penultimately "reduced to" (be replaced by) products of *unassisted* labour'.

Now, Marx detected such an assumption underlying Ricardian-socialist reasoning when he criticized them for 'underestimating the importance of past materialized labour' (see pp. 55–6, 63–9). As we shall see in chapter 5, section 3 and in chapter 8, section 3, von Bortkiewicz used such a Ricardian-socialist assumption in his analysis of value and price in the Marxian system generalized to allow extended reproduction. That on the basis of proposition 2, the Ricardian-socialist proposition is valid has been explicitly noted by mathematical economists (Georgescu-Roegen, 1971, p. 290; Samuelson, 1971, pp. 400–401).

The assumption that all products are penultimately reducible to products of unassisted labour, is also the distinguishing feature of several modern 'Austrian' or 'neo-Austrian' models of production (see Hicks, 1970; Nuti, 1970).

However, whether or not we believe in an anthropological record which says that the first stone-age axe was made by 'unassisted labour', there is no doubt that the ('horizontal') physical structure of production in the nineteenth-century capitalism of the *Communist Manifesto* onwards *excludes*, as *observable reality*, proposition 2. There is also a self-contradiction involved in assuming that an economy where all products *are* so reducible, *can* be a capitalist economy *at all*, i.e. an economy where capitalists claim a (positive) share of the net product as profit-income. Thus, if corn were produced by unassisted labour, cloth and iron by corn plus labour, why should any labourer part with any portion of the net product as profit collected by capitalists?

So it is clear that an 'Austrian' (Ricardian-socialist) model is admissible for analysing problems of capitalism only if it is a valid 'parable' in terms of definition 2 (chapter 1, section 3) i.e. *if* it predicts results (about capitalist exploitation) which are also predicted by *non*-Austrian models of capitalist production.

The question therefore boils down to this: in a 'real-life' model of capitalist production, where (a) there are *no* products reducible penultimately to products of unassisted labour, and (b) no production is possible without paying profits to capitalist owners of the means of production (see chapter 6, section 6) does proposition 1 hold, i.e. is 'labour the only ultimate source of wealth (value)'?[2]

The answer is a categorical No. The fundamental reason is that in *no* 'real-life' capitalist model can labour be the 'only factor', which it should be, for simplicity, in any neo-Austrian model (as it *is* in Hicks, 1970, p. 258).

The technicalities of this negative answer are connected *first* of all, with the presence of scarce land owned by capitalist landlords, which *cannot* be got rid of as Ricardo and the Ricardian socialists tried to do in their analysis of capitalism. (The reasons for this statement will be discussed in chapter 6, section 3. Marx's *disagreement* with the Ricardian socialists on this point will be noted in pp. 63–9.)

Secondly, in a non-Austrian model of capitalist production, as defined in the question above, the following statements hold.

2. In the question, (a) does not, of course, rule out products of unassisted labour which are final consumer goods.

Statements

1 Commodities are *not* reducible to uniquely determined quantities of direct and indirect labour 'contained' in them, given by technology alone.

2 Direct and indirect labour 'contained' in commodities produced by a *given technology* fluctuate according to the pattern of *income-distribution* between workers and capitalists.

3 The pattern of fluctuation mentioned in statement 2 is *haphazard*, i.e. the total labour 'contained' in a commodity may increase, or decrease, or at first increase and then decrease, and then increase again, as different patterns of income-distribution with the same technology are considered.

The technical literature on what is somewhat unhappily called 'reduction to dated quantities of labour' (Sraffa, 1960, Part I, chapter 6)[3] must be consulted to validate statements 1–3.

The fundamental difficulty is that in a 'real-life' model of capitalist production of commodities by means of commodities, even if we ignore land,[4] 'reduction to total (direct plus indirect) labour quantities "contained" in a commodity', is given by an expression like the left side of equation **1**:

$$L_a w + L'_a w(1+r) + L'_a w(1+r)\{L''_a(1+r)\} + \ldots + L'_a w(1+r)\{L''_a(1+r)\}^n = Ap_a,$$ **1**

where:[5]

1 Commodity A (e.g. iron) has its unit price p_a, input (in natural units) into industry A is A_a, into industry B is A_b etc.,

3. The reference to 'dated' labour is unhappy and incongruous, since horizontally interdependent production in the *same* period is under consideration.

4. And intrinsic joint production of the wheat-and-straw type, which ought *not* to be ignored, and is not ignored in complete models used in later chapters.

5. The notation is Sraffa's, which is unorthodox, but is slowly coming into use. The equation is a slightly corrected version of Sraffa's 'reduction equation' (Sraffa, 1960, Part I, ch. 6, section 46, p. 35). See chapter 6, section 4, for a numerical example which makes the notation more comprehensible.

and its gross output in physical units (i.e. $A_a + A_b + \ldots$) is A, and its gross output in money terms is Ap_a. Commodity A is produced with the help of direct labour L_a (expressed as a fraction of the social labour force L) plus inputs of commodities B, C,..., etc. expressed as B_a, C_a etc. which are all reducible, however (but only at infinity) to fractions of social labour L, which is usually normalized so that $L = 1$.)

2 L_a' and L_a'' are constants (with $L_a' \neq L_a''$ and $L_a' < L$, $L_a'' < L$), whose magnitudes are determined by the physical input–output relations of the entire system of interdependent production.

3 r is the uniform rate of profit, and w is the share of wages expressed as a fraction of the 'standard national income' (which also serves as the numeraire for unit prices, and is made equal to 1 as another normalizing assumption).

4 The relation $r = R(1-w)$ holds, where R is the 'maximum rate of profit', or the lowest profit-rate corresponding to $w = 0$, which is compatible with all-positive prices, and is uniquely determined for a given technology.

5 1, 2, ..., n represents successive rounds of the 'reduction operation' (which can go on to infinity) as we replace physical commodity inputs by labour and physical commodity inputs which have produced the inputs.

Now, with the help of definitions and assumptions 1–5, it is easy to see that all the terms on the left side of the equation 1 except the first, form a converging infinite series whose common ratio is less than 1, after either w or r have been assigned a fixed value, and the other has been determined with the help of the $r = R(1-w)$ relation. But this means that although total labour 'contained' can always be calculated, its value will differ according to an exogenously fixed income-distribution pattern. *In other words, statements 1 and 2 hold.* (They would *not* hold, nor would statement 5 hold, *only* if we had a *non*-capitalist model of production of commodities by means of commodities in which $r = 0$ and $w = 1$. We are not concerned with such a model in Part One.)

In spite of the non-uniqueness of total labour 'contained' in commodities (i.e. in spite of statements 1 and 2), we could perhaps still say the Ricardian-socialist dictum that labour is the only source of wealth and value holds *approximately*, if statement 3 above did not come in the way. But it does: any hope of saying that the summed infinite series on the left side of **1**, and *a fortiori*, total labour 'contained' in Ap_a, is the greater, the larger is the profit rate r, is barred by statement 3.

To see this (it is *not* self-evident), we have to note that by manipulation, the relation $r = R(1-w)$ – which is a fundamental relation in the Sraffa system – yields (Sraffa, 1960, p. 35):

$$w = 1 - r/R. \qquad\qquad 2$$

Substitution of **2** into **1** yields:

$$L_a(1-r/R) + L_a'(1-r/R)(1+r) + L_a'(1-r/R)(1+r) \qquad 3$$
$$\{L_a''(1+r)\} + \ldots + L_a'(1-r/R)(1+r)\{L_a''(1+r)\}^n = Ap_a.$$

Now, in **3**, if a higher r *raises* the sum of total (direct plus indirect) labour 'contained' in Ap_a, by increasing $(1+r)$, $(1+r)^2, \ldots, (1+r)^n$, it *reduces* the sum of total labour contained by *decreasing* $(1-r/R)$ (since R is a constant, and r is, by definition, less than R). Thus, we have statement 3 not only confirmed, but amplified (Sraffa, 1960, p. 35).

Statement

4 As the rate of profit rises, the value of each of the labour terms is pulled in opposite directions by the rate of profits and the wage, and it moves up or down as one or the other prevails.[6]

We conclude that the derivation of the Ricardian-socialist proposition 'labour is the only source of wealth (value)' from

6. The curious fact, discovered by Sraffa (Sraffa, 1960, pp. 35–7) that the only monotonicity possible is that of a continuous *fall* in the value of a well-defined class of 'labour terms' as the profit-rate *rises*, is of no interest in the present context.

an Austrian-type model of capitalist production is a *false* parable. The proposition itself, which is an *ex natura factual* statement about a capitalist model of production, is factually false. It is therefore *not* a sound basis for an acceptable Ricardian-socialist theory of capitalist exploitation.[7]

Why on capitalistic competitive assumptions, there are no unequal exchanges between buyers and sellers of labour-power

The Ricardian-socialist theory of 'unequal exchanges' in *competitive* markets for labour-power favouring capitalists (Thompson, 1824, ch. 1, section 10, pp. 78–83, ch. 5, p. 364) is also open to objection as an *alternative* basis, independently of the one discussed in the previous section, for the Ricardian-socialist theory of capitalist exploitation.

The argument seems to be that the workers are 'at the mercy' of the capitalists, who own the means of subsistence and the physical materials needed for production (Engels in Preface to Marx, 1957, p. 13, quoting Thompson, 1824). But in *capitalistic* production (in contrast to 'petty commodity production' where owners and labourers are the same) the capitalists are *also* 'at the mercy' of the workers, in so far as they cannot produce and earn profit-incomes without employing workers.

In short, the institutional datum, that workers own no means of production, or of subsistence, is not enough, on *capitalistic* competitive assumptions, to 'prove' exploitation.

Thus, the Ricardian-socialist theory of capitalist exploitation is unacceptable because it is deficient with respect to ingredient 1 (chapter 2, section 2) of a theory of capitalist exploitation (i.e. a *definition* of capitalist exploitation), and lacking in ingredient 3 (i.e. a theory as to why there is a positive rate of capitalist exploitation in long-run equilibrium).

7. Discussions with Sukhamoy Chakravarty and correspondence with Maurice Dobb on related matters have helped clarify issues discussed in this sub-section. However, the conclusions reached are not necessarily theirs.

Marx, Marxists and the Ricardian socialists

There is a widespread tendency to underplay Marx's objections to the Ricardian-socialist ideas just criticized. This is partly because Marx and Engels were restrained in their criticism of the Ricardian socialists, as indicated by Marx's favourable references to Bray (see p. 55) and Engels's favourable references to Thompson (see p. 62). They concentrated their criticism on Ricardian-socialist ideas appearing in the writings of Proudhon (Marx, 1964), Rodbertus (Engels, 1957; Marx, 1957), of the German Lassalleans (Marx, 1949). They were also more concerned with criticizing the Ricardian-socialist demand that labour should receive 'the whole produce' in the context of a *socialist* society. But Part III of Marx's *Theories of Surplus Value* does give Marx's critical assessment of the Ricardian socialists (as already noted in p. 55 above), though only the anonymous authors of the general preface to the Marxism-Leninism Institute edition of this work seem to have noted it (Marx, 1964, p. 30).

Of course, it is generally recognized in the literature that Marx argued *against* the view that workers under competitive capitalism were victims of 'unequal exchanges', and he maintained, instead, that, on competitive capitalist assumptions, the worker *does* receive 'the value of his labour-power' (Schumpeter, 1954, p. 121). Marx is absolutely explicit on this point (e.g. Marx, 1950b, section 7, p. 385), though he did add that the 'surplus' part of labour only 'appears' to be paid for, but is 'in reality' unpaid labour (Marx, 1950b, section 9, pp. 388–9). (It is clear that the difference between the Ricardian socialists and Marx on this point is more than a mere formality, contrary to what Dobb seems to suggest (1968, p. 61). It arises because the Ricardian socialists ignored the problem of capitalist 'mystification' which Marx emphasized.)

It is also recognized (though more rarely, e.g. Schumpeter, 1956, p. 8), that in contrast to the Ricardian socialists, Marx stressed the 'historical necessity' of the capitalist as promoter of accumulation until the 'productive forces' and other 'superstructural prerequisites' mature for a revolutionary transition to socialism (Marx, 1954, chapters 24 and 32). It is worth noting that Marx even had a serious, nonsophistical, definition of the '*productivity* of capital' which was, however, an *anti*-capitalist one, fully compatible with his basic postulate that capital represents a *coercive* social power – 'capital is . . . productive (a) as a force compelling surplus labour, (b) as the absorber and appropriator (personification) of the productive powers of social labour and of the general social productive forces, such as science' (Marx, 1964, Part 1, Addenda 12, p. 380).

But there is the impression, which does not in the end seem justified, that Marx agreed that 'labour is the only source of (wealth or) value' (Schumpeter, 1954, pp. 479–80), and that for this reason, he can be called the 'greatest of the Ricardian socialists', though he got the idea directly from Ricardo,[8] and *not* from the English 'Ricardian socialists' proper. Veblen also agreed that for Marx, too 'labour is the only source of wealth or value',[9] though he traced it to Marx's neo-Hegelianism, and *not* to Ricardian-socialist writings, to which, according to him, Marx's writings bore only a 'superficial' resemblance (Veblen, 1906, pp. 577–8). The modern writer Mandel (1968, vol. 2, p. 712) also takes it for granted that Marx adopted this doctrine, without discussing its lineage.

There is also indirect evidence that the doctrine 'labour is the only source of value' is assumed implicitly at least in almost all modern expositions of Marxian value-theory. Thus, Dobb, in his classic restatement of Marxian political economy, writes, with reference to Marx's value theory: 'To say that commodities had certain exchange values was an alternative way of saying that the labour force of society was divided between occupations in a certain way . . .' (Dobb, 1968, p. 61). Since the 'labour force of society' consists of

8. Schumpeter points out, however, that the idea seems to have entered economic literature with Galiani (Schumpeter, 1955, p. 302), a late eighteenth-century writer, who is also referred to by Marx as having realized that 'value is a relation between persons' (Marx, 1954, p. 74).

9. Veblen stresses, however, a *related* Ricardian-socialist doctrine, viz. 'the labourer's claim to the whole of his product'.

'living labour', this is only a slightly oblique way of saying that exchange values in equilibrium allocation of the 'labour force' are equal to 'labour-contained' quantities. As we have seen above (pp. 56–62), this is the Ricardian-socialist proposition 1 – labour is the only source of value – which holds only on the (unrealistic and untenable) proposition 2 – all products are penultimately reducible to products of unassisted labour.[10] Paul Sweezy, in the earlier one of his two restatements of the Marxian theory of capitalism (Sweezy, 1949),[11] has also claimed that the dictum 'labour is the only source of value' is true if we isolate the 'qualitative' value problem from the 'quantitative' one (Sweezy, 1949, chapter 2, sections i, iv and vi).[12]

Now, this near-unanimous verdict of the authorities, which has hardly been challenged for nearly seventy years, is certainly *not* based on a hasty misreading of Marx.

In lectures to workers in 1847 and 1865 (Marx, 1950a; 1950b) and in *Capital*, volume one (Marx, 1954, p. 46), there are categorical references to the role of human labour as 'creator' of exchange values, of exchange values being equal to 'crystals of social labour' which commodities contain etc. (There is even the assumption, unambiguously made, in *Wage Labour and Capital* (Marx, 1950a, section 2), that production is carried on by unassisted labour.) It is also true that Marx says in his first research-level work, his 1859 *Critique of Political Economy* (Marx, 1970, p. 35) that 'it is a tautology to say that labour is the only source of exchange values and consequently of wealth, in so far as the latter consists of exchange values'.

But, firstly, Marx insisted that this tautology did *not* hold

10. Actually, Dobb implicitly adopts this assumption also when he interprets Marx's 'prices of production' as being equal to 'wages plus an average or normal profit' (Dobb, 1968, p. 62).
11. His more recent restatement (Baran and Sweezy, 1966) will be discussed in chapter 9 of this book.
12. In this book, Sweezy pioneered with another 'false parable' which gives 'labour as the only source of value' along with a *positive* profit-rate: the case of 'equal organic composition' of variable and constant capital' (Sweezy, 1949, pp. 70, 109–111) to which a brief reference will be made again in chapter 5.

when, with a positive profit-rate ('surplus value'), non-uniform 'organic composition of capital', and scarce land are considered. He developed his 'prices of production' theory and his theory of 'market values' in *Capital*, volume three, to handle such cases (to be discussed in chapter 5).

Secondly, in the key chapter entitled 'Conversion of Surplus Value in Capital', in *Capital*, volume one, Marx emphatically rejected the notion (attributed by him to errors in the writings of Smith and Ricardo, which were repeated by John Stuart Mill) that 'all surplus value that is changed into capital becomes variable capital' (Marx, 1954, pp. 590–1). He maintained, instead, that 'so far from this being the case, the surplus value, like the original capital, divides itself into constant and variable capital, into the means of production and labour-power' (Marx, 1954, pp. 589–90). Marx adhered more or less consistently to this view when he defined surplus value as what is left of the value of the product, after deducting *both* constant and variable capital (e.g. *Capital*, volume three, chapter 9).[13] This Marxian view played an important role in his analysis of the reproduction process. (Marx emphasized his differences with Sismondi on this point, and accused him of not 'saying *one* scientific word, . . . contributing one iota to the clarification of the problem' of 'the relation of capital to revenue' (Marx, 1957, Part 3, ch. 19, section 3, p. 391; see also Lenin, 1963; Chakravarty 1969, pp. 13–14). But the clear implication of this Marxian doctrine on the theory of capital and reproduction for the theory of *value* is that variable and constant capital are jointly productive of value and surplus value.

13. Of course, there *are* a few passages in which Marx defines 'surplus' in Ricardian-socialist fashion, as the value of output minus variable capital (ignoring constant capital), e.g. 'productive labour, in its meaning for capitalist production, is wage-labour which, exchanged against the variable part of capital . . . reproduces not only this part of capital (or the value of its own labour-power), but in addition produces surplus value for the capitalist' (Marx, 1964, chapter 4, sec. 1). Passages like this one may cause confusion, which should be cleared up, and not made the excuse for overlooking essential differences between Marx and the Ricardian socialists.

Thirdly, and finally, in his last major work on economic theory, *Critique of the Gotha Programme* written in 1875 (Marx 1949a, p. 17) Marx *denounces* the formulation of the German socialist Ferdinand Lassalle that 'labour is the source of all wealth' as a 'bourgeois idea' because, to attribute 'supernatural creative powers to labour' is to conceal the fact that 'labour depends upon nature', and that this suits the capitalists who have made themselves the owners of the 'material conditions of labour'.

In the foregoing, a subtle distinction between the propositions 'labour is the source of all wealth' and 'labour is the source of all exchange values', made by Dobb (1968, p. 55) and Medio (1972, p. 315), has been disregarded. Dobb makes a sharp contrast between Marx's acceptance of 'capital or rather the concrete instruments in which stored-up labour was embodied [as] creative of wealth or riches' (or utilities), and his alleged denial of 'land or capital [as] productive of value'. But in the very first sentence of *Capital*, volume one, Marx says 'the wealth of those societies in which the capitalist mode of production prevails, presents itself as an "immense accumulation of commodities"'. He adds in the next page: 'the utility of a thing makes it a use value. . . . In the form of society we are about to consider, they are in addition, the material depositories of exchange value' (1954, pp. 35–6). In short, Marx in *Capital*, volume one, analysed a 'pure' capitalist society, in which wealth (other than 'free goods') or use values (utilities) appeared as commodities having exchange value. In such a society, if constant capital is creative of utilities, it is also creative of exchange values, like variable capital (labour) and (scarce) land.

Dobb (1968, p. 55) seeks to deny the proposition just presented with an analogy which seems to be false:

Ricardo [did not] deny that land even uncultivated might yield utilities. But this was not to say that land or capital were productive of value. In fact, the more lavish was nature with the fruits of the earth, the *less* value were the latter likely to have and the *less* chance was there that land would yield a rent.

No doubt Ricardo affirmed that land yielded utilities, but land rent did not 'enter into' price (a theory which will be discussed in chapter 6, section 3). But this clarifies nothing about Marx's views on land or capital being a source of use value and/or of exchange value. In fact, on Marx's assumption of a 'pure' capitalist society, *if* land is a 'source of use value', it is *also* a source of exchange value (implied in Marx, 1957, chapter 7, section 1, and more explicitly in Marx, 1949a, p. 17).

Conclusion

Fortunately, the misconception about Marx's stand *vis-à-vis* the dictum that 'labour is the only source of value' is not universal. The importance that Marx attached to fixed capital used in production was noted in the modern literature as early as in 1938. Leontief, who was, we are informed by Samuelson (1971, p. 424) taught by von Bortkiewicz, noted, in 1938, the apparent paradox in the fact that 'the dean of bourgeois economists (Bohm-Bawerk) insisted on theoretical reduction of all capital goods to pure labour; he was opposed by the formidable proponent of the labour theory of value (Marx) in the role of a defender of the independent primary function of fixed capital' (Leontief, 1966, pp. 77–8).

More recently, in 1960, Sraffa noted that Marx denied the existence of 'ultimate' commodities produced by pure labour without means of production except land, and that on this denial was based Marx's emphatic rejection of Adam Smith's 'claim ... that the price of every commodity "either immediately or ultimately" resolves itself (... without leaving any commodity residue) into wages, profit and rent' (Sraffa, 1960, p. 94).

Actually, of course, there is no paradox involved in these differences between Smith and Bohm-Bawerk on one side and Marx on the other. As Marx said in the neglected passage in the *Critique of the Gotha Programme* (1949a, p. 17) referred to above, the attribution of supernatural creative powers to labour suited bourgeois interests who benefited from the doctrines of Smith and Bohm-Bawerk. On the other hand,

Marx, by emphasizing the role of constant (circulating and fixed) capital, along with variable capital (labour) in capitalist production, by no means attributed any supernatural 'value-creating' role to the capitalist (see chapter 4). Still less did Marx attribute such a role to the capitalist landlord, who did not, according to Marx, have even the historically 'transient' role of the industrial or commercial capitalist (see chapter 5, section 4).

4 Modern neo-Marxian theories and capitalist exploitation

In modern controversies on the theory of capital and distributive shares (referred to in section 2 above) a revulsion against notions of 'class harmony' in competitive capitalism is strongly reflected.

Sketches of theories of capital and distributive shares have been put forward which incorporate notions of 'class conflict' even under *competitive* capitalist conditions. For this reason, they are distinct from the more amorphous 'politically neutral' theories of distributive shares under capitalism which stress the role of 'monopoly' elements (to be discussed in the next section).

However, these theories are distinct also from the Marxian theories (though they are in some respects analytically superior), and are also *incomplete* as theories of capitalist exploitation.

The central feature of these theories is the 'perennial gale' of worker–capitalist class antagonism. This is derived, in the first place, from an *inverse* wage–profit relation (given the technology), which is now recognized (see chapter 7, section 2) as one of the basic theorems of economic theory, on the same footing as the proposition that two and two makes four. In the second place, the importance of this finding is not submerged by the fact that with improving technology, *both* workers' wages and capitalists' profits *may* rise. *Before* and *after* the improvement, the distributive shares will be fixed, at least in *money* terms, 'exogenously' by the terms of the class struggle. Moreover, it has been pointed out (Nuti, 1970), that by pressing Keynesian short-run analysis into service and by relying on the 'money illusion', capitalists can, through monetary manipulation, 'impose' the pattern of distributive shares in 'real' terms desired by them.

These theories are understandably attractive for those who are weary of the 'class harmony' message of a bourgeois-apologetic interpretation of neo-classical marginal productivity theories of distribution, or are dissatisfied with the rather aimless 'anti-monopoly' edge of these theories when extended to the case of 'monopolistic competition' (as we shall see in the next section, these theories could justify a struggle against the workers organized in 'monopolistic trade unions' as much as against capitalist trusts).

These theories also mark an analytical improvement on Marx's theory in two respects. First, they establish, rigorously, that 'capital is not a quantity but a social relation', whereas Marx only asserted that capital is a (coercive) social relation, but in his production models, capital is *both* an unchanging quantity (invariant with respect to the profit-rate) *and* a coercive social relation (Bhaduri, 1969, p. 534). Second, these theories are based on a rigorous mathematical proof of the inverse wage–profit relation, already referred to, which Marx asserted rather than proved (see chapter 7, section 2).

But these neo-Marxian theories of capital and of distributive shares contain only incomplete fragments of a theory of capitalist exploitation under competitive conditions.

The first ingredient missing in these theories is a *definition* of capitalist exploitation, i.e. ingredient 1 (chapter 2, section 3). This is essential to convert a theory of class conflict into a theory of capitalist exploitation. (In its absence, distributive shares may be altered through fierce class struggle, but it would be impossible to tell who was exploiting whom.) Nell (1967, p. 19) is the only writer who makes an explicit value judgement defining capitalist exploitation as occurring whenever a share of the net product is claimed by the capitalists, since 'the only service the owner of capital renders to industry is the service of permitting it to be owned by him'. This is the Ricardian-socialist value judgement which asserts the workers' claim to the 'whole produce' (Thompson, 1824, chapter 1, section 10). It is less acceptable than the weaker, 'prescriptive' propositions on which Marx's and post-Marxian definitions of capitalist exploitations, to be considered later, are based.

The second missing ingredient is ingredient 3, i.e. a reason as to *why* the profit-rate, and, *a fortiori*, the rate of capitalist exploitation, must be *positive* in long-run equilibrium under competitive conditions. No better candidate for this role seems to have been found so far than a self-perpetuating long-run Malthusian equilibrium wage at a subsistence level (Samuelson, 1971, pp. 415, 419, 422; 1972, p. 53). But there are technical difficulties with a minimum-of-subsistence wage notion fitted into a steady-state, golden-age, permanent equilibrium – in such equilibrium, the profit-rate *could* be zero (Samuelson, 1971, pp. 407–8). Moreover, it would make a neo-Marxian theory decidedly *non*-Marxian because natural (demographic) factors, instead of *capitalist coercion* (a 'man-made' problem) would be responsible for the exploitation of workers. Indeed, logically, such a theory of 'capitalist exploitation' would hardly be distinguishable from an exploitationless class-harmony based on long-run equilibrium of neo-classical bourgeois apologetics. Robinson's reliance (1965, pp. 178–81) on 'human nature and the structure of society' to close this gap in the theory is hardly a solution of the problem, since the meaning of the phrase (which probably *is* no more than a phrase) is not at all clear.

5 The Pigovian theory of exploitation

As indicated in chapter 2, section 4, ingredient 1 (the defin-itional assumption) in the Pigovian theory of exploitation is the value judgement that there is exploitation whenever the unit price of a 'factor' is less than the value of its marginal physical product.

However, it is just *this* value judgement which is the basic weakness of the theory. Its weakness with respect to ingredient 2 – a proof of 'existence' (and 'uniqueness') of equilibrium in a Walrasian general equilibrium model including mono-polies – has been removed by recent progress made by Inada

(1966) and Batra (1972). It must also be counted a weakness if, when interpreted as a theory of exploitation, it states no reason as to why, in long-run equilibrium, the rate of exploitation *must* be positive.

The value judgement – 'there is exploitation whenever the unit price of the factor is less than the value of its marginal physical product' – is completely *arbitrary* and completely *general*. It is almost impossible to interpret it as a theory of *capitalist* exploitation, or even as a theory of 'monopoly-capitalist' exploitation, which is what might seem, from common sense, to make it superior, as a 'realistic' theory of capitalist exploitation, to all others.

Why is this value judgement a completely *Robbinsian* one (of the type discarded by our 'rule of theorizing', rule 1 chapter 1, section 1)? Because it is *not* unanimously acceptable on strictly ethical grounds. Even if unit prices of factors *were* equal to the value of marginal physical products, and there is no 'exploitation' in the Pigovian sense, the 'ethical justness' of the marginal productivity mode of distribution would not be irrefutably proved (Samuelson, 1971, p. 423). It was pointed out long ago (Lerner, 1939, pp. 558, 565–6) that the Pigovian definition sanctifies what may be objectionable on ethical grounds, viz. income inequality favouring the 'elite' in a socialist society where there is no private property in the means of production.

The point just made draws attention to the completely *general* scope of the Pigovian definition of exploitation. Exploitation is regarded solely as an outgrowth of 'monopoly' elements in a system (whether socialist or capitalist). On this basis, in a capitalist society, either workers, or capitalists or landlords could, in principle, be declared to be the 'victims of exploitation'. Thus, we have the statement in Robinson's standard discussion of the theory: 'In so far as labour is strongly organized in trade unions while the supply of land to a particular industry is often perfectly [14] elastic, it is probable

14. An obvious misprint occurred in the original in that the word 'imperfectly' was printed instead of 'perfectly'. This I have changed.

that land is more exploitable than labour' (Robinson, 1969, ch. 27, especially section 7, p. 319). In the passage that follows immediately – 'but the factor of production which is at once the poorest and the most exploitable is unorganized unskilled labour' – there is a dubious attempt to pass off the Pigovian general theory of 'monopolistic exploitation' as a theory of *capitalist* exploitation, on the basis of the 'facts' of the case.

The attempt is dubious for more than one reason. First, it combines ('conflates') two definitions of exploitation which have, strictly speaking, nothing to do with one another (viz. the Pigovian definition, and a definition which says whenever there is income-inequality, the higher income-earners are 'exploiting' the lower-income earners). Secondly, this double definition being the basis, even if unskilled workers were identified as the 'most exploited' class in capitalist societies, it could easily be argued, in strict logic that 'for equal welfare of the worst-off individuals, the second worst-off individuals etc. . . . maximize the welfare of the best-off' (i.e. the 'mono-poly-capitalist' individuals). (This is John Rawls's well-known maximin rule in its lexicographic version (Rawls, 1971, pp. 42–3; Sen, 1970, p. 138). Nor will the alternative 'make the worst-off best-off' reduce 'exploitation' defined in terms of income inequality, unambiguously (Sen, 1970, p. 139).

Thus, unlike the other theories discussed in this chapter, the Pigovian theory of exploitation is not a socialist theory, and is 'neutral' in the struggle between capitalism and socialism. It turns out to be a 'toothless' theory from the viewpoint of an anti-capitalist, militant, class-struggle, which is the central message of the 'neo-Marxian' theories discussed in section 4, though Robinson seems to be riding *both* these horses at the same time (Bose, 1972, pp. 219–20).

A Marxian assessment of the alternative non-Marxian theories of exploitation, attempted in this chapter, is a controversial matter on which we have not heard the last word. However, if the suggestion that they are ill-defined and unsatisfactory is accepted, they cannot kill interest in the Marxian and post-Marxian theories of capitalist exploitation, to which we turn in the next four chapters. (Applications of the post-Marxian theory to deal with state monopoly-capitalist and private monopoly-capitalist phenomena, much emphasized in the Pigovian theory, will be found in chapters 9–11.)

4 Marx's 'De-mystified' Theory of Value, Capital and Exploitation:

A Bird's Eye View

1 Introduction

The previous chapter may have left the reader dissatisfied with non-Marxian theories, and also curious about the Marxian theory of capitalist exploitation which, he will perhaps now allow, differs from the non-Marxian theories in essentials.

In this chapter, we do to the Marxian theory what we did to the non-Marxian theories in the previous chapter, that is, make a critical assessment on the basis of the general criteria for assessing alternative theories formulated in chapter 1, section 3. This chapter, then, contains a synoptic statement and assessment of the Marxian theory, purged of Ricardian-socialist admixtures, followed by the sketch of a post-Marxian reconstruction. The rest of Part One is devoted to an elaboration of the contents of this chapter, some of which goes into some technical details.

2 A concise statement

The Marxian theory of capitalist exploitation is elaborate but water-tight, with a structure consisting of the four essential ingredients, listed in chapter 2, section 3, considered to be common for all theories of capitalist exploitation.

Purged of Ricardian-socialist admixtures (for reasons stated in chapter 3, pp. 63–9), the Marxian theory consists of the following basic ingredients.

Statements

1 Definitional propositions:

(a) The institutional specification of a capitalist society as one in which workers 'own' only their 'labour-power' or capacity for labour, and the capitalists own all the means of production (as also the wage-fund for labourers, and, in *Capital*, volume three, scarce land). (This is the basis of the coercive power of capital, even when 'labour-power' is bought and sold in the labour market under strictly competitive conditions.)

(b) The labour-power of the 'productive labourers'[1] is a commodity (marketable product) which, when used in the production process, along with the instruments and 'subjects'[2] of production supplied by the capitalists (and preserved or replaced in the production-process), produces a *surplus value*,[3] which the capitalists use their coercive power (acquired when they 'bought' labour-power) to appropriate.

(c) The appropriation of surplus value by capitalists represents *exploitation*, not only because it is contrary to the socialist 'sense of morality' (which Marx shared), but because Marx's analytical theory of capitalism predicts the 'inevitable revolutionary collapse of the capitalist system', and its replacement by an exploitation-free socialist society (Engels, n.d., pp. 12–13).[4] (The institutional specification (a), and the definitional propositions (b) about surplus value and (c) about exploitation, together yield the Marxian proposition that

1. Marx's '*un*productive labourers' are labourers engaged in the pure process of circulation, e.g. in accounting, book-keeping, marketing, conversion of products into money, money into means of production etc. (Marx, 1959, ch. 17, pp. 283–4).
2. Defined, roughly, as land and raw materials (Marx, 1954, ch. 7, section 2).
3. Defined as the excess of the product of the total number of labour-hours a capitalist acquires the right to make use of when he 'buys' labour-power, over the product of the labour-hours he 'pays for' (as wage advances) to restore the labourer's capacity for labour (Marx, 1954, chapter 7, section 2).
4. We disregard, of course, the argument sometimes used by Engels that the 'inevitable collapse' was also a *fact of life*, proceeding 'before our eyes'. Such affirmations of subjective faith, or propagandist clarion calls about events play no essential role in the pure logic of Marxian theory.

there is exploitation when the surplus value (or the sum of property incomes) is positive in long-run competitive equilibrium.)

2 Propositions which attempt to incorporate capitalist exploitation, as defined by statement 1, in a general equilibrium theory of production and circulation, with a solution, as a 'first approximation' in *Capital*, volume one (Marx, 1954) in terms of long-run equilibrium values coinciding with 'labour-embodied costs', and a *final* solution in *Capital*, volume three (Marx, 1959) in terms of equilibrium values coinciding with 'prices of production', a uniform average profit-rate, and differential, absolute and 'monopoly' rents for scarce lands.

The method employed by Marx was explicitly to take into account the well-known complications Ricardo ran into in his attempts to show that long-run equilibrium values coincided with, or were mainly determined by 'costs' measured in terms of labour required in production. These complications arose once simplifying assumptions were relaxed to admit fixed and circulating capital of varying 'durability' (and varying rates of turnover) which were combined in varying proportions in producing different products (Sraffa, 1951, section 5). (Marx explicitly took into account complications introduced by scarce land which Ricardo essentially tried to abstract from even in his final model, with the help of his theory of differential rent.)

Marx reduced all these complications to the *single* complication arising from the *non-uniformity*, in different industries or branches of the economy (including agriculture) of the '*organic composition of (total) capital*', expressed in terms of the ratio of the labour-embodied in wage-goods ('variable capital') to fixed and circulating capital ('constant capital'). In the context of free transferability of resources, including labour, over the long-run, the equilibrium condition of a uniform profit-rate is then imposed. The result is the 'transformation' of outputs expressed in labour-embodied 'costs' plus notional (potential) *non*-uniform profit-rates (reflecting non-uniform organic composition of capital) *into* outputs expressed in 'prices of production' (which are labour-embodied 'costs' adjusted to ensure a uniform profit-rate) (Marx, 1959, chapters 8–10, in Parts 2 and 4).

3 A statement of two, more or less independent reasons as to *why* surplus value (or profit-incomes as a simplified indicator of surplus value) *must* be positive over the long-run, and exploitation must occur, in a competitive capitalist economy. (The first of these reasons has to do with the Marxian theory of a 'labour reserve army' under capitalism, which Lange incorporated in *his* theory of capitalist exploitation (as noted in chapter 3, section 2). The second has to do with the Marxian postulate about the basic motive-force of capitalist production, viz. the 'passion for accumulation'. *Both* these theories – which are quite unrelated to each other – are discussed further in chapter 6, section 6, where reasons are given for discarding the first and adopting the second.)

3 A concise assessment

An investigation, whose main results are presented in the rest of Part One, and extended in Parts Two and Three of this book, suggests that there is nothing very wrong with Marx's definition of exploitation under competitive capitalism (the amendment made in chapter 6, section 6 when defining capitalist exploitation in 'post-Marxian' terms is minor).

This is also true of ingredient 3 (chapter 2, section 3) in the Marxian theory, i.e. his reason for maintaining that capitalist exploitation must occur in long-run equilibrium under competitive conditions (as already indicated in the last section. This too will be discussed in chapter 6, section 6).

It is also claimed in chapter 7 that at least one long-run tendency under capitalism predicted by Marx, viz. the inverse relation between wages and profits deserves serious attention as an empirically testable hypothesis.

In short, it is found that ingredients 1, 2 and 4 of the Marxian theory of capitalist exploitation under competitive conditions stands up well to criticism, even if ingredient 3, i.e. his attempted reconciliation of his theory of capitalist exploitation with a theory of long-run equilibrium values under competitive capitalism, does not.

Indeed, it turns out (details are given in chapter 5) that Marx's 'transformation problem', whose solution was to provide, or so Marx thought, a finally corrected 'de-mystified' post-Ricardian general equilibrium system incorporating capitalist exploitation, is both a *falsely*-constructed problem, and also an *irrelevant* one, at least so far as a theory of capitalist exploitation is concerned.

The criticism just made has nothing to do with several minor faults found with Marx's attempted solution of the transformation problem on which writers have concentrated for nearly 100 years. The first of these is the generally admitted formal mistake Marx made in his own attempt at solving the problem. He recognized the need for, but did not work out, a procedure for the simultaneous determination of the unknowns in 'prices of production' models. This particular mistake is easily remedied, and *has* been remedied in various 'algebraic' solutions of the problem in the past half-century or more. The second, much stressed by some writers, is the assumption of an 'equal rate of surplus value' in all branches of the economy (Samuelson, 1957, p. 890; Sweezy, 1949, chapter 4, p. 65). The third is the assumption of 'equality of total values and total prices' of all commodities produced by the system made by Marx and some contributors to the debate on the transformation problem (Winternitz, 1948; Sweezy, 1949, pp. 115–23). These are *not* the crucial defects.

Nor is the 'transformation problem' of Marxian exploitation theory to be regarded as a falsely-constructed problem because of the objection that to calculate 'labour-embodied values' one *must* first know 'prices of production' so that the entire procedure is meaningless (Robinson, 1950, p. 362). For reasons which have been touched upon in chapter 3, section 3 and will be referred to again in chapter 5, this is simply not true, mathematically speaking. (The problem *is* a mathematical one, whether one likes it or not, and whether or not one is willing to give Marx credit for rare mathematical insight.)

The real trouble is that both Marx's own construction of his 'transformation' problem, as well as post-Marx 'corrected' solutions of the problem, violate rule 1 (chapter 1, section 3) – the 'is' propositions admitted . . . in an economic theory must exclude mythical (fictional) terms which are not . . . observable in fact or in principle.

Now, as noted in chapter 2, section 2, Marx set himself the aim of 'de-mystifying' capitalist realities, as the cornerstone of a *materialistic* interpretation of history (as opposed to one based on Hegelian idealism). In a more general way, Marx and Engels believed in the 'primacy of matter over mind' (Engels, 1949, p. 337). Unlike the 'mechanistic materialists' they emphasized that reality was 'matter in motion', i.e. it consisted of 'processes'; but they added that 'it was necessary first to examine things before it was possible to examine processes' (Engels, 1949, p. 351). They *unambiguously* upheld the materialistic aphorism 'mercilessly to sacrifice every idealist crochet which could not be brought into harmony with the facts conceived in their own and not in a fantastic interconnection' (Engels, 1949, pp. 349–50).

It is therefore ironical that the same Marx constructed his 'transformation problem' – whose solution was to be a master-stroke of 'de-mystification' – on the assumption that 'indirect labour' embodied in commodity inputs required for producing commodities were as easily observable as 'direct labour' and commodity inputs (in their natural units). But this is simply not true (see chapter 3, section 3 and chapter 5). All that modern theory has proved, and proved *conclusively*, is that 'indirect' labour-embodied quantities are 'operational' in the sense that they are empirically *calculable*, provided only that directly observable quantities of 'direct' labour (e.g. in man-hours) and commodity inputs in their natural units (e.g. tons of iron ore) are known. Moreover, modern theory has also proved that 'indirect' labour-embodied calculations will *not*, as Marx assumed, consist only of pure labour cost, but *include* surplus labour on account of 'surplus value' or profit in a capitalist competitive model with positive profit (Sraffa, 1960, ch. 3, section 14, p. 12).[5]

Post-Marx 'corrected' solutions of the transformation problem have retained Marx's assumption just criticized. Moreover, as we shall see in chapter 5, section 5, they do not seem to have a method of handling scarce land, so that they violate rule 6 (chapter 1, section 3) which permits *abstraction from* scarce land provided only that successful 'transformation' is also demonstrated in a final model which *includes* scarce land. Thus these post-Marx solutions, though logically impeccable, and fitted out with 'existence' proofs, are as irrelevant for a theory of capitalist exploitation under competitive conditions as Marx's own.

However, the century-long 'transformation debate' has produced three results on the credit side of the ledger.

First, it has been proved, conclusively, that corresponding to each possible level of (positive) profit-rate, there is a unique solution in terms of all-positive prices, for any viable[6] technology represented by a set of production equations of commodities by means of commodities (including direct labour) in which all the constants are expressed in natural physical units. As we shall note in chapter 14, section 1, Marx's presumption that a solved 'transformation problem' could validate his theory of capitalist exploitation was somewhat like the discovery of America by Columbus (who was looking for, but did not find, India). It has applications for assessing the performance of a *socialist* economy: comparing the benefits of alternative price formulae which are available to a centralized socialist economy (but not to a capitalist economy), e.g. alternative price-systems based on incomes distributed according to material costs, wage costs, or to

5. Only if the profit-rate is notionally (and artificially in a capitalist economy which must have a positive profit-rate) at zero, will 'labour-embodied' coincide with 'labour cost' (Sraffa, 1960).
6. Which produces a surplus of at least one commodity and a deficit of none (Sraffa, 1960, chapter 1, section 3, p. 5, n. 1).

stock of capital (Kyn, Sekerka and Heijl, 1967, sections i and ii; Brody, 1965, pp. 58–66).

Second, a rather more promising outcome than the proof of the existence of alternative price formulae usable in a socialist economy, is the discovery, attributed to von Bortkiewicz (Pasinetti, 1960, p. 128, quoting Sraffa), of sectors of an economy whose products – 'luxury goods' (von Bortkiewicz), 'non-basics' (Sraffa) – do not determine the (uniform) rate of profit and all prices in the system. This lends precision to the old, but inchoate notion going back to the physiocrats, and very much in evidence in Marx, of 'unproductive labour' engaged in 'unproductive' production processes. As we shall see (chapters 9–13) this notion has a wide range of applications in contemporary economies, whether capitalist or socialist.

Third, the post-Marxian 'transformation debate' has *not* yielded a proof that Marx's failure, or the failure of later writers on the subject, to reconcile his notion of capitalist exploitation with an acceptable theory of long-run equilibrium values under competitive capitalist conditions is *intrinsic*. On the contrary, analytical interest in the Marxian effort has been kept alive by a narrowing of the issues, and by strong pointers to a truly 'corrected' theory thrown up by the debate. (These pointers originate in the incisive criticisms of both Marx and his critics, made *both* by the 'constructive' authors of the post-Marxian algebraic solutions, notably by von Bortkiewicz, and also by the destructive sceptics, notably Samuelson.)

4 A sketch of a post-Marxian reconstruction

The pointers thrown up by the 'transformation' debate are that instead of getting bogged down in solving 'transformation problems' (which are irrelevant for proving capitalist exploitation), an attempt should be made to incorporate Marxian capitalist exploitation in a *post*-Marxian general interdependence or general equilibrium model of competitive capitalism,[7] by concentrating on *three* essentials.

7. Why the post-Marxian model of general interdependence is

Rules

1 The model must be based on the notion of simultaneous determination of the unknowns of the system (as modern, multisector models are).

2 The constant terms in the system must be expressed as observable quantities of various commodities (including direct labour-power), appearing in their natural units (so that the need to transform imaginary, unobserved 'indirect labour' quantities into their equilibrium prices is done away with).

3 Proofs of existence (and, preferably, of uniqueness) of long-run equilibrium must be worked out to cover cases of fixed capital and scarce land used in production (because a theory of exploitation which does not take these into account is incomplete, and may be false).

A special type of multisector general equilibrium model, dating from the publication by Sraffa of his *Production of Commodities by Means of Commodities* in 1960, meets the requirements just listed. (So also, to some extent, do other classes of modern linear multisector models of capitalist production (e.g. Schwartz, 1961). Why the models of Sraffa's theory of interdependent commodity production is preferred in the present study, is discussed in chapter 6, section 1.)

The commodity production theory, as indicated by several references already made in this study, has had an indirect or direct impact on Marxian economic theory in *three* ways so far.

First, there are attempts to interpret it in such a way as to validate, more or less, Marx's *own* method of reconciling (competitive) capitalist equilibrium and exploitation theory (Meek, 1961; Dobb, 1967, p. 258; 1970, p. 12; 1972, pp. 208–20; Medio, 1972, pp. 312–44). (In some of these interpretations (e.g. Dobb, 1972, pp. 214–15) it is von Bortkiewicz's 'reconciliation', with the help of a neo-Austrian model of equilibrium, which is distinct from Marx's own, as

referred to as a 'general equilibrium' model, in spite of major differences with neo-classical general equilibrium models, is explained in chapter 1, section 5.

we shall see in chapter 5, section 3, that is validated, rather than Marx's.) Why these interpretations are disregarded in the present study is explained, partly in chapter 5 and in the critique of the Ricardian-socialists in chapter 3, section 3.

Some very recent attempts at apparent validation of Marx's 'reconciliation' procedure with the help of *non*-Austrian models of production amalgamated with an assumption about a composite 'subsistence' wage-good may be said to belong to this type of interpretation of Sraffa's or von Neumann's modern models of interdependent production (Samuelson, 1972, pp. 409–10, 420–21; Morishima, 1973, Part 2, sections 5 and 6). In the first exercise, its status as a mere curiosum (and *not* a valid parable according to definition 2, chapter 1, section 3) of Marx's method of 'reconciliation' validated on these terms is *rightly* stressed on the ground that it does not survive the dropping of simplifying assumptions which abstract from use of scarce land, heterogeneous labour etc. In the second, the stress is on the inferiority of the 'validated' Marx model to the von Neumann model which does *not* provide for a uniform rate of exploitation in all sectors of the economy and insists on handling capital goods as joint products etc. (Morishima, 1973, Parts 1 and 5, sections 13 and 14). (In the second exercise, for some unexplained reason, the objection that the von Neumann model itself is no more than a curiosum, since it disregards the use of scarce land in production pointed out long ago (Champernowne, 1968, p. 237) is ignored.) Thus, these exercises merely give the Marxian reconciliation of exploitation and equilibrium theory a long rope; they do not validate it. However, these explorations in the formal properties of the models of modern mathematical economic theory are exceptionally thorough. They yield, as by-products, insights into 'dual duality, of one between physical and value systems, and the other between physical and price systems' (Morishima, 1973, Part 1, Introduction), the 'exploitation frontier' (Morishima, 1973, Part 2, section 6), alternative tax policies for a socialist economy (Samuelson, 1971, Part 1, pp. 402–4). Some of these are used in later chapters of this book.

The second interpretation of modern commodity-production theory is represented by 'neo-Marxian' theories of (competitive) capitalist equilibrium which place central emphasis on the role of the worker-capitalist class struggle, which is also a central feature of Marxian capitalist exploitation theory. They originate in Sraffa's own early interpretation of his commodity production theory to explode the apologetic notion of capital as a fixed 'quantity' determined independently of the profit-rate, which is to be found in some versions of Walrasian and Austrian theories of competitive capitalist equilibrium (Sraffa, 1960, p. 38; 1962, pp. 477–79; 1963, pp. 305–6, 325). These theories represent a major advance on Marx's own theory. But why they are incomplete as theories of capitalist exploitation under competitive conditions has been discussed already in chapter 3, section 4 and need not be repeated here.

However, there is a third possible interpretation of modern commodity-production theory. By this interpretation, its results can be used to construct a *post-Marxian*, properly 'de-mystified', integrated theory of value, capital and exploitation (Bose, 1971, pp. 313–15, pp. 320–34).

Ingredient 1 of such a post-Marxian theory, i.e. its definitional propositions, can consist of Marx's own definitional propositions (given in section 2), with *two* amendments.

First, in statement 1, (a) and (c) are retained, but (b) is replaced: surplus value is now re-defined to mean aggregate 'excess production'[8] or the surplus product of the system of interdependent commodity production taken as a whole, i.e. the excess of the output of at least one commodity (and a deficit of none) over the (aggregate) inputs of these commodities.[9]

8. This differs from the 'surplus product' in Marx's – or in some of the later 'transformation' models – which is defined as what is left over after deducting the added-up values of wage-goods and producer goods consumed or used in each sector (as well as in the aggregate in the whole economy), everything being expressed in terms of embodied-labour.

9. See Bose, 1971, p. 314; Samuelson, 1971, Part II, p. 418. The point was made earlier by Robinson, 1950, p. 362.

The second amendment replaces statement 3 by statements 1–5 (chapter 6, section 6) to specify *why*, in a post-Marxian equilibrium–exploitation model, the profit rate and land rents *must* be positive, why wages cannot swallow up the whole of the net product or 'excess production' of the system, and why exploitation *must* occur in long-run competitive capitalist equilibrium. (The commodity-production theory itself leaves this issue completely open, by merely saying that either the wage share or the profit-rate must be taken as a datum, so that there can be a determinate solution of the simultaneous equations system (Sraffa, 1960, p. 33.) The effect of this second amendment is to 'close the gap' in the post-Marxian theory by relying solely on the capitalists' 'passion to accumulate' stressed by Marx.

Investigations made in chapter 6, section 2–5 suggest that a post-Marxian theory has no serious trouble with *its* ingredient 2, i.e. a set of propositions validating an integration of competitive-capitalist equilibrium–exploitation theory, to replace the troublesome statement 2 proposition of the Marxian theory.

Thus, the post-Marxian 'de-mystified' theory of value, capital and exploitation under competitive conditions is satisfactory as regards its ingredients 1–3. As we shall see in Part Two, it also has ingredient 4, i.e. a number of applications (predictions) about capitalist and socialist societies, not excluding an explanation of the 'geneses' of capitalist colonialism, imperialism, neo-imperialism and a *non*-imperialistic monopolistic capitalism.

5 Reconciliation of Marxian Capitalist Exploitation–Equilibrium Theory:

A Critique

1 Background

As already indicated in chapter 2, section 1, Marx linked his capitalist exploitation theory with a competitive equilibrium theory so as to demonstrate that capitalism was a workable system of exploitation of man by man, comparable to feudalism. This was essential from the standpoint of Marxian 'scientific socialism'. The idea that 'private vices [could be] public virtues' as Mandeville wrote in 1723 (Harth, 1970, p. 76) and could serve as the basis of a community's economic life, instead of (feudal) authoritarianism or ('utopian socialist') altruism, had first to be established *before* 'capitalist vices' and the capitalist system could be attacked.

The pursuit of this aim, which Smith and Ricardo had also set before themselves, but for other reasons, led straight to what is now identified by modern economic theory as the (mathematical) problem of the 'existence' of solutions of simultaneous equations systems which represent models of general economic equilibrium.

Smith had already identified the *existence* of such an 'existence problem', when he started with a 'labour (cost) theory of value' for the 'early and rude' state of society, but quickly switched to a 'cost-of-production theory of value' for a nonprimitive capitalist society. (Of course, Smith lingered for not more than a page over this 'existence problem' of premodern equilibrium theory.) Whether one treats this as a sign of wisdom (as Samuelson, 1971, p. 404, does) or of complacency, or unsophisticated naivete, depends upon how far one is troubled by modern doubts about neo-classical descendants of Smith's 'cost-of-production theory' which recognize capital as a factor of production defined independently of the profit (interest) rate, and rely on Walrasian *tatonnement* in the 'search' for equilibrium.

2 The Ricardian 'transformation' problem

Ricardo grappled harder and longer with the 'existence problem' in a nonprimitive capitalist society. He thought the problem could be simplified to some extent by abstracting from scarce land even in a capitalist society, on the basis of a theory of 'differential rent'. But he admitted that the reality of unequal proportions in which (circulating and fixed) capital goods are combined for the production of different products makes long-run competitive equilibrium values diverge from the 'labour-cost' values which rule in Smith's 'early and rude state'. But he asserted, apparently without any proof, that the divergencies would not be large enough to matter. In this way, Ricardo recognized, but minimized, a 'transformation problem' analytically linked to the 'existence problem' of general economic equilibrium.

Now, modern mathematical economics has proved conclusively that Ricardo was wrong on both counts. Why a differential rent theory cannot successfully 'get rid of' the problem of scarce land will be discussed in chapter 6, section 3.

Why there is no basis for approximate (up to '93 per cent') 'labour-cost values' to rule in a competitive capitalist equilibrium can be understood merely by extending statements 1 and 2 (chapter 3, section 3), about Ricardian-socialist theories, to cover the Ricardian version of the 'transformation problem'.

The results of these statements can be generalized.

Statement

1 In a non-Austrian general equilibrium model, where all products are not penultimately reducible to products of unassisted labour, (a) if the composition of 'constant capital' differs (or the proportions in which different products expressed in their natural physical units are combined as means of production used are different in different industries) (b)

but where there are no 'ordinary' joint products of the wool-and-mutton type, the following results will hold:

Long-run equilibrium values will diverge from 'labour cost' in an irregular, haphazard way, whenever the profit (interest) rate is positive;
There is no basis for saying that the divergence will be less the nearer (or farther) the profit (interest) rate is from zero;
There is no basis for saying that the divergences will not, in general, be large enough to prevent a reasonable 'approximation' to 'labour-cost values'.

An amplification of the statement to cover three fine points are of some (though purely formal) interest.

First, it can be shown that if the only joint products used, represent fixed capital equipment emerging as joint products along with the main products they help to produce, the system behaves as if there are no joint products, and the statement holds without modification.

Second, however, if the system admits 'ordinary' joint products of the wool-and-mutton type (i.e. assumption (b) does not hold), then even with a zero profit-rate, there is no guarantee of the 'convergence' of the infinite series in the reduction equation (chapter 3, section 3) (Sraffa, 1960, chapter 9, sections 66, 68, pp. 56, 58–9).

Third, there are two freakish exceptions to the statement. The first one occurs when Ricardian 'proportions' differ between industries but the Marxian 'organic composition of capital' (to be discussed in the next section) does not. (In general, when Ricardian 'proportions' differ, so does the organic composition of capital. But freakish exceptions can be constructed, though nobody seems to have found it worth while to publish any.) In such a case, *even with a positive profit (interest) rate*, long-run equilibrium values always coincide with Ricardian 'labour costs', whatever the profit-rate. A second exception arises if we work with a two-commodity model, consisting of a wage-good 'corn' and a luxury good 'gold', gold being used as an 'invariant' measure of value. In this example, gold is *made* to serve as an 'invariant measure' because it is *assumed* (quite arbitrarily) that 'at any time and place [it] always requires the same quantity of labour to produce', its period of production is taken to be the same as that of corn, and the monetary unit is the quantity of gold which is produced by the labour of one worker in the given period of production' (Pasinetti, 1968, p. 125).[1]

3 The Marxian version of the 'transformation problem'

Marx, as noted in chapter 4, section 2, tried to solve both the Smith–Ricardo version of the 'existence problem' and Ricardo's 'transformation' problem by a reconstructed Marxian 'transformation problem'.

In this reconstructed version, *both* scarce land (which Ricardo had ignored), and the 'unequal proportions' which he had tried to take into account, were explicitly admitted. The method adopted was to reduce *both* these aspects of capitalist reality to the *single* generalized problem of *lower-than-average* 'organic composition of capital' in agriculture and *unequal* 'organic composition of capital' in industries. (The Marxian 'organic composition of capital' refers to the proportion in which constant (i.e. circulating and fixed) capital and variable capital (i.e. wage advances) are combined in production, with both constant and variable capital being expressed in terms of 'labour-embodied' quantities.) The assumptions are then made of the free transferability of resources (including labour-power) between industries to ensure an equal profit-rate everywhere in equilibrium, and restricted transfer of resources between agriculture and non-agriculture to ensure 'absolute rent' (resulting from lower-than-average organic composition of capital in agriculture) being earned by capitalist landlords in agriculture.

Marx's master-stroke, or so he thought, was to insert into this, as an essential part of the long-delayed solution of these problems of classical political economy, his notion of capital

1. For a full discussion of the subject-matter of this section, see Samuelson, 1957, p. 888; Sraffa, 1960, ch. 3, section 14; Bose, 1964, pp. 722–8.

as a coercive social power, which capitalists exercised to appropriate surplus value (which was the source of profits, interest and rent).

As we shall see in the next section, Marx's intended 'master-stroke' did not quite come off. It turns out that from the point of view of solving the 'existence' and 'equilibrium' problems, the 'transformation' problem was falsely-constructed, a hindrance and not an aid. Fortunately, a post-Marxian solution of the 'existence' and 'exploitation' problems, which has nothing to do with the 'transformation' of Marxian values into Marxian 'production prices' or 'absolute rents' is perfectly possible. (Also possible is a 'subsistence wage' validation of Marxian exploitation theory, already referred to in chapter 4, section 4, which also does without 'trans-formations' of Marxian values into prices.) However, the century-old debate on the Ricardo–Marx 'transformation problem' has produced theorems which are of interest to the mathematically-inclined, and which have promising ap-plications in understanding problems of capitalist and socialist societies (some of which are discussed in Part Two).

4 The debate on the 'transformation problem'

Marx sketched in outline his plan of a joint solution of the existence of equilibrium (in terms of long-run 'production prices' for industrial products which were linked with 'absolute rents' earned in agriculture whose products were sold at 'market values') between 'transformation' and 'exploitation' in a capitalist competitive model in a letter written to Engels on 2 August 1862 (Marx, 1938b, pp. 129–33).

In the years since then, many writers have found fault with Marx's procedure in this matter at many points. But there are *three* crucial defects (the first of which has been overemphasized and the other two underemphasized) which make controversy over others derived from these – the assumption of an 'equal rate of surplus value' (Samuelson, 1957, p. 890; Sweezy, 1949, p. 65) or the equality of 'total values and total prices' (Sweezy, 1949, pp. 115–23, Winternitz, 1948, pp. 163–84) – nearly meaningless exercises in 'over-kill'.

Marx's 'incomplete' transformation

The *first* of these, treated as a purely formal defect and easily remedied, was Marx's highly idiosyncratic procedure in solving his transformation problem. This procedure was the transformation of inputs of wage-goods ('variable capital') plus means of production ('constant capital') and their sum, called the 'cost-price', all expressed at long-run values equal to 'embodied-labour cost', *into* outputs at long-run values equal to their 'prices of production', linked with a uniform average rate of profit in spite of varying organic composition of capital (Marx, 1959, chapters 9, 10 and 45).

Marx admitted that the procedure was not exact, that a 'production price' which diverges from 'labour-embodied cost values' may become an element in the 'cost-price' of a commodity, but maintained that his procedure was passable since it 'remains true, nevertheless . . . that the cost-price is smaller than the price of production' (Marx, 1959, Part 2, ch. 9, p. 162). But since the truth of this statement was itself derived from Marx's transformation procedure, and not independent of it, the argument seems to have been circular. Nor is Marx's procedure valid in the special cases covered by his numerical illustrations of 'transformation of values into prices', i.e. cases of *non*-interdependent commodity production (Meek, 1967, p. 150, n. 24). Even if inputs are more like neo-classical 'factors' and do not reappear as outputs, in one and the same system with non-uniform organic composition of capital, in general there cannot be input prices at Marxian 'labour-cost values', output prices at Marxian 'production prices' and an equal rate of profit.

However, history has been kind to Marx. Already in the passage just quoted, he admits, in effect, that long-run equilibrium values or prices (using these two words interchangeably) of inputs which enter the 'cost-price', and of outputs (which are formed by 'cost-price' plus an average profit-rate) are, in any exact model, *simultaneously determined*. In other words, he recognized, though *insufficiently*, and implicitly, what the semi-socialist Walras recognized explicitly in 1874 to begin an analytical breakthrough, viz. the use of simultaneous equations systems in solving problems of general economic equilibrium (Walras, 1954). Of course, it is now generally acknowledged that Walras only scratched the surface of the 'existence problem', and that there was no solution of the problem in its Walrasian version available even as recently as 1934 (Dorfman, Samuelson and Solow, 1958, pp. 349–51; Hicks, 1967, pp. 77–81). There seems to be no evidence that Marx or Engels took any notice of the work of Walras, maybe because Marx had already completed his theoretical work before his health began to fail in 1870, four years before the publication of the *magnum opus* of Walras.[2] Later Marxists were hardly attracted by Walras's 'semi-socialism' (Schumpeter, 1955, p. 888), and were repelled by the categorically anti-socialist politics of a prominent successor of Walras, Vilfredo Pareto.

In any case, whatever the limitations of Walras's initial break-through, once the seed of an idea had been planted, it was only a question of time before somebody (it turned out to be Dimitriev (1898), whom von Bortkiewicz (1907) acknowledged to be his master), used the technique of simultaneous equations to attack Ricardo's 'transformation' problems.

2. The neglect of Walras's work by Marx is really surprising, since Marx was exceptionally meticulous in taking note of contributions to economic theory, regardless of viewpoint, at least up to those who were writing in the middle of the nineteenth century. Alternative speculative hypotheses are:

1 Marx was totally unaware of a 'mathematical gap' in his theory, so that he was not on the look-out for mathematical contributions towards a solution.

2 After the 1830 European bourgeois revolutions, Marx did not expect any scientific elements to survive in the run-of-the-mill 'syncretic' and 'apologetic' 'vulgar economy' in the service of the bourgeoisie, which he thought would dominate (see chapters 16 and 17 for more on this).

Whether Marx's *knowledge* of Walras's theory helped him to reach this conclusion, or whether he did not take the trouble to study Walras because he had already reached this conclusion, we shall only know for certain when complete works and correspondence of Marx are published.

(In fact Dimitriev showed a greater insight into the mathe-matical-economic problems involved in the 'existence' question than did Leon Walras, when he disputed the Wal-rasian dictum that equality of the number of equations and unknowns is a necessary and sufficient condition for the existence of equilibrium solutions (Dobb, 1970, p. 212).) Soon, von Bortkiewicz followed up by recasting *Marx's* transformation problem in the form of sets of simultaneous equations, in which the constants were the 'embodied-labour' contents of both inputs and outputs, and the uniform profit-rate and the prices of production were the unknowns. Further work on the transformation problem has produced the theorem: 'if, in the system of labour values, the rate of surplus value is positive, then, in the system of prices of production, the rate of profit is positive', which is exactly what Marx had claimed to be true, and is now generally acknowledged (e.g. Samuelson, 1971, p. 422; Morishima, 1973, Part 3, section 7).

Are labour-contents of commodities 'observable'?

However – and this brings us to the *second* weakness in Marxian transformation procedures – von Bortkiewicz's corrected version of the Marxian transformation was as firmly anchored as Marx's own 'labour theory of value' of *Capital*, volume one, as well as *his* version of his prices-of-production theory of *Capital*, volume three, to the assumption that total labour embodied (i.e. both direct and indirect labour embodied) in commodities is known from *direct observation*. Why such an assumption cannot be entertained has been gone into at length in chapter 3, section 3 in the context of the Ricardian-socialist doctrine that labour is the only source of value, and need not be repeated. But Marx, who *rejected* this Ricardian-socialist doctrine, *defended* the assumption that total labour embodied in commodities is known from direct observation in the context of his 'trans-formation' procedure. Marx and Engels (and modern Marxist writers) have defended the assumption with two mutually exclusive arguments – both cannot be true, and neither makes much sense – viz. that values antedate prices of production 'not only theoretically but also historically', *and also* that labour values are concepts which approach reality (prices of production) asymptotically, never coinciding.

The first of these arguments is *asserted* by Marx (1959, ch. 10, p. 174). Engels in his *Supplement* to *Capital*, volume three (Marx, 1959, p. 874) argued in support that labour quantities embodied in goods traded were fairly accurately known to peasants and craftsmen in the Middle Ages in Germany. But this would have relevance only in a very undeveloped *capitalist* economy in which very few, very primitively produced raw materials and tools – or very long-lasting tools whose replacement and depreciation charges could be ignored – were combined with direct labour-power in all its production processes. But this is emphatically *not* the kind of capitalist economy, modelled on the historical realities of British nineteenth-century capitalism (Marx, 1954, p. 8) that Marx's *Capital* was supposed to analyse.

The second argument – the 'asymptotic approach' of the concept of Marxian 'labour-cost values' to reality in the form the Marxian production prices – was put forward by Engels in a letter (Engels, 1938, pp. 527–8). But the context suggests that Engels is advancing, knowingly, a Hegelian rather than a strictly Marxian argument. In so far as he *is* advancing a Marxian argument, he seems to be discussing the general problem of the statistical (measurable) accuracy of economic observations, e.g. how far, in actual fact, the profit-rate can be verified to be 'exactly' equal in every branch of the economy. Of course, *by definition*, since Marx's 'production prices' are 'labour-cost values' adjusted to give an equal profit-rate everywhere in a regime of unequal organic composition of capital, the problem of 'observability' of labour-cost values could be *reduced to* a question of the degree of accuracy of statistical observations. But to do so, one must be sure that 'labour-cost values' are in the *first place* observable; which brings the argument back to its starting-point.

Von Bortkiewicz had no use for the arguments just examined.

He defended *his* assumption of observability of labour-embodied values with the mathematically sophisticated argument that the total labour embodied in commodities could always be *calculated* by summing finite series representing indirect labour requirements. This is only so, he recognized explicitly, for the assumption that *all* units of constant capital (both circulating and fixed) are ultimately produced by unassisted labour (von Bortkiewicz, 1907, pp. 13–14, 18).

Actually, as we have seen in chapter 3, section 3, such an extreme Ricardian-socialist or 'Austrian' assumption is *not* essential to justify the observability in principle of total labour-embodied quantities (and Marx explicitly rejected such an assumption). If we drop the assumption of reduction of all commodities to unassisted labour-power, but follow von Bortkiewicz's 'reduction' procedure of replacing commodity inputs into each commodity by direct labour-power and commodities required to produce these inputs etc. in an endless chain, we get a convergent infinite series which can be summed up to give the total labour-content of each commodity. Moreover, as we shall see in chapter 6, section 4, summing up for a few rounds will give a good approximation. The only difficulty is that the 'reduction method' fails in the context of joint production, e.g. of wheat and straw, or wool and mutton (Sraffa, 1960, pp. 58–9). But in such cases, too, an alternative method is available, the method of 'sub-systems' which will give the labour-contents at least in some cases (Sraffa, 1960, pp. 89; Bose, 1964).

However, all this does not really matter and is beside the point. A solid objection to the suggested procedure of von Bortkiewicz – going first from commodities expressed in their natural physical units to 'labour-embodied' quantities and then on to 'prices' – is that there is no sense in taking such a circuitous route, although it is formally possible, for reconciling Marxian exploitation with long-run equilibrium values linked with an equal profit-rate (but non-uniform organic composition of capital). This is one of those cases where there is no doubt that the principle of Occam's razor, or rule 5 (chapter 1, section 3), *should* apply. One can go straight from commodity inputs and outputs (including direct labour-power as primary commodity inputs) in their natural physical units – which are directly observable – to production prices linked with a uniform profit-rate. It has already been noted in chapter 4, section 4 that this is possible if a 'subsistence wage' notion is adopted. It will be shown in chapter 6 that it is also possible in a post-Marxian theory *without* adopting such a notion. (Other explicitly linear, modern, Leontief-type theories also do this, with or without adopting 'subsistence wage' notions (e.g. Johansen, 1961, pp. 21–2; Schwartz, 1961, pp. 3–55.)

Von Bortkiewiez's 'withholding' theory of capitalist exploitation

However, von Bortkiewicz's own theory of competitive capitalist exploitation was a very special one, which differs from all those just mentioned, and is crucially connected with his Ricardian-socialist assumption that all products are reducible to products of direct, unassisted labour-power. The proof starts with his important proposition (see chapter 4, section 3) that the profit-rate is *independent* of production conditions of luxury goods (defined as goods which do not enter into the production of other goods as raw materials or wage-goods). He then adds the assumption that all non-luxury goods are wage-goods (p. 15). He then concludes that the origin of profits must clearly be sought in the wage relationships and not in the ability of capital to increase production (p. 32), and that some of the produce of labour (i.e. luxury products) is *withheld* by capitalists as profits (p. 33).

It is clear that this theory of capitalist exploitation falls to the ground if we reject, as we do for reasons given in chapter 3, the Ricardian-socialist proposition that in a capitalist society all products are reducible to products of unassisted labour-power. Only on this assumption can it be said that labour employed in the wage-goods sector *alone* produces the entire surplus of the system. If capital goods are in fact needed to produce wage-goods in a capitalist society – so that *not all* non-luxury goods are wage-goods – then, on this reasoning, both labour-power and capital goods employed in both the wage-goods and the capital-goods sectors are 'productive'.

Two crucial defects of Marx's transformation procedure have been discussed in this section. Before we pass on to the third, in section 6, we have to pay some attention to the literature on the 'inverse transformation' problem, including a solution to this problem, which, at one time, was thought to have been the last word on the subject.

5 The 'inverse transformation problem' and its solution

Work on the 'inverse transformation of prices to labour-embodied values' seems to have started as long ago as 1905 (see reference to Tugan-Baranowsky's work, published in German, in Samuelson, 1971, p. 426). In the modern version (Morishima and Seton, 1961), the constants are the wage and non-wage factor incomes and outputs at current prices; Marxian labour-embodied values emerge as the solution. However, *some* assumption about the sector-wise 'rate of surplus value' (whether equal or unequal) is essential for the 'inverse transformation'. But if neither the amount of surplus value nor the amount of variable capital can be *observed* (and neither the wage-goods at current prices, nor the value-added at current prices approximate to them), it is hard to decide, in general, what the pattern of the ratio of these two quantities at the 'rate of surplus value' should be. (Assumptions attributed to Okishio by Morishima and Seton (1961, p. 206), get round the problem precisely by assuming the observability of the wage bill and surplus value and wage-goods consumed in each sector in terms of Marxian 'values', so as to get an equal rate of surplus value and complete 'inverse transformation'.)

If this is so, the 'inverse transformation' exercise will also *not* be based on observable data and will take us no farther in solving the basic problem of Marxian political economy, viz. the reconciliation of the theories of capitalist exploitation and of long-run equilibrium values under competitive capitalism.

6 The problem of scarce land

Something must now be said about the *third* crucial defect in Marx's attempts to construct an exploitation-based model of competitive-capitalist general economic equilibrium, which has hardly been noticed until recently (Samuelson, 1959, Appendix, pp. 1–35). As already noted in section 3, Marx's handling of the problem of scarce land is merely an application of his method of handling models with unequal organic composition of capital in different branches of the economy. (In fact, the letter written in 1862 to Engels (Marx, 1938b) shows that Marx used the concept of unequal organic composition of capital (defined in terms of 'labour-embodied' quantities of constant and variable capital) to analyse land rent, *before* he used it to deal with Ricardo's complications originating in the problem of non-uniform capital-composition in manufacturing industry.) So, the criticisms made in section 4 against Marx's own setting-up of the 'transformation problem' extend to his method of handling the problem of scarce land.

Later writers, starting with von Bortkiewicz, seemed to have ignored the problem of scarce land and of land-rent altogether. No explanation is given. But the omission itself cannot be ignored. It is likely that their cross-bred Marx–Walras models cannot handle the problem by using either Marx's or Walras's methods, unlike the strict modern mathematical version of the Ricardian model, which *does* have an independent method of handling scarce land, though only by ignoring substitutability in production and consumption, which is unacceptable in a realistic 'final' model (Pasinetti, 1968, p. 133).

7 Conclusion

The upshot of the critique presented in this chapter is that the 'corrected' solutions of Marx's 'transformation problem' do not do much better than Marx's own solution in presenting a properly de-mystified theory of long-run equilibrium values under competitive capitalism, with the exploitation of workers by capitalists, on the basis of the coercive power of capital, in the centre of the picture.

So we turn, in the next chapter, to a post-Marxian theory of capitalist exploitation which makes use of modern commodity production models of general economic equilibrium, originating in the work of Sraffa.

6 A Post-Marxian Theory of Capitalist Exploitation

1 Introduction

It has been pointed out in chapter 4, section 4, that Sraffa's theory of interdependent commodity production (henceforth, 'commodity-production theory' for short), provides a suitable basis for a post-Marxian theory of capitalist exploitation under competitive conditions, which has each of the four ingredients listed in chapter 2, section 3 as necessary for *any* theory of capitalist exploitation.

It has also been claimed there that this post-Marxian theory has no difficulty in assimilating, with minor adaptations, the definitional propositions of the Marxian theory of capitalist exploitation. In fact, the definitional propositions of the Marxian theory, suitably rephrased and renumbered, become the post-Marxian definitional propositions.

Definitional propositions

1 The institutional specification of a capitalist society as one in which workers 'own' only their labour-power, and the capitalists own all the means of production (as also the wage-fund for labourers and scarce land).

2 Surplus value is defined to mean the value of the aggregate 'excess production' or surplus produced by the system taken as a whole, i.e. the value of the excess of output of at least one commodity (and a deficit of none) over the aggregate input of these commodities (including wage-payments and rents payable to landlords).

3 The appropriation of surplus value (in the form of profits and rents) earned by capitalists represents *exploitation* of

workers by capitalists, not only because it offends the 'socialist sense of morality', but because this post-Marxian theory of capitalist exploitation can be extended to give an economic theory of socialism (chapter 14) and of a transition to socialism (chapter 13).

Success of this post-Marxian theory with respect to ingredient 2 (chapter 2, section 3) – a reconciled equilibrium–exploitation theory, which is the Achilles' heel of the Marxian theory – was also claimed, but the discussion postponed to this chapter, which is concerned with *three* points.

First, the specifically Marxian properties of the commodity production theory are identified in detail (section 2) to reinforce the claim that the theory of the present chapter can legitimately be called a post-Marxian theory, i.e. an extension of the Marxian theory.

Second, in discussing ingredient 2 of the post-Marxian theory, we face up to the fact that there has been no systematic discussion so far on the proof of the 'existence' of equilibrium in the commodity-production model, on the 'search' for (or the 'identification of') an equilibrium which has been proved to exist, and on the 'realization' or 'preservation' of such an equilibrium. All these are explained in Walrasian theory essentially by relying on a *tatonnement* (groping, or trial-and-error) procedure, with or without an auctioneer, for which there is no place in the commodity-production theory. These problems are discussed in sections 3–5.

Third, the chapter concludes (section 6) with a discussion of ingredient 3 of the post-Marxian theory, i.e. the incorporation of capitalist exploitation in a competitive-capitalist model by making explicit a reason why the rate of profit or of exploitation must be positive in long-run equilibrium.

The Appendix to chapter 6 is a brief excursion into the possible relevance of some of the findings of the modern mathematical political–economic theory of collective choice, which uses novel tools of analysis borrowed from modern symbolic logic, to a discussion of the unsolved problems of the Marxian theory of capitalist exploitation. It is interesting to find that this points to an *alternative* post-Marxian approach to a solution of these problems which has the added advantage (from a Marxian standpoint) of including an explicitly stated political dimension in the formulation of the problem.

2 Marxian properties of modern commodity-production theory
Ricardian features

Modern commodity-production models are Ricardian rather than Marxian, in so far as we have to start with the data (product inputs, inputs of direct labour-power and product outputs) expressed in their own natural units, to derive the unknown equilibrium values under competitive capitalism. This is Ricardian rather than Marxianp rocedure. Von Bortkiewicz, whose contribution to the Marxian 'trans-formation-problem' debate has been noted in chapter 5, section 5, pointed out that his acknowledged mentor Dimitriev *ignored* Marx's transformation problem, and used algebraic methods to show that prices are determined by the technical conditions of production represented by inputs, outputs, etc. expressed in their natural physical units (but also ignored the Marxian theory of exploitation) (von Bortkiewicz, 1907, pp. 22–3).

With commodity-production models, there is no com-pulsion[1] to transform labour-embodied values into 'pro-duction prices' (or vice versa), in order to derive long-run equilibrium values under competitive capitalism, or to incorporate a theory of capitalist exploitation in it. (Yet, as a formal exercise (or for discussing alternative price-policies in a *socialist* economy (see the Appendix to chapter 13), commodity-production models could be used to show that prices coincide with 'embodied labour' if the profit-rate is zero, and scarce

1. In Sraffa's exposition of his commodity-production theory, the transformation of 'labour-embodied values' into prices of production which diverge from them when the profit-rate is positive, seems to play an essential role in the proof of the existence of solutions in terms of all-positive prices (Sraffa, 1960 ch. 5, section 39, pp. 27–8). But more direct mathematical proofs, which are independent of 'transformations' seem to be available (Newman, 1962; Burmeister, 1968; Bose, 1971, pp. 323–4).

land is ignored, and also that prices will be invariant at labour-embodied values, if the social surplus is allocated among enterprises in proportion to the size of the wage incomes, i.e. by a flat rate tax on the national wage bill. Such exercises establish the common features of Ricardian and Marxian models of interdependent production.)

On the other hand, there are several Marxian properties of these commodity production models which make them particularly suitable for our purpose (though some are also properties of other modern linear economic models).

Closedness, circularity and partial decomposability

The first Marxian property of modern commodity-production models is the use of the notion of interdependent commodity production to derive long-run equilibrium values. The notion originates in the writings of the Physiocrats, but was refined and developed by Marx in *Capital*, volume two (though neither used it to derive long-run values under competitive capitalism). Modern input–output economics (originating in the work of Leontief) has developed the notion in a more extreme form than modern commodity-production theory – to postulate *closed* systems (with no inflows from outside the system, since labour-power is replaced by wage-goods consumed in fixed proportions and scarce land is ignored) – to discuss many problems of capitalist and socialist economies, but not mainly to derive long-run values under competitive capitalism, or to incorporate in it a theory of capitalist exploitation.

Two specific peculiarities of the commodity-production models should, however, be noted (which also makes these models stand closer to Marxian than to alternative modern models). First, commodity-production models (except the *beginning* model in Sraffa's book, 1960, ch. 1) are *not* completely circular, hermetically *closed* models, but are 'open' in the sense that they explicitly admit direct labour-power and scarce land as 'unproduced' primary resources which are inflows from nature. This is fully in line with Marx's emphasis (1949a, p. 17) on the role of nature and not only labour (which is also a part of nature)[2] as a source of wealth and value. This, in conjunction with the strong emphasis on the 'passion to accumulate' among capitalists (section 6), makes the post-Marxian theory founded on commodity-production models immune to the criticism against other 'closed models' that they are based on an incorrect interpretation of the facts (Georgescu-Roegen, 1966, pp. 97–8).

A second peculiarity of interdependent commodity-production models has to do with the 'partial decomposability' of these models. This means that these models contain *both* 'basic' produced commodities and 'non-basic' produced commodities (or a special type of 'non-basic', viz. 'unproduced' scarce land). 'Basic products' are those that enter directly or indirectly, as raw materials or machines, or consumer goods consumed in fixed proportions, into the production of all commodities produced by the system (Sraffa, 1960, pp. 7–8, 10, 51, 74). 'Non-basic products' are those that do *not* do so (though they may be not only final consumer goods, typically luxury products, but also producer goods as long as they do not enter into the production of basics, or, if they do, are 'unproduced' scarce land). As we shall see, in chapters 9–13, these concepts of commodity-production theory lend precision to the Marxian notion of the role of labour processes involving 'productive' and 'unproductive' labour-power.

The notion of a maximum potential rate of profit

The notion of a maximum potential rate of profit compatible with all-positive prices is the sheet anchor of the proofs of existence and of uniqueness in commodity-production models. Marx spoke of such a maximum rate of profit corresponding to a hypothetical zero wage in *Capital*, volume three (Marx, 1959, p. 242) and that this was not casual is underlined as it is derived from the assumption that Marx implicitly made (see

2. In making this point, Marx goes *beyond* William Petty's dictum that labour is the father and nature the mother of value, in stressing the role of nature.

chapter 3, section 3) that under capitalism, production of commodities does not originate in production by unassisted labour-power. (If it did, at a hypothetical zero wage, the rate of profit would be infinite.)

In commodity-production models, the notion of the maximum potential rate of profit compatible with all-positive prices plays a crucial role in giving us a price theory where prices are determined without demand functions (as we shall see in greater detail in section 5).

As several modern writers have pointed out, the mathematical basis of the notion was laid by theorems by the mathematicians Perron (1907) and Frobenius (1908 and 1912) about 'characteristic roots' or 'eigen values' in the theory of matrices (Gantmacher, 1959, chapter 3; Debreu and Herstein, 1968; Newman, 1962, pp. 65–6). However, Sraffa (1960, p. vi), who first worked out the implications of the notion of a maximum potential rate of profits in the 1920s, definitely acknowledged it to Marx (Sraffa, 1960, p. 94).

How much credit one is willing to give Marx for having anticipated a provable theorem in mathematics and used it (though for a limited purpose) in economic theory, depends partly on the rating that one is willing to give to Marx's mathematical ability. On this point, opinions are sharply divided. Engels claimed Marx was 'well versed in mathematics.' (Engels, 1947, p. 19). Von Bortkiewicz thought Engels was being ironic, and rated Marx's mathematical ability very poorly (von Bortkiewicz, 1907, p. 55), though the modern mathematician May (1948, pp. 596–9) has not given von Bortkiewicz himself a high rating as a mathematician, against protests by Samuelson (1971, pp. 415–16, 25). Samuelson, who has stressed Marx's 'incapacity in algebra' relentlessly for the past fifteen years during the rise of modern mathematical economics, has lately conceded that Marx had 'mathematical ability but lacked mathematical training', which is why he had trouble with algebra (Samuelson, 1972, p. 52). Evidently, the verdict can never be final, and depends partly on where one draws the line between 'insight' and 'guess work' and a real 'breakthrough' both in economic theory and in mathematics.

In any case, a final verdict on Marx and the 'maximum rate of profit' notion can be left to historians of economic doctrines. What matters is that Marx's use of this notion – albeit for the limited purpose of a dispute with Adam Smith on the particular question of how far the price of every commodity resolves itself entirely into wage, profit and rent (Sraffa, 1960, p. 94) – introduced it to economic theory, although its wider implications were not realized until recently, when the modern commodity-production theory was established on its basis.

The 'standard commodity' as numeraire

A third point of contact between modern commodity-production theory and Marxian economic theory is the use of the 'standard commodity' as a numeraire – as an 'auxiliary device' (Sraffa, 1960, p. 31) up to a certain stage of the analysis of equilibrium conditions. Of course, it is Ricardo who searched for an 'invariant' numeraire, which is what the 'standard commodity' is. But Marx also continued the search, and thought he had concluded it when he assumed, in his 'prices of production' theory, quite *arbitrarily*, that the numeraire, gold, was produced under conditions of the 'average organic composition of capital' prevailing in the economy.

The nature of capitalists' income

A fourth, distinctly Marxian property of modern commodity-production models has to do with the analysis of capitalists' income. As already indicated several times in earlier chapters, there is no place in the commodity-production model for capital regarded as a quantity of 'waiting'. Furthermore, these models rule out notions of the incomes of capitalists regarded as rentals for capital service collected by owners of capital goods, which are visualized in other modern mathematical models (e.g. Morishima, 1966, pp. 520–25). Such a 'rental' concept applied to capitalists' incomes would explain them as originating in surpluses accruing to the owners of capital goods as a result of the 'natural' inelasticity of the supply of capital goods (because, presumably, taking all capital goods together, *all* of them cannot be substituted by direct labour-power even in the long-run; the long-run supply curve of capital goods cannot be horizontal with their owners having transfer earnings equivalent to the earnings of direct labour-power which has replaced all capital goods). This would give a purely 'institutional' theory of capitalist exploitation if we postulate that there is no inherent reason why the ownership of capital goods should not be socialized, so that rentals accruing on capital goods are not appropriated as private capitalists' incomes. However, such a theory would make use of the Marshallian apparatus of demand–supply analysis to validate a theory of capitalist exploitation under competitive conditions. Such a theory will be discussed in Part Three, but it is enough to note at this point that modern commodity-production theory, by doing without such an approach, is decidedly closer to the Marxian theory of capitalist exploitation under competitive conditions.

The handling of demand, scarce land and an inverse wage–profit relation

A fifth similarity between commodity-production models and the orthodox Marxian models is to be found in the handling of demand. Commodity-production models have no 'demand equations' or ('objective functions') to determine equilibrium values. Actually, the inclusion of such equations would make the equations systems of commodity-production theory inconsistent. This is in sharp contrast, not only to orthodox neo-classical theory (in both its Walrasian and Marshallian variants) but to modern linear theory (Hicks, 1967) which, at any rate up to the late 1950s, treated price determination without specification of demand conditions as an imaginary (and impossible) case of a capitalist economy in which the profit-rate is zero but more recently also covered cases of a positive profit-rate (Koopmans, 1951, chapters 7–10; Samuelson, 1961, section 7–9; Morishima, 1958a; 1958b; Morishima and Murata, 1968; Stiglitz, 1970). The matter will be discussed further in section 5 and referred to in chapters 9–11.

Suffice it to note at this point that modern commodity-production theory is more radical in 'doing without demand functions' than the Marxian theory, in which there is scope for incorporating demand functions to explain short-run deviation of 'market prices' from 'production prices' or 'market values' (Marx, 1959, chapter 10; Sweezy, 1949, Part I, chapter 3, section 3).

The sixth similarity between commodity-production and Marxian theories is to be found in the fact that it is commodity-production theory which has pioneered with a rigorous attempt (which, however, is not entirely convincing, as we shall see in section 3) to bring scarce land into the model of general economic equilibrium, in contrast to other linear models (e.g. of the von Neumann type) which do not. This is a Marxian preoccupation, contrary to the general impression derived from the abstraction from the role of scarce land in *Capital*, volume one, for in *Capital*, volume three, Marx makes ample amends.

Finally, it is modern commodity-production theory which has pioneered with a rigorous proof of the proposition that there will, with given technology, and also, on certain assumptions, with improving technology, be an adverse wage–profit relation in a capitalist economy. As we shall see in chapter 7 of this book, this was also an important Marxian prediction.

The Marxian properties of modern commodity-production theory listed in this section justify the decision to call the theory of capitalist exploitation under competitive conditions presented in this chapter a post-Marxian theory. Of course, this is only *one* possible application or extension of the theory. The author of the commodity-production theory has himself concentrated, as noted earlier, in 'de-mystifying' the concept of capital,[3] while others, the 'neo-Marxians' have used it to incorporate the notion of 'class struggle' as against

3. It is only fair to say here that Piero Sraffa, in private correspondence with me at an early stage of my work along lines indicated here, has said that he does not agree with the interpretation of his theory given in this book.

'class harmony' in a theory of general capitalist equilibrium under competitive conditions.

3 Proofs of the existence of equilibrium in simple and complex commodity-production models

In this section, we first try to make sure that the 'existence proofs' of commodity-production theory exist for the simplest versions of the model, which assume indecomposability or 'irreducibility' (i.e. assume, in the terminology of section 2, that there are only 'basic' products), abstract from joint production, from heterogeneous labour, use of fixed capital, scarce land etc. We then discuss solutions to some (selected) problems which arise, when some of these simplifying assumptions are dropped.

To clear initial doubts, we note that in the *simplest* case, there is general agreement that a rigorous mathematical proof of the existence and uniqueness of solutions with strictly all-positive prices, a positive (uniform) profit-rate and a non-negative wage is available (Sraffa, 1960, Part I; Schwartz, 1961, Part A; Newman, 1962; Morishima, 1964, p. 195; Burmeister (quoting results presented at a 1963–4 seminar by Samuelson), 1968, p. 83). Later in this chapter we shall rely on Sraffa's version of the proof, which is distinguished, among other things, by a proof of positivity of prices which *starts* from the *necessary* positivity of all prices of basics when the profit-rate is zero and prices are equal to 'labour cost', and then states that as prices are 'transformed' by a cut in the wage, 'no price can become zero or negative before any other, so that no price can become negative at all' (Sraffa, 1960, pp. 27–8).

What has just been said is true, whether wages are advanced, as with Marx and in Garegnani's adaptation of the commodity-production model (Garegnani, 1966), or are paid *post factum* at the end of the production period, as with Sraffa (1960, p. 10) and Pasinetti (1966). It is true, whether the number of techniques[4] *available* exceeds or equals the number chosen for

4. Defined as a collection of methods of interdependent production, equal to the number of commodities in the system, which combine,

use (and this holds both for single products and joint products systems) (Bose, 1965, p. 774).

Moreover, although there have been no detailed investigations into these matters, no insuperable difficulties are likely to be faced when transportation, trading, stock-carrying or banking services are introduced into the model (on transportation, see Schwartz, 1961, chapter 1, pp. 12–13).

As indicated in chapter 3, section 4, there is an 'unclosed gap' in commodity-production theory as far as the matter of income distribution is concerned. There is much discussion of this aspect of the theory and it is likely that a full answer to the problem will be found along lines suggested by Nuti (1970), by postulating that the worker–capitalist class struggle fixes the inversely related money wage and profit (interest) rate, but that the interaction of real and monetary phenomena fixes the 'real' wage-rate.

We turn now to more complex versions of the commodity production model in which some of the simplifying assumptions are dropped.

Partial decomposability

It has been noted in section 2 that the main prototype of a commodity production model is a 'partially decomposable' model, containing some 'basic' products which enter, directly or indirectly, into the production of all other products in the system, and some 'non-basic' products which do not. This prototype is important, because, as we shall see in chapters 10–13, contrasting implications of assumptions of 'indecomposability' and of 'partial decomposability' provide insights into a number of problems of capitalist and socialist economies.

An objection has been raised (Newman, 1962, p. 66) that commodity-production systems become *inconsistent* when they are made 'partially decomposable', with the inclusion of non-basics. But in the counter-example demonstrating this, inconsistency seems to arise because (a) it is a two-commodity

as input or output, some or all commodities in the system in different proportions.

example, and (b) direct labour terms are not included explicitly in the equations (though they always *are* shown explicitly in all commodity-production models with 'excess production', or 'production with a surplus'. It is easily checked that if the direct labour terms *are* shown explicitly, there is no problem even with a two-commodity model (see the numerical example in Bose, 1965, Appendix I, section 4, p. 785).

In general, it is conceded that indecomposability is *not* needed to assure consistency or to give strictly positive prices (Burmeister, 1968, p. 84).

However, Sraffa has himself acknowledged that in a partially decomposable system with non-basics, there is no guarantee that all non-basic prices will be strictly positive (Sraffa, 1960, p. 28, pp. 90–91). Remembering that, by definition, at least one basic enters (in positive quantity) into the production of every non-basic, and that at no possible (non-negative) level of the wages or the profit-rate, is it possible for the price of any basic to be non-positive, it is obvious that the price of a non-basic can never be zero. But there may be the problem of a non-basic price becoming infinite or negative. The problem can be summed up in the following statements:

Statements

1 The method of production of a non-basic has no influence on the general rate of profits (and, via the profit-rate, on *all* prices) (Sraffa, 1960, p. 25).

2 But the 'own rate' of surplus production of a non-basic which enters into its own production may be much lower than the maximum potential profit-rate of the system, e.g. a species of corn, sown as seed produces a crop which is only 10 per cent in excess of the quantity of seed input, when the maximum profit-rate of the system is, say, 15 per cent.

3 In the case of a non-basic of the kind specified by statement 2, as the wage is reduced and the profit-rate is raised above zero, its price rises without limit, becoming infinite when the

profit-rate of the system is 10 per cent, and negative when the profit-rate rises above 10 per cent.

This problem is an awkward one for commodity-production theory. For, although interdependence in production is of the essence in this theory, enterprises controlling processes or 'industries' are independent of one another, and no enterprise will produce a product whose notional equilibrium price is negative. On the other hand, it is hard to imagine how negative-priced non-basics will be bought as inputs by other enterprises. So a commodity-production system containing such a nega-tively-priced non-basic has no economic meaning.

We may ignore partially decomposable systems containing *such* non-basics as rare and ignorable.

Assumptions

1 No non-basic enters into its own production, nor into the production of any other non-basic which has entered into its own production.

If this assumption is adopted, food-grains consumed in fixed proportions as parts of a composite wage-good will have to be classified as 'semi-basics' (as in chapter 13). They represent the only cases of non-basics entering as seed into their own production that one can readily think of. Most other non-basics are 'luxury goods' proper, which do *not* enter into their own production, directly or indirectly, although they may enter, as raw materials, into the production of other non-basics which are final consumer goods.

Homogeneous and heterogeneous labour

It would be a fatal flaw in the commodity-production theory, if the assumption of homogeneous labour (retained through-out by Sraffa, 1960, but *not* by Schwartz, 1961, pp. 34–5) were indispensable for proving the existence of equilibrium solutions.

In fact, it is a simplifying assumption, which can be dropped without loss. Along with homogeneous unskilled labour-power as a primary factor, we could insert in the production equations a number of types of skilled labour-power (or embodiments of 'human capital') 'produced' by an equal number of sectors. The efficiency-level of each category of skilled labourers could then be taken as a definite fraction (or multiple) of their initial efficiency-level, as they grow older. A rise in efficiency-levels through greater experience, or learning by doing, can be provided as easily as decline due to age, through the inclusion of appropriate joint-production processes in which skilled labour of a particular category is produced jointly with the main product, in the same way as durable fixed capital, to be considered under 'Fixed capital' below.

There is a last-ditch stand against this solution (which he correctly attributes to Marx) by Samuelson (1971, pp. 404–5). His argument is that it is impossible to ignore differences in the efficiency-levels of men and women doing the same job, and between men (or women) of the same age-group, doing the same job, originating in genetical differences. (The argument, in its extreme form, is that to ignore these differences is to assume, in effect, that all men (or women) are genetically identical or monozygotic twins, derived from a single fertilized egg!) The conclusion drawn by Samuelson is that nothing short of Walrasian full-demand equilibrium will do (i.e. that commodity-production theory for *this*, among other reasons, is at best an interesting continuation of the Ricardo–Marx 'false start').

However, this verdict against modern commodity-production theory is unconvincing. Since it is conceded that *skilled* labour categories can be derived as 'produced' labour, in processes in which 'homogeneous' unskilled labour is a primary input, the issue is whether genetically heterogeneous unskilled labourers can still represent homogeneous unskilled labour. Thus, the point, ultimately, *is* (only) a matter of genetics. Now, it is true that only in the case of monozygotic twins can we be *sure* that any differences between them *must* be due to the environment (Bodmer, 1972, p. 95). But, because of constant interaction between genes and environment during development, there is an essential indeterminacy between genotype (the genes) and phenotype (adult characteristics as observed) – and 'genes cannot explain anything' (Hambley, 1972). (Moreover, genetic variations might determine innumerable differences between individuals of the species (as well as between ethnic groups), with respect to skin-colour, eye-colour, etc., which are *not* determinants of efficiency-levels in most cases.) Thus, Samuelson's argument must be rejected on *factual* rather than on methodological grounds.

Fixed capital

Now, to bring in fixed capital, we may assume, as Marx does (Marx, 1954, ch. 9, section 1, p. 213, quoting Malthus), that mechanized processes produce used machines (e.g. partially or wholly worn-out weaving machines) along with the main product (cloth). (The method was first proposed by Torrens, then adopted by Ricardo (and Malthus) in the early nineteenth century, was forgotten and reintroduced into the literature by von Neumann and Sraffa. Torrens had a 'capital theory of value', which was the polar opposite of Marx's labour theory of value of *Capital*, volume one. By borrowing from him, Marx demonstrates his methodological pragmatism.)

Used machines (or, for that matter, used buildings) remain the property of the enterprise at the end of the production cycle, whether they are then sold in the second-hand market or are retained and at least sold sometimes, so that a second-hand market in machines (and buildings) exists, and machines are *not* generally 'non-movable' (as they are assumed to be, quite arbitrarily, and purely for analytical convenience, in some recent work on the 'non-substitution theorem' (Morishima and Murata, 1968, p. 78; Stiglitz, 1970, pp. 546–7)). So there is a gain in generality if we treat used capital equipment as joint products, along with what they produce.

But should we, in this type of model, use the von Neumann procedure (1968, pp. 221–9) of treating machines of the same type but of different ages as different machines, each with its own price? If we do this, then in order to equalize the number of equations and unknowns, we might have to make artificial assumptions which are hard to justify, e.g. the assumption that machines of each type are of balanced age composition, or that the number of mechanized processes (a number fixed arbitrarily by the life span of machines) must produce goods which are also produced by other processes in the system or sell only second-hand machines.

Instead of making such artificial assumptions, we could revert to Marx's notion that capitalist enterprises calculate the rate at which machines depreciate in physical terms, on the basis of the life expectancy of a capital asset (Marx, 1954, ch. 8, p. 203; 1957, ch. 8, pp. 157–8). (This method, with acknowledgement to Marx, has been suggested in Bose, 1971, section 10, p. 325, and without acknowledgement by Samuelson, 1971, section 14, p. 425.) On this basis, a new machine going in as input would emerge as an output equal to, say, nine-tenths of a machine, along with what it produces. There is no need to make simplifying assumptions which are necessarily made in many modern mathematical growth models, viz. decline in efficiency at a constant rate, 'radioactive decay', or 'sudden death' etc. The decline in efficiency may be at a nonconstant rate, according to intensity of use, or age, depending upon the nature of the machine or the capital equipment. (Of course, it is essential to assume, as Marx and von Bortkiewcz did, that all machines and buildings have a finite life span which can be estimated approximately.) No other assumption is then needed to make the number of machines (and their separate prices, taken as unknowns) equal to the number of processes (and corresponding equations). Since every process is mechanized and each machine will have to be produced, every process will be a joint-production process, and the number of such processes will be equal to the number of products in the system, and to the rank of the system. (Peculiar problems which may arise with 'ordinary joint products', from the viewpoint of the purely mathematical properties of the system, to be discussed below, will *not* arise when capital equipment of *declining* efficiency is treated as a joint product, for reasons indicated there. They arise only if we make the impossible assumption that used machines 'appreciate', instead of depreciating, in *physical* terms!)

Scarce land

In a commodity production model with scarce land, we could assume that there is no general ordering of lands in terms of fertility or advantage of location, independently of the product prices and land rents (and the profit-rate), though different kinds of land are physically distinguishable in some sense. This seems to be the only correct assumption. The only alternative seems to be the artificial assumption that all land is used to produce one (maybe a composite) product, but few writers have discussed this problem of economic theory. (Samuelson, 1959, pp. 1–35; Frisch in a little known paper quoted by Samuelson, 1959, p. 21; Sraffa, 1960, ch. 11; Pasinetti, 1968, p. 133, are rare exceptions.)

If we *do* assume that there is no general ordering of scarce lands, given independently of profit-rate and prices, then, if we want land rents to be determined by the solution of a system of simultaneous equations, we might think of making the assumption that the number of processes is equal to the number of qualities of land plus the number of products. This would mean, for example, that if there are one hundred products and fifty kinds of land, there must be exactly fifty extra processes which produce a product also produced by some other process (if we want to stick to commodity-production models and not adopt linear-programming solutions of the type indicated by Samuelson 1959, pp. 28–34).

One way of avoiding such arbitrary assumptions is to assume instead that (positive) land rents are fixed by bargains between landlords and capitalist tenants in a *competitive* land market, and appear as data in the system of simultaneous equations, so that the number of processes *and* of equations is equal to the number of products (since the essential technical properties of the production equations would remain unchanged, the proof of existence of solutions in the no-land case carries over). A limit to the rise in land rents would be imposed by the need to maintain a positive wage, and a positive profit-rate, which is sufficient to allow capitalist reproduction on an extended scale. A lower limit which keeps land rents positive would be set by the consideration that landlords must have some incentive to let out the land (since, unlike capitalists who cannot produce without employing workers, and so cannot displace workers, landlords *can* displace capitalist tenants and produce by employing hired labour). This has some support from Marx's categorical statement that private property in land 'creates an obstacle to the investment of capital' and that landlords must have some incentive to let out the land (Marx, 1959, ch. 45, pp. 732–4) which would explain why, when land is scarce in relation to the demand for it, even in a competitive land market, positive rents must be paid and received for the use of land. However, there will remain an 'unclosed gap' in a fully-fledged theory of income-distribution incorporated in commodity-production theory, unless we further specify that land rents are either paid in kind or their values are determined independently of the wage–profit share-out, on the basis of what is known and accepted about landlords' consumption in traditionally fixed proportions, and on the assumption that landlords, being spendthrift, save and invest a negligible part of their incomes. In short, we reduce *all* land rents to Marx's 'monopoly rents', so called to distinguish them from differential and absolute rents for which also there was a place in Marx's theory (1959, ch. 50, pp. 839–40). Marx's use of the term 'monopoly' in this context does *not* imply any departure from competitive conditions in the land market, and is perfectly compatible with it. It refers to the institutional monopoly over land enjoyed by landlords as a class, which entitles them, even when there is a competitive land market, to make *deductions* from real wages and profits for collecting rents.

4 The 'search' for equilibrium: the reduction to 'dated labour' as a substitute for Walrasian tatonnement

Solving 'existence' problems without demand functions is all very well, but can the 'search' for equilibria, or the 'identification' of equilibrium prices, whose existence is proved, be conducted without demand functions?

As already indicated, in commodity-production models, it

is possible, in principle, to separate three problems connected with equilibrium – the 'existence', the 'identification' and the 'realization' – each of which can be, indeed must be, solved separately. The separation of the last two problems which are lumped together in modern Walrasian analysis as the 'stability' problem, has heuristic value in revealing, as will be shown in chapter 10, the *raison d'être* of colonialist, imperialistic and neo-imperialistic policies adopted by capitalist economies, to solve the third problem on this list. In this section, we concentrate on the second – the 'identification' problem.

The 'existence' problem can be formally solved for commodity production models by the usual method of solving simultaneous equations in which the number of equations and the number of unknowns are equal, and the rules of rank are satisfied, though a polynomial has to be solved to choose the maximum rate of profit compatible with all-positive prices, and the relation $r = R(1-w)$ has to be used, to eliminate 'extra' unknowns.

But the individual capitalists in a competitive situation cannot be expected to construct full simultaneous equations systems for the entire economy and to solve them, as a behaviourist assumption. So the fact that solutions for such systems representing the economy *exist*, does not tell us much about the procedure of 'search' for equilibrium actually adopted in practice. In Walrasian theory, this problem is avoided by postulating the existence of an auctioneer in each market, who cries out provisional prices, on the basis of which contracting and 'recontracting' goes on, until equilibrium solutions are found.

Modern commodity production theory has an ingenious answer to this problem, to which Dobb has drawn attention in a letter to the present writer. This is none other than the 'reduction operation' method of solving simultaneous equations systems discussed by Sraffa, and used in another context in chapter 3, section 3 of this book.

Reference to this alternative method of solving simultaneous equations would be otiose, and rule 7 (chapter 1, section 3) for judging alternative economic theories would be of no help, were it not for the fact that it yields the insight that each individual capitalist might identify long-run equilibrium values (corresponding to a given technology and income distribution) by summing convergent infinite series, which, moreover, have the convenient property of converging fairly rapidly.[5] This has the implication that if each individual capitalist knows the inputs of direct labour-power into the commodity he produces, into the commodities he uses as inputs, into these inputs, and so on for a few stages, and also the profit rate corresponding to a given technology and income distribution, he can discover the long-run equilibrium prices of his product after summing up for a few stages, up to a sufficient degree of approximation. This is illustrated by 1–4.

Equation 1 represents the value-equations of a two-commodity[6] indecomposable system consisting of two 'basic' commodities, A and B, each of which enters both production equations directly as raw materials or constituents of a composite wage-good. The notation is Sraffa's: p_a, p_b represent product prices per unit, r the profit-rate and w the wage share; the constants are quantities of commodities A and B and direct labour-power (the latter expressed as a fraction of the social labour force employed in each industry, with the aggregate social labour force made equal to one).

$$(1p_a + 1p_b)(1+r) + \tfrac{1}{3}w = 3p_a, \tag{1}$$

$$(1p_a + 1p_b)(1+r) + \tfrac{2}{3}w = 3p_b. \tag{2}$$

Since 1 has been made (*only* for convenience of calculation) a 'standard system' (in which aggregate commodity inputs

5. Dobb's conviction that the series *is* rapidly converging is evidently based on modern empirical studies of the Soviet economic structure (Ellman, 1972, chapter 6, pp. 78–9), but can probably be extended to refer to modern capitalist economic structures whose purely physical technological properties are similar.

6. Since with more than two commodities we shall get an expression of the same form as 3, the argument will hold for any number of commodities.

and outputs of the system as a whole are combined in the same proportion), it is easy to read off the maximum potential rate of profit of the system as

$$R = 1p_a + 1p_b\left(\frac{1}{2p_a + 2p_b}\right) = \frac{1}{2}.$$

Now, if the 'going profit-rate'[7] $r = \frac{1}{4}$, then, by the relation $r = R(1-w)$, we derive $w = \frac{1}{2}$.

If we then replace in **1** each commodity input by direct labour-power, and the commodity inputs required to be combined with it to produce that commodity input, and so on, we have a reduction equation in which all the terms after the first two terms belong to an infinite series, with the common ratio $\frac{5}{6}$, so that it is converging:

$$\frac{1}{3} \cdot \frac{1}{2} + \frac{1}{3} \cdot \frac{5}{4} \cdot \frac{1}{2} + \frac{1}{3} \cdot \frac{5}{4} \cdot \frac{1}{2} \cdot \left(\frac{2}{3} \cdot \frac{5}{4}\right) + \frac{1}{3} \cdot \frac{5}{4} \cdot \frac{1}{2}\left(\frac{2}{3} \cdot \frac{5}{4}\right)^2 +$$

$$... + \frac{1}{3} \cdot \frac{5}{4} \cdot \frac{1}{2}\left(\frac{2}{3} \cdot \frac{5}{4}\right)^n + ... + 3p_a. \qquad \textbf{3}$$

If we now apply the formula for summing infinite converging series, **3** reduces to

$$\frac{1}{2}\left(\frac{1}{3} + \frac{5}{2}\right) = 3p_a. \qquad \textbf{4}$$

This gives the solution $p_a = 17/36$.

A similar reduction equation corresponding to **2** gives $p_b = 19/36$.

It is easily verified that the two values for p_a and p_b together constitute the solution of the simultaneous equations system **1** and **2**.

These solutions could be obtained from the 'reduction equations' up to a high degree of approximation by summing up for a few stages (instead of applying the formula for summing infinite series). Thus, in **3**, summing up to the seventh

7. The 'going profit-rate' represents the maximum profit-rate that can be earned by using any one of the set of available techniques, after wages have been paid. The profit-maximizing capitalist will reject all techniques which give a lower profit-rate after wages have been paid.

stage gives a good approximation to within 76·36 per cent of the exact equilibrium value of p_a.

Thus, it is clear that the 'reduction to labour quantities' is an alternative to the Walrasian *tatonnement* as a method of 'search' for equilibrium prices by 'atomistic' individual capitalists. The method has, moreover, the advantage of dispensing with the Walrasian notion of an auctioneer dominating each market, which may be considered artificial (or superseded on the principle of Occam's razor by the 'reduction method').

If used fixed capital, treated as joint product, is counted as a fraction (in physical terms) of new capital equipment of the same type (as proposed in the section on 'Fixed capital' above), the 'reduction equation' for each product would still consist of positive terms only, and would converge. So the 'reduction operation' solves the 'search' problem in complex, realistic models as well as in simplified ones.

Of course, the method cannot be used in cases of 'ordinary' joint products like wool and mutton, wheat and straw, etc. (Sraffa, 1960, pp. 56, 58) because the 'reduction equation' would then have to include 'negative quantities of labour, for which no reasonable interpretation can be suggested' (Sraffa, 1960, p. 59).

However, unlike the 'reduction operation' which is *totally* unusable with 'ordinary' joint products, the alternative construct of 'sub-systems' *is* usable as a substitute, at least in some cases (Sraffa, 1960, p. 89; Bose, 1964).

This method pictures a situation in which individual capitalist farmers, producing, say, wheat and straw (which *must* emerge as a by-product), use two different methods of production, each method involving the use of a different product (say, a different kind of fertiliser) as input, and producing quantities of wheat and straw in different proportions. If the capitalist farmer runs two farms, A and B, in each of which he uses both methods (in two different plots) he can choose the 'process intensities' in Farm A in such a way as to produce a net output in the farm consisting of straw only (the joint output of wheat, in this farm, being equal to the quantity of wheat used as seed for employing both methods of production). The direct labour-power employed in Farm A can then be attributed, straightaway, to the production of the quantity of net output of straw in the farm. Once the direct labour-content of straw is calculated in this way, it is easy to find out the direct labour-content of wheat. (Each of the two farms will, of course, use third products, e.g. fertilisers, as inputs, which, if they are single-products, will have their 'labour-contents' calculated by the 'reduction operation'.)

Now, the 'sub-systems' construct, just sketched, *may* provide a substitute for the unusable 'reduction method' when there are 'ordinary' joint products. But it may fail in some cases, where all-positive sets of 'sub-systems multipliers' needed for constructing sub-systems may not exist. Although the matter has not been discussed in publications, it seems that *only* in the case of single-products systems is the existence of *all-positive* sets of sub-systems multipliers *guaranteed*. With 'ordinary' joint products, there is no such guarantee: the set of sub-systems multipliers may be all-positive, but it may also be semi-positive (i.e. contain both positive and negative sub-systems multipliers). But negative sub-systems multipliers imply the existence of 'negative' industries, which make no sense.

To fill this residual gap in commodity-production theory, we may suppose that joint production methods which require the use of semi-positive sets of sub-system multipliers are discarded as unusable, and that substitute methods with all-positive sets of sub-systems multipliers are always available, to allow common products such as wheat and straw, or mutton and wool, to be produced and marketed. (Alternatively, we may ignore the problem, in the sense that even if straw is the joint product of wheat, only the wheat is marketed, the straw is used to thatch the roof etc., and the entire direct labour-power employed in farming is attributed to wheat production.)

5 The role of demand

As already stated, commodity-production theory has no use for demand functions; with their inclusion, its equation systems would be over-determined. However, shifts in the commodity composition of aggregate demand, with the commodity composition of aggregate output remaining the same, could occur (or, what is the same thing, shifts in the commodity composition of aggregate output may be caused by technological change, commodity composition of aggregate demand remaining the same). Such shifts would be reflected in commodity-production models in a disequilibrium condition with non-uniform profit-rates within the industry.

When this happens, it can be shown (rigorously) that an inter-industry transfer of resources, *without change in technique*, can always adapt the output pattern to the demand pattern.

Assumptions

1 Processes are mechanized, with fixed capital treated as joint product in the manner suggested in section 3 on 'Fixed capital'.

2 Homogeneous labour is used.

3 'Ordinary' joint products of the wheat and straw variety are insignificant.

4 Land is either free, or rent of scarce land is fixed as suggested in section 4 on 'scarce land', so that scarce land does not have to be shown explicitly.

5 Universal constant returns to scale prevail.

On these assumptions, all-positive sets of 'adaptation multipliers' can always be found, which, when applied to the industry equations (all of which together represent a chosen, profit-maximizing technique), adapt outputs to demands, restore the uniform profit-rate at the same level as before, on the basis of unchanged relative prices.

But when we assume, more realistically, that labour is heterogeneous, and/or 'ordinary' joint products are *not* ignorable, only semi-positive sets of 'adaptation multipliers', which are unusable because they refer to 'negative' industries, may be available. Furthermore, if we allow even *some* exceptions to assumption 5, even all-positive 'adaptation multipliers', when there are no joint products etc., are meaningless.

These results, pertaining to commodity-production models, have not been published, presumably because they merely restate the known results of the 'nonsubstitution theorems' of modern Leontief matrices, referred to in section 2 above. In other versions of modern linear economic theory, these results pose no serious problem, because they incorporate demand or objective functions, which can be relied upon to deal with cases where the 'nonsubstitution theorem' does *not* hold.

But in commodity-production models, in which, as already stated, demand functions are *excluded*, they leave a gap, because in the *final* commodity-production models, assumptions 2 and 5 cannot hold strictly, even if the other assumptions do. Moreover, even in the 'simplest' case, where assumptions 1–5 *all* hold, 'adaptation' imposes a cost on those who make temporary losses (as will be shown in numerical illustrations in chapter 10) before the process of adaptation is completed. The problem is solved if we do not insist on abstracting from contrived 'institutional change' as a remedy for economic problems when mathematical solutions 'within the same institutional framework' are economically meaningless. This is what is attempted in chapter 10, where the geneses of institutional changes represented by historically identifiable policies of capitalist colonialism, imperialism and neo-imperialism are traced back, partly, to demand–supply adjustment problems discussed in this section.

6 The incorporation of a positive rate of capitalist exploitation in a commodity-production model of competitive equilibrium

It remains to round off this chapter by giving a 'post-Marxian' theoretical explanation as to why wages, profits and rents should all be positive in long-run competitive equilibrium represented by a commodity-production model.

Explanations can be given in terms of the physiologically determined minimum-of-existence subsistence wage of Malthus (as in some neo-Marxian theories of exploitation) or strictly in terms of the Marxian labour reserve army ensuring an equilibrium wage which is less than the full-employment wage (which Lange used).

Both these explanations ensure positive profits by imposing a maximum limit on a (positive) wage, so that property incomes are also positive, and labourers are 'exploited'. But the first explanation makes natural factors (the 'population principle') ultimately responsible for workers' exploitation. The second rests essentially on the assumption that technical improvements introduced by the capitalist accumulator are on balance of the 'labour-saving' type, plus an implicit assumption that the labour surplus induced by labour-saving improvements is not offset by a slow-down in the number of new entrants into the labour force in the capitalist sector, due to demographic factors. Both these explanations de-emphasize the coercive 'man-made' power of the capitalists over workers. Moreover, not enough is known, as yet, both about the nature of technological progress and about demographic factors involved in the growth of the labour force, to force us to choose either one or the other of these explanations.

An alternative explanation can be given, on the basis of the following Marxian propositions about the basic motivation of capitalist production, and the nature of technological progress, with capitalist development appearing as a succession of long-run equilibria with given techniques.

Statements

1 The basic motivation of capitalist production and circulation is accumulation for expanded reproduction: 'Accumulate, accumulate! That is Moses and the prophets. . . . Accumulation for accumulation's sake, production for production's sake . . . [is the] formula [which expresses] the historical mission of the bourgeoisie' (Marx, 1954, ch. 24, section 3, p. 595).

2 It follows from statement 1 that the capitalist system would never come into existence in the first place, if the profit is non-positive (for the rate of profit is the 'fundamental premise and driving force for accumulation . . . the vital fire of production' (Marx, 1959, p. 254), and would certainly come to an end if it fell to zero although it may also end when the profit is still positive, if 'conditions ripen' to make the function of capital accumulation on the basis of private enterprise obsolete (Marx, 1954, ch. 32).

3 It follows from statements 1 and 2, that the following equilibrium conditions must hold:

The share of land rents in the surplus product of the system must be such as to leave the maximum potential rate of profit (corresponding to a hypothetical zero wage) positive; The share of wages out of the maximum potential profit margin must be such as to give a positive actual rate of profit, after wages have been deducted.

4 But (a) a possible secular rise in living standards of workers (Marx did not exclude this possibility altogether, though he did not quite predict it (Marx, 1954, ch. 6, p. 171; ch. 25, section 4, p. 645)) and (b) increasing scarcity of land due to expanded reproduction, would tend to raise real wages and land rents, and press against available profit-margins.

5 However, the 'passion to accumulate' would stimulate capitalists to introduce technical improvements which are land-saving in character, and which increase labour productivity (by promoting 'capital-saving' as well as 'labour-saving' technical improvements distributed over various sectors). This would maintain a positive rate of profit (and of accumulation).

The reader will notice that there is no mention of the much-discussed 'profit-maximizing' motive in statements 1–5. But, as was made clear in section 5 above, this motive *must* be postulated in a commodity-production model to make choice between alternative techniques determinate. It is also the basis on which, if there are demand–supply discrepancies, inter-industry transfer of resources take place until a uniform profit-rate is established.

However, as we shall see in chapter 9, except under ideal conditions, profit-maximization by decentralized capitalist enterprises in a competitive situation does *not* maximize the rate of capital accumulation in the economy as a whole. The geneses of imperialist, neo-imperialist and non-imperialist policies of advanced capitalist societies can be partly traced back to this chronic contradiction between private and public capitalist self-interest.

Appendix:

The Modern Theory of Collective Choice and the Marxian Theory of Capitalism

1 Introduction

The modern theory of collective (social) choice, which originates in the work of Kenneth Arrow (1970) is of interest to students of the Marxian theory of capitalism for several reasons.

First, it rejects, partly by criticism and partly by a value judgement, approaches to the problem of social choice under capitalism which are decidedly anti-Marxian because they stifle, or curb, social criticism of income distribution or property ownership under capitalism from the standpoint of members of the exploited classes of society. One of these rejected approaches 'assumes' that society (*a fortiori*, a capitalist society), has a personality and a preference pattern of its own, which must prevail over individual preferences (see a critical reference to this approach in Sen, 1970, p. 1). The second is the approach based exclusively on the principle of 'Pareto-optimality', which cannot diagnose any increase or decrease, or even absence of any change in welfare, if all workers are made better off by a process which would also make a single capitalist feel worse off (see a critical rejection of this approach in Sen, 1970, pp. 21–2).

Second, it makes the forthright assertion, backed by some theoretical constructs, that there is no essential distinction between voting and the market mechanism in a capitalist society (Arrow, 1970, pp. 5–6, Kramer, 1969, p. 1). This, too, is very much in line with a Marxian dictum, which goes back to Engels and Lenin (1947) that voting offers no essential escape from the results of the capitalist-controlled market mechanism.

Third, in line with what has just been noted, it includes, as a value judgement with which the equilibrium condition of a competitive capitalist society is to be reconciled, the question of 'dictatorship' or 'non-dictatorship' (understood in a personal sense to refer, for example, to modern fascist dictatorships in capitalist societies), which introduces what is welcome from the Marxian viewpoint, i.e. an overtly political element in the discussion of capitalist equilibrium conditions.

Fourth, the modern theory of collective choice made a far-reaching contribution by reopening the question of the optimality of a competitive capitalist equilibrium in any sense other than Pareto optimality. Much faith was put in the forties on using a social welfare function for the society as a whole, and deriving competitive conditions as a part of optimal resource allocation in terms of maximizing the value of social welfare as defined by such a function. Arrow's impossibility theorem proved that it is impossible to relate individual preferences to social preferences satisfying four reasonable conditions (this difficulty applies to competitive capitalist conditions as well).

Conditions

1 Unrestricted domain, i.e. the condition that the method of going from individual preferences to social preferences must work for every logically possible configuration of individual preference orderings.

2 The 'weak Pareto principle' that, if everyone prefers X to Y, then society must also prefer X to Y.

3 Independence of irrelevant alternatives, which says that social choice over a set of alternatives must depend upon the orderings of individuals *only* over *those* alternatives: rankings of all other alternatives are irrelevant to social choice.

4 Non-dictatorship which states that there should be no individual, such that, for every possible configuration of individual preferences in the domain of the group-decision rule, if that individual prefers any alternative X to any other alternative Y, then society also prefers X to Y

The entire vast literature on collective social choice, which has grown up over the last twenty-five years, can essentially be interpreted as an attempt to establish the compatibility of competitive capitalist equilibrium, with alternative assumptions about the realities of capitalist society (or, as we shall see in chapter 14, of modern socialist societies). Much of this literature has been devoted to a discussion of 'escape routes' from Arrow's impossibility result, proved in terms of normatively laid-down conditions. More recently, there is literature, published in a 'positivist' tradition, which identifies social decision (voting) rules used in practice in real life, and discusses, using rigorous logical methods, their implications, especially the problems created by sincere and insincere voting (Farquharson, 1969; Pattanaik, 1972).

2 The modern theory of collective choice and the Marxian theory of capitalism

However, in spite of the reasons listed in the previous section for cross-fertilization of the modern choice-theoretic and Marxian critiques of competitive capitalism, very little progress has been made in this matter. (Indeed, *no* attempt seems to have been made at all, except for a tentative one by Amartya Sen (1967b).)

Promising political-economic interpretations of the results of the Arrow impossibility theorem were held up because of a tendency to put into separate compartments the discussion of

Social welfare functions in terms of Arrowian (or substitute) conditions;
The modern discussion of competitive equilibrium in the neo-classical tradition; and
The problems of competitive-capitalist equilibrium in a Marxian model.

By contrast, discussion about the relevance of Arrow's results for Marxian discussion about a *socialist* economy began early (Arrow, 1970, pp. 84–5 and Sen, 1967b, concentrate on this).

Furthermore, the political-economic interpretation of the

Arrow results – assessing the problems of a capitalist society made on the basis of a similarity in the preference patterns of individuals (or the condition of 'single-peakedness') – was rather narrowly restricted at first (Arrow, 1970, p. 74) to cases where, with a common desire for freedom and national power, and the acceptance of inequality to increase total output, the method of majority-decision would make this agreed on ordering the social order. These cases seem to leave no scope for a competitive-capitalist equilibrium (of a political–economic nature) established in the context of class-struggle and exploitation, which was the main focus of Marxian (and modern neo-Marxian) interest. On a superficial view, the interpretation of the 'single-peakedness' condition in terms of 'a common desire for national power' seemed to limit the application of choice-theory results to problems of a capitalist society to the exceptional (and relatively uninteresting) situation where the class-struggle, the outgrowth of capitalist exploitation, was held in abeyance. This restricted application of the 'single-peakedness' condition, more than anything else, seems to have been responsible for the almost total absence of cross-fertilization between the modern theory of collective choice and the Marxian theory of capitalism.

3 Possibility results incorporating class conflict, capitalist exploitation and workers' apathy

Arrow's condition of 'single-peakedness' was extended by Inada (1964), and generalized by Sen (1966) into the 'value restriction' condition, and finally interpreted by Sen:

. . . if one assumed that individuals are divided into specific classes with a certain coincidence of interests *within* each class, and certain contrasts of interests *between* classes, the need for considering every logically possible combination of individual preferences [i.e. condition 1] becomes redundant (1967b, p. 12). [Sen went on to add] It is very easy to show that if the community is divided into *two* classes with exactly *opposite* interests, no problem whatsoever can arise in moving from individual preferences to social choice, satisfying all [other] conditions of Arrow [except the now redundant condition 1 of unrestricted domain].

Thus, on this interpretation of the Arrow 'single-peakedness' condition, and the generalized Sen 'value-restriction' condition, a sharply polarized capitalist society – in which there is a head-on collision of preferences and interests between capitalists and workers (and all secondary conflicts of class interests have been subordinated to this major conflict between the *two* dominant classes) – can exist in 'equilibrium', fulfilling all the Arrow conditions (except the first), including the personal 'non-dictatorship' condition.

However, it is clear that such a sharply bi-polarized capitalist society would be one in the grip of a 'revolutionary crisis', i.e. a capitalist society which 'fulfils itself', as it were, by making it impossible for the capitalist social structure to be sustained, and providing the basis for a transition to a socialist society (Dahl, 1968, p. 80; Lenin, 1947, p. 112; 1965, vol. 9, pp. 48–52; Pattanaik, 1971, p. 96).

Furthermore, while this interpretation does incorporate the Marxian notion of worker–capitalist class conflict in the centre of the picture, to get a possibility result, it does not *necessarily* incorporate the notion of capitalist *exploitation* of workers. At least hypothetically, the 'opposite interests and/or values' (Pattanaik, 1971, p. 96) of workers and capitalists could be a case of opposed consumer interests (the capitalists' meat being poison to the worker and vice versa). To convert the Arrow–Inada–Sen result into a theorem about capitalist exploitation, we would have to adopt some definition of capitalist exploitation, along the lines indicated in chapter 6, section 1.

A second escape from Arrow's impossibility result may validate certain kinds of rational choice in a society, including a capitalist society. By utilizing a solution to a bargaining problem in game theory given by Nash (1950), Sen shows how the problem of interpersonal comparison of utilities can be solved, but the social ordering that results is loaded in favour of the *status quo*, and the (fixed) 'threat advantages' of the bargainers. He goes on to infer that, applied to the case of worker–capitalist bargaining in the labour market in the context of unemployment, the Nash solution would mean that 'workers were exploited because their bargaining-power was poor' (Sen, 1970, pp. 118–21). Whether the inference holds on the assumption of shifting 'threat advantages' does not seem to have been investigated.

A third route of escape from Arrow's impossibility result has been suggested recently, which is also of interest from the viewpoint of the Marxian analysis of capitalism (Hinich, Ledyard and Ordeshook, 1972, section 1). According to this result, which is discussed mainly in the context of political voting, rather than market choice, but should extend to both, 'citizens' failure to reveal their preferences (i.e. their abstention from voting) gives a sufficient condition of escape from Arrow's impossibility result' (Hinich, Ledyard and Ordeshook, 1972, pp. 144–5). The problem of aggregation of individual preferences becomes simpler in this context, because the diversity of preferences expressed by individuals gets considerably reduced when a significant section of society abstains from voting. This can be interpreted to say that Arrow's condition 1 (i.e. 'unrestricted domain') can be rendered irrelevant by the apathy or 'alienation' of some who 'withdraw' from political (or market) processes, so as to give a definite outcome in an Arrowesque capitalist model.

Since it is sections of workers rather than capitalists (and those sections of workers who are organized in trade unions and political parties) who are likely to 'withdraw' in this way, this result might explain the *domination* of a typical modern capitalist society by capitalists without the aid of a regime of personal (fascist) dictatorship.

However, this interpretation has nothing directly to do with any theory of capitalist *exploitation* of workers, unless 'nonvoting' by unorganized workers is attributed to total revulsion against capitalism caused by an understanding which *defines* capitalism as a system of exploitation, either on Lange–Lerner assumptions (chapter 3, section 2) or on the basis of the propositions given in section 1 of chapter 6.

4 Conclusions

We conclude, tentatively, that, like the modern commodity-production theory, discussed in detail in chapter 6, the modern theory of collective choice has produced a number of results which can be interpreted to support neo-Marxian trends in economic theory, which incorporate the notion of class conflict in the explanation of competitive capitalist equilibrium. Some of its results also seem to be interpretable to support an alternative *post-Marxian* theory of capitalist exploitation (alternative to the theory of chapter 6, which has grown out of modern commodity-production theory). This alternative post-Marxian theory uses tools of analysis which have nothing to do with the Marxian tools of analysis, unlike the commodity-production theory (though there are a few similarities pointed out by Sen (1967b, pp. 13–24)). On the other hand, it brings together, within a single frame-work of analysis, as is also attempted in Marxian political economy, political and market processes (including, by a short extension, 'controlled' market processes).

Furthermore, as we shall see in chapter 14, it throws some light on a fundamental problem of the Marxian theory of a *socialist* society, viz. the problem of taking economic decisions by 'political processes' working *outside* the market mechanism, but *utilizing* the market mechanism for *implementing* the decisions taken.

7 Long-run Tendencies of Capitalist Development:

Marxian and Post-Marxian Predictions

1 Introduction

An integrated Marxian or post-Marxian theory of value, capital and exploitation is expected to be logically acceptable. But it is also expected to make interesting, empirically verifiable predictions about long-run tendencies in capitalist development. Indeed, both its critical opponents (e.g. Samuelson, 1970, pp. 620–23) and its more or less critical defenders (e.g. Lange, 1935, section 3, pp. 73–4; Dobb, 1968, pp. 64–6) have made such predictions the acid test of the relevance of the Marxian theory.

In this stand taken by opponents, and conceded by defenders, the emphasis seems to be misplaced. A logically valid theory of capitalist exploitation which is linked with a notion that a socialist society can replace it, is itself significant, quite apart from whatever other predictions it might make about the 'process of capitalist evolution'. It tells us, for instance, that when people (Russian, Chinese or Vietnamese) make (or tolerate the making of) a Communist revolution to put an end to capitalist exploitation and establish a socialist society, they are not victims of an irrational, romantic, delusion, they are not chasing a chimera. It tells us something about the sanity of human beings involved in revolutionary mass upheavals.

However, both the Marxian and post-Marxian theories of capitalist exploitation (chapters 5 and 6), *also* make specific predictions about long-run tendencies under capitalism. In this chapter, we concentrate on those of the much-discussed Marxian 'long-run tendencies' which are at least partially confirmed by the post-Marxian theory of chapter 6. In Part

Two, we shall examine some other predictions, viz. the emergence of capitalist colonialism etc., which have already been referred to several times in earlier chapters.

2 The inverse wage–profit relation

A long-run 'law of motion' of competitive capitalism, predicted by Marx on the basis of his 'first approximation', i.e. that commodities sell at their 'labour-embodied values' (usually referred to in the modern critical literature as the 'simple labour theory of value'), is partially confirmed by the rigorous analysis of modern commodity-production theory.

In his *Wage Labour and Capital*, section 4, based on lectures delivered before an audience of workers in 1847, Marx wrote:

What, then, is the general law which determines the rise and fall of wages and profit in their reciprocal relation?

They stand in inverse ratio to each other. Capital's share, profit, rises in the same proportion as labour's share, wages, falls, and vice versa. Profit rises to the extent that wages fall; it falls to the extent that wages rise (1950a, p. 89).

Now, it is confirmed that Marx's reference to this 'law' occurs in the very first version of *Wage Labour and Capital*, published in December 1849 (Marx, 1963, vol. 1, p. 219).[1] Thus, Marx's publication of this 'law' antedates the publication of von Thünen's natural-wage theory based on recognition of such an inverse wage–profit relation in his *Isolierte Staat* (von Thünen, 1850). (However, perhaps the first-ever categorical *assertion* that wages vary inversely as profits (an idea which is found in particular contexts in Ricardo's writings) is to be found in an 1825 publication by Thomas Hodgskin (1963 edn, p. 27), the Ricardian socialist.

It is not clear why reference to this 'general law' was omitted both from the fuller version of Marx's 'simple labour theory' in *Capital*, volume one, and from the exposition of the prices-of-production theory in *Capital*, volume three. But it was *retained* in a revised version of *Wage Labour and Capital*,

1. I am grateful to David McLellan, a well-known modern authority on the young Marx, for confirming this, and supplying the reference to the French edition of Marx's works, edited by M. Rubel.

prepared by Engels, and described by him in his Introduction as 'not the pamphlet as Marx wrote it in 1849, but approximately as he would have written it in 1891' (Engels, 1950, p. 67).

What may, or may not, explain Marx's hesitation in including a reference to this 'general law' in his definitive work, *Capital*, is the fact that it is clear from the context that in his *Wage Labour and Capital*, Marx was of the view that this inverse relation holds, not only with *given* technology, but with *improving* technology.

But it is easily checked that the relation is strictly true only if we abstract from 'ordinary' joint production (Sraffa, 1960, p. 62), which may not matter, and assume given technology[2] which we cannot, for a typical capitalist economy, nor did Marx.[3]

Moreover, it can be established, with the tools of modern commodity-production theory, that with improving technology, the inverse wage–profit relation holds strictly only for 'sufficiently large' improvements in technology. Otherwise, both the real wage-rate and the profit-rate will rise, unless the rise in the real wage-rate is large enough to wipe out the effects of technological progress in yielding a rise in the profit-rate.

It is worth noting, in passing, that the results just stated have been confirmed by using the modern linear theory of Leontief matrices (Samuelson, 1957, section 2, pp. 892–5; 1960, p. 720). It has also been elaborated recently for 'subsistence wage' neo-Marxian models (Samuelson, 1972, pp. 53–7).

2. Sraffa, 1960, pp. 38–40. A more elaborate 'envelope curve' depicting wage–profit-rate possibilities with a given set of available techniques is drawn in Pasinetti (1966). With improving technology, these envelope curves would shift to the right (if the wage-rate is shown on the vertical, and the profit-rate on the horizontal axis).
3. In *The Manifesto of the Communist Party*, written about the same time as *Wage Labour and Capital*, in 1848 (Marx and Engels, 1950, vol. 1).

3 A post-Marxian verdict on the 'tendency for the rate of profit to fall'

While Marx's contribution to the discovery of the inverse wage–profit-rate relation with given technology has received no recognition (an exception is Bose, 1971, section 9, pp. 329–31), the main target of attack by critics has been the Marxian version of the theory of the 'tendency' for the average rate of profit to fall in the course of capitalist development.

The Marxian version of the theory (unlike, for instance, the Ricardian version, in which the tendency derives from diminishing returns from land) is derived strictly from the assumption that technological progress under capitalism makes for a rise in the '*social* organic composition of capital' (i.e. the ratio of aggregate constant capital to aggregate variable capital in the system as a whole), which sets up a *basic* tendency for the rate of profit to fall. It is quite clear that Marx thought this 'basic tendency' would be in fact stronger than the 'counteracting causes' holding it in check (Marx, 1959, ch. 14, p. 227).[4]

Now, Marx meant by the rise in the 'social organic composition of capital' *both* (a) a greater rate of growth (in *physical* terms) of machinery and raw materials, compared with the rate of growth of wage-goods (also measured in *physical* terms), and (b) a rise in the aggregate organic composition of capital in terms of 'labour-embodied values' as well as 'prices of production' (Marx, 1959, ch. 13, pp. 208–10), since, according to *his* 'transformation' procedure, the totals of constant and variable capitals for the system as a whole in 'value' terms were equal to these totals in 'price' terms.

However, in commodity-production models, on which the post-Marxian theory of chapter 6 (and of this book) depend, there is no suggestion of any plausible reason for thinking the

4. This passage in *Capital*, volume three, should dispose of suggestions that Marxian 'tendencies', such as the 'tendency for the profit-rate to fall' were *not* firm, empirically verifiable predictions, but guarded, inconclusive dialectical statements which could be superseded as often as they prevailed.

Marxian version of the theory of the long-run 'tendency' for the average rate of profit to fall is valid.

In commodity-production models, a greater rate of growth of machinery and raw materials compared to wage-goods produced and consumed in physical terms *need not* mean a rise in the reciprocal of the maximum potential rate of profit of the system (this is because units of fixed capital are treated as inputs which reappear as joint products after use). And even if it *does* mean a rise, the actual rate of profit may still not decline, i.e. the rate of profit with a positive wage may not fall.

Thus, there does not seem to be a rigorous analytical basis for the prediction that the long-run profit-rate will have a 'basic tendency' to decline in the course of capitalist development. However, this is no great calamity, as we shall see in Part Two of this book. Marx's main interest in this 'tendency' was to emphasize the 'self-contradictions' or 'internal contradictions' of capitalist development (Marx, 1959, ch. 15, section 2, pp. 242–5). The post-Marxian theory of capitalist exploitation of chapter 6, which grows out of modern commodity-production theory, dispenses with any 'falling profit tendency', but predicts 'internal contradictions' in the process of capitalist accumulation, which explain several contemporary phenomena in advanced and backward capitalist economies (chapters 10 and 11).

8 Parables in Economic Theory

1 Introduction

If the post-Marxian theory elaborated in chapter 6 is more or less accepted, the conclusion is that the Marxian theory of capitalist exploitation under competitive conditions is proved with the help of a completely realistic commodity-production model which contains no irremovable artificial assumptions, 'artefacts' or empirically unobservable entities. Chapter 7 showed that the post-Marxian theory of capitalist exploitation also confirms, partially, but significantly, an important Marxian prediction about long-run tendencies under capitalism; the chapters of Part Two will show that a few more Marxian insights are given a definite meaning with the help of the post-Marxian theory in interpreting important institutional developments in capitalist and socialist societies of various types.

If this is the case, we can say, with the benefit of hindsight, that Marx's 'labour theory' in *Capital*, volume one, referred to in statement 2 (chapter 4, section 2) is a valid parable in terms of our definition 2 (chapter 1, section 3) which says that a parable in economic theory is a model in which artificial, initial assumptions about unobservable objects are deliberately introduced to predict a result which survives the dropping of these assumptions. In other words, in *Capital*, volume one (and also in the *Wage Labour and Capital*, published earlier, referred to in chapter 7) the artificial assumption that total labour embodied in commodities is empirically observable, is deliberately introduced to produce a result, that capital is a relation of exploitation, which survives the dropping of this assumption. (How far there is evidence that Marx himself, deliberately and knowingly, introduced this artificial assumption, will be discussed in a moment.)

Much the same can be said about von Bortkiewicz's 'transformation' model (see chapter 5, section 4), which also included total labour-embodied quantities supposed to be known from direct observation, but led to the important conclusion (see chapter 4, section 3) that conditions of production of 'luxury' goods do not affect the general rate of profit. Von Bortkiewicz acknowledged the idea to assertions in Ricardo's *Principles* (1951, vol. 1, pp. 118; 132, 205; von Bortkiewicz, 1952, p. 32). Von Bortkiewicz was right in pointing out that Marx (whose notion of 'unproductive labour' was, as we have said in chapter 4, section 3, made concrete by von Bortkiewicz's conclusion) tended to dispute this conclusion. However, generalized for commodity-production theory as the proposition that conditions of production of 'non-basics' do not affect the general rate of profit, the von Bortkiewicz proposition helps us to interpret a number of institutional changes in capitalist or socialist societies, as we shall see in Part Two. Thus, for reaching *this* particular conclusion (about the role of 'non-basics'), the von Bortkiewicz transformation model stands as a valid parable, as defined in chapter 1. (This remains true, although, as we have noted in chapter 5, section 4, von Bortkiewicz's own 'deduction theory' of capitalist exploitation, which he tried to deduce from his 'transformation model' with the help of the further artificial assumption that all goods are either wage-goods or luxury goods, is not confirmed by any 'realistic' commodity-production model which must include the assumption that goods which are neither wage-goods nor luxury goods exist, and that they are not produced by unassisted labour.) However, unlike Marx, von Bortkiewicz does not seem to have been aware that he was making an artificial assumption when he assumed the observability of total labour embodied in commodities when working out the 'transformation' to 'prices of production'.

2 Marx on the role of unobservable 'labour-embodied' terms in economic theory

There is evidence that Marx recognized that in a full model of capitalism, in which 'prices of production' rule, 'by the transformation of values into prices, the basis of the determination of value is itself removed from direct observation' (Marx, 1909, ch. 9, p. 198).[1] Moreover, as we have noted in chapter 3, there is a close analytical connection between the Ricardian-socialist dictum that 'labour is the source of all wealth (value)' – which Marx denounced as a 'bourgeois idea' (chapter 3, section 3) – and the assumption that labour embodied in commodities is known from direct observation (chapter 3, section 3).

There is also the evidence that Marx justified the use of such artificial notions partly at least because he was not only interested in working out a theory of capitalist exploitation for its own sake, but in teaching it to a large audience (especially of workers) who would use it as a guide to (revolutionary) political action. Thus Marx expected the workers' press in nineteenth century Germany to act as the principal defenders of his economic theories against bourgeois critics (Marx, 1954, p. 16). He also recognized that once one assumes the observability of labour-contents of commodities, it is easy to make a distinction between 'necessary' and 'surplus' labour-time under capitalism. This makes the 'fact' of workers' exploitation under capitalism as transparent as the 'extraction of surplus labour' under feudalism (Marx, 1954, ch. 9, section 1, p. 217). (Marx even admitted that the 'extraction of surplus labour' from producers is clear beyond doubt, or is self-evident, only in a particular type of feudalism, viz. the 'labour rent' system under serfdom (Marx, 1959, ch. 47, section 2, p. 772).)

Thus, there are hints in the evidence just cited that Marx not only recognized the artificiality of the assumption of the

1. In Marx (1959), i.e. the Moscow edition of Marx's *Capital*, volume three, this sentence is given as: 'The transformation of values into prices of production serves to obscure the basis of determining value itself' (p. 166).

observability of labour-contents under capitalism, but that he used the assumption as a 'parable' for simple exposition of his theory of capitalist exploitation in a manner which makes it easily comparable to more 'obvious' systems of exploitation of producers.

But Marx and Engels seem to have been undecided on this point. Even when they *did* recognize that the labour-contents of commodities were *not* directly observable (unlike the Ricardian socialists or von Bortkiewicz, or modern Marxian writers who never seem to recognize this, as we saw in chapter 3), they seem to have thought that this artificial, non-observable entity is nevertheless *indispensable* for a theory of capitalist exploitation.

Thus, Engels gave his general approval to the following summary, by the historian Werner Sombart, of the role of value in the Marxian system: 'Value is *not manifest* in the exchange relation of commodities produced capitalistically; it does not live in the consciousness of the agents of capitalist production; it is *not* an *empirical*, but a *mental*, a *logical* fact ... ' [my italics] (Marx, 1959, p. 871).

Now, it is hard to conceive of 'mental' or 'logical' facts.[2] But it is clear that if the post-Marxian theory of capitalist exploitation elaborated (and defended) in chapter 6 is accepted, artificially conceived non-observable labour-contents of commodities are *not* needed for a valid theory of capitalist exploitation, and should be dispensed with on the principle of Occam's razor, i.e. rule 1 (chapter 1, section 3). (The only non-empirical assumptions needed are prescriptive statements defining capitalist exploitation, as we noted in chapter 6, section 1.)

On this view, Marx's 'first approximation', the 'simple labour theory' of *Capital*, volume one, will then fall into place as a valid 'parable' in economic theory, as defined in chapter 1, section 3. However, it was obviously impossible to assert this, until the modern commodity-production theory could

2. However, belief in such 'facts' is in the tradition of Platonic 'realism', and has been reaffirmed in modern times by so eminent a philosopher as Kurt Godel (Nagel and Newman, 1968, p. 99, n. 32).

provide the tools with which the Marxian theory of capitalist exploitation could be validated *without* using the artefact of labour-contents of commodities known from direct observation.

The case seems in some respects similar to the concept of the 'ether', which has subsequently been discarded as being artificial, but on the basis of which, the equations explaining electromagnetic radiation were worked out by Clerk Maxwell, and had great influence on the developments of modern physics. (The analogy has been discussed in the economic literature recently by Harrod 1968, pp. 181–2.) It is somewhat ironical, that the labour-content of capitalistically produced commodities can also be compared to phlogiston, a non-existent chemical that, prior to the discovery of oxygen, was thought to be released through combustion. It served as a link in the chain of advancing knowledge which led to the discovery of oxygen. Engels claimed (Marx, 1957, pp. 14–15) that Marx's concept of 'congealed labour' contained in commodities was like *oxygen*, which revolutionized chemistry. But from the standpoint of the present study, it is more like the phlogiston concept, which nevertheless fulfilled a historical role by posing a problem of identification of a chemical substance which led to the discovery of the empirically verified 'fact' of oxygen.

Of course, these parallels with developments in physics and chemistry should not be taken too far. In the natural sciences, when a proper theory supersedes a parable which has outlived its usefulness in most cases – apparently the kinetic theory of gases could be an exception (Samuelson, 1965, pp. 1167–9) – *all* the assumptions and results of the theory consist of empirically observable entities. But in theories of capitalist exploitation, as noted in chapter 2, section 4 (and the post-Marxian theory of chapter 6 is no exception), the entire theory cannot be reduced to a question of empirically observable 'facts'. There must be room for prescriptive statements among the definitional propositions of the theory.

Part Two

Problems of Contemporary Capitalist and Socialist Economies:

A Post-Marxian Analysis

9 Applications, Extensions and Properties of Partially Decomposable Models

1 Introduction

As already noted in chapter 8, a post-Marxian theory of capitalist exploitation is of interest chiefly for its own sake. It tells us that revolutions against capitalist exploitation which have actually occurred, are not devoid of rational motivation. Can the economic model on which the theory is based tell us more, and qualify as a post-Marxian political economy?

It is unlikely that the model will have applications and extensions which tell us much that is new on problems of 'quantitative economics', with which most modern economists have been mainly concerned. As we saw in chapter 7, the post-Marxian theory makes no empirically testable prediction about the long-run rate of profit in the course of capitalist development. Nor does it say anything new on, say, the 'index number problem', i.e. the 'problem' (if it is one) that all intertemporal and interspatial comparisons of complex economic magnitudes are necessarily relative. (An early critic of modern commodity-production theory demanded of the theory that it supply a new 'solution' of the index number problem, with the help of its 'standard system' construct (Reder, 1961, p. 692). But this, of course, is not possible.)

It is not unnatural to expect the commodity-production model of the post-Marxian theory of capitalist exploitation to explain the institutional changes in advanced and backward capitalist and socialist societies, i.e. the mutation of the political-economic model in these societies.

The reader will find that chapters 10 and 11 deal precisely with the geneses of such institutional changes as the emergence of capitalist colonialism, imperialism, neo-imperialism etc.

in the advanced capitalist societies, and of radical capitalism in backward capitalist societies. (A radical state-capitalist strategy in a minority of backward economies which are oil-rich is considered in chapter 11.)

Chapters 13 and 14 discuss the geneses of socialist economic models of different types and their economic rationale.

What about the thesis of the 'breakdown of capitalism' from the standpoint of strict economic determinism, which Marx and Engels (or, for that matter, Lenin, Stalin, Mao Tse-tung or Ho Chi-Minh) did *not* have, but Rosa Luxembourg did? An investigation undertaken in chapter 12 of this book suggests that it is *possible* to define the conditions of capitalist breakdown (for *both* advanced and backward capitalist societies) by adopting choice-theory political-economic models to discuss the problem.[1] (The conclusion does not, of course, suggest a theory of 'economic determinism' at work in a process of capitalist breakdown.)

What about the assertion, by some self-professed Marxists, as well as by non-Marxists or anti-Marxists, that *all* societies[2] which had accomplished a revolutionary transition to socialism were in danger of going into, or had in fact gone into, reverse gear, in a step-by-step process of restoration of capitalism, or in a chameleon-like 'change of colour' to revert to capitalism? Not so pointedly articulated, but more widely felt, is the view that socialist societies, stricken with *anomie*, i.e. a state in which the normative standards of conduct and belief in a society are weak or lacking, are ripe for the restoration of capitalism. These ideas have been in the air long enough, and have been controverted by recorded facts long enough, to make it worth while to formulate a socialist breakdown (or non-breakdown thesis) in terms of analytical

1. The reasoning is on the basis of an adaptation of the two-person, non-zero-sum game known as the 'prisoners' dilemma' in modern game theory.
2. Yugoslavia since 1948, Hungary since the 1950s, the Soviet Union, Czechoslovakia and China since the early 1960s, i.e. *all* socialist societies without exception, according to their critics, or defenders, or both.

models, and to test the models for logical possibility or impossibility.

Such a thesis of capitalist restoration does not seem to be testable with the help of models of interdependent, partially decomposable production structures. But it *is* testable with the help of tools of the modern theory of collective choice discussed in the Appendix to chapter 6. (A beginning is made in this direction in chapter 13, section 6.)

2 Properties of commodity-production models with heuristic powers vis-à-vis institutional change under capitalism and socialism

Most of the subject-matter in Part Two consists of the interpretations of the properties of interdependent commodity-production models, especially of the partial decomposability of the general prototype of such models. These interpretations are made, as we shall see, on the basis of the properties of interdependent commodity-production models taken in association with some reasonable assumptions about the political environment which are implicit, or are made explicit, as in chapters 10–15. Only in chapter 14 is restricted use made of the properties of commodity-production models.

It is therefore necessary to give a set of definitions and propositions about such commodity-production models, for ready reference.

Properties of indecomposable economic models of production and consumption

Definitions

1 An interdependent commodity-production model is *indecomposable* if all commodities in the system enter, directly or indirectly into the production of all commodities, as is the case in equations **1a** and **1b** (which represent the same system, with the same production equations, expressed in 'standard' (**1a**) and in 'nonstandard' (**1b**) proportions as far as the aggregates of the system are concerned). Since neither labourers, nor capitalists, nor landlords, all of whom must be represented in a capitalist model, can live on air, consumption

by these classes, in fixed proportions, must be included among the expressions on the left-hand side, if an indecomposable model is to be economically meaningful:

$$(2p_a+1p_b)(1+R) = 5p_a,$$ **1a**

$$(1p_a+2p_b)(1+R) = 5p_b,$$

$$(3p_a+3p_b)(1+R) = 5p_a+5p_b.$$

$$(2p_a+1p_b)(1+R) = 5p_a,$$ **1b**

$$(2p_a+4p_b)(1+R) = 10p_b,$$

$$(4p_a+5p_b)(1+R) = 5p_a+10p_b.$$

In **1a** and **1b** the notation is the orthodox Sraffa notation of modern commodity-production theory, used in chapter 6, section 4, except that the 'labour terms' have been left out of the equations, because they are not needed. It is easily checked (from Sraffa, 1960, ch. 4) that both in **1a** and **1b**, the production conditions of *all* commodities in the system enter into the determination of the 'maximum rate of profit' (which is the only possible rate of profit in an indecomposable system under definition 1).

2 The maximum rate of profit R in an indecomposable system of interdependent production (and consumption) is the ratio of the excess (surplus) production of each commodity in the system to the aggregate means of production (consisting of all commodities) employed in production. To illustrate, in **1a**, the value of R can be read off straightaway, without solving for prices:

$$R = \frac{2p_a+2p_b}{3p_a+3p_b} = \frac{2}{3}.$$ **2a**

In **1b**, solving for prices, we have $p_a = p_b = 1$, so that:

$$R = \frac{1p_a+5p_b}{4p_a+5p_b} = \frac{2}{3}.$$ **2b**

A distinction should be drawn between the maximum rate of profit in an indecomposable commodity production system, and the 'aggregate rate of surplus value' of the system.

3 The aggregate rate of surplus value $ARSV$ of an indecomposable system of interdependent production and consumption is the ratio of the surplus production of each commodity *plus* the commodities consumed in fixed proportions by capitalists (*including* capitalist landlords) to the aggregate inputs (*excluding* capitalists' consumption in fixed proportions) of the system. Thus, in **1a**, if capitalists consume $0 \cdot 5p_a + 0 \cdot 5p_b$ in the aggregate,

$$ARSV = \frac{2 \cdot 5p_a + 2 \cdot 5p_b}{2 \cdot 5p_a + 2 \cdot 5p_b} = 1. \qquad \text{3a}$$

On the other hand, in **1b**, if capitalists consume $0 \cdot 5p_a + 0 \cdot 5p_b$, putting $p_a = p_b = 1$, we have

$$ARSV = \frac{1 \cdot 5p_a + 5 \cdot 5p_b}{3 \cdot 5p_a + 4 \cdot 5p_b} = \frac{7}{8}. \qquad \text{3b}$$

4 The aggregate capital accumulation rate $ACAR$ in an indecomposable system is the ratio of aggregate surplus to the aggregate inputs of the system. In **1a** it is easy to see that

$$ACAR = \frac{2p_a + 2p_b}{3p_a + 3p_b} = \frac{2}{3}. \qquad \text{4a}$$

In **1b** with the solution $p_a = p_b = 1$, we have

$$ACAR = \frac{1p_a + 5p_b}{4p_a + 5p_b} = \frac{2}{3}. \qquad \text{4b}$$

Propositions

It follows immediately from definitions 1–4 that, in an indecomposable system of interdependent production and consumption, the aggregate capital accumulation rate $ACAR$ is *equal* to the maximum profit-rate R, and *both* these rates are *less* than the aggregate rate of surplus value $ARSV$.

1 As we shall see in chapters 10 and 11, this property (which does *not* hold for partially decomposable systems, as noted below), makes an indecomposable system an 'ideal' capitalist system. However even such 'ideal' capitalist systems have a problem of 'demand-supply disproportions' originating in shifts in the fixed proportions in consumption (i.e. a change in

consumer tastes) and in production (i.e. a change in technology).

2 This problem arises because in an indecomposable system of capitalist production, any change in consumer tastes or in technology, involving the use of new products, or a change in the fixed proportions in consumption and/or production in any industry, changes R and all prices, and *a fortiori* the *ACAR* and the *ARSV*.

This proposition merely follows from the proof of the uniqueness of a maximum rate of profit compatible with all-positive prices in an indecomposable system (Sraffa, 1960, chapters 3–5), except that in the indecomposable system (definition 1), consumption in fixed proportions has been explicitly admitted. We shall see in chapter 10 that the proposition helps explain 'colonialist' policies in early capitalism.

3 Partially decomposable models

It has been said more than once in earlier chapters that the general prototype of a capitalist economic model has a partially decomposable structure. Some definitions are now given for partially decomposable models of production and consumption.

Definitions

5 A partially decomposable production structure contains both basic and non-basic commodities.

6 Basics are produced commodities which enter, directly or indirectly, into the production of all commodities in the system, as raw materials, capital equipment, or as consumer goods which are consumed in fixed proportions, and enter into the production of other basic commodities.

7 Non-basics are commodities which do not enter, directly or indirectly, into the production of all commodities, i.e. they do not enter into the production of basic commodities. Some non-basics are final consumer goods (consumed in variable proportions), others are producer goods which enter, as raw materials or capital equipment, into the production only of

other non-basics, except themselves (see assumption 1, chapter 6, section 3).

8 In a partially decomposable system, consisting of basics and non-basics, R is the ratio of surplus production of basics to the aggregate input of basics in the system (Sraffa, 1960, ch. 4, p. 25). Thus the production conditions of non-basics, reflected in their production equations, do not affect the determination of the maximum rate of profit of the system.

9 In a partially decomposable system, consisting of basics and non-basics, the $ARSV$ is the ratio of the surplus production of each commodity (basic and non-basic) in the system, to the aggregate inputs of all commodities (basic or non-basic) entering as means of production in the system.

10 In a partially decomposable system, consisting of basics and non-basics, the $ACAR$ of the system is the ratio of the aggregate surplus of all basics and non-basics, *except* 'pure' non-basics, which are final consumer goods consumed in variable proportions, to the aggregate inputs of basics and non-basics in the system.[3]

Equation **5** illustrates a partially decomposable model, consisting of one basic good A, a non-basic producer good C which enters only into the production of a non-basic final consumer good D:

$$(2p_a+0p_c+0p_d)(1+r)+\tfrac{1}{3}w = 5p_a,$$

$$(2p_a+0p_c+0p_d)(1+r)+\tfrac{1}{3}w = 6p_c,$$

$$(0p_a+5p_c+0p_d)(1+r)+\tfrac{1}{3}w = 3p_d,$$

$$(4p_a+5p_c+0p_d)(1+r)+w = 5p_a+6p_c+3p_d.$$

$\qquad\qquad\qquad\qquad\qquad\qquad\qquad\qquad\qquad\qquad\qquad$ **5**

3. The $ACAR$ as defined here, is based on an exact specification of the Baran–Sweezy notion of the 'economic surplus' of the system, as distinguished from its 'surplus value'. But in this book, only advertising expenses with respect to non-basics (counted as a part of sales-promotion expenditure), is counted as a part of the 'economic surplus', whereas in the Baran–Sweezy–Phillips calculation, *all* advertising expenditure is so counted (Baran and Sweezy, 1970, pp. 23–4, 365).

If we assume that workers consume composite wage-goods (which may vary in different industries, but appear as basics in 5 because every product is a basic), then, as capitalists consume in variable proportions, we can put $r = R$ (and $w = 0$), and derive $r = R = \frac{3}{2}, p_a = 1, p_c = \frac{5}{6}, p_d = 125/36$.

With this solution, we have

$$R = \frac{3p_a}{2p_a} = \frac{3}{2} \qquad \qquad \text{6a}$$

$$ARSV = \frac{1p_a + 1p_c + 3p_d}{4p_a + 5p_c} = \frac{3}{2} \qquad \qquad \text{7a}$$

$$ACAR = \frac{1p_a + 1p_c}{4p_a + 5p_c} = \frac{11}{49}. \qquad \qquad \text{8a}$$

On the other hand, we could assume, instead, that *both* workers and capitalists consume in variable proportions. We could then put $r = \frac{3}{4}$, and, by the formula $r = R(1-w)$ derive $w = \frac{1}{2}$. Filling in the labour terms, we derive $p_a = \frac{1}{9}, p_c = 5/54$ and $p_d = 107/324$, giving:

$$R = \frac{147}{98}, \qquad \qquad \text{6b}$$

$$ARSV = \frac{129}{98}, \qquad \qquad \text{7b}$$

$$ACAR = \frac{22}{98}. \qquad \qquad \text{8b}$$

An 'under-accumulation' problem

Equations **6a–8a** and **6b–8b** seem to underline a possible contrast between indecomposable and partially decomposable models. As we have seen, for indecomposable models (proposition 1) the $ACAR$ is always *equal* to R, which, in turn, is less than the $ARSV$. Now, **6a–8a** and **6b–8b** refer to a numerical example of a partially decomposable model in which the $ACAR$ is *less* than R and the $ARSV$.

It is, of course, impossible to generalize from a single numerical example. But it so happens, that we know from definition 6 above, that the following proposition holds.

Proposition

3 In a partially decomposable system, the *ACAR* is always less than the *ARSV*.

This proposition follows immediately from definition 6, which says that the *ARSV* is simply the expression for the *ACAR*, modified to include in the numerator the (positive) quantity of non-basic 'luxury' consumer goods multiplied by the (positive) price of the non-basic good.

But why should the *ACAR* be less than *R*, as it is in **6a** and **7a** and in **6b** and **7b**? It is clear that in these numerical expressions, the accidental quantitative magnitudes of *A*, *B*, *C* and *D*, as well as their prices, have determined the results.

However, it should be recalled that by definitions 1–3, in a partially decomposable model, basics are essential for the production of non-basics, but non-basics, even if *some* of them are producer goods (*all* of them *cannot* be) are *not* needed for the production of basics.

Thus, in a partially decomposable model like **5**, there may be non-basics which are producer goods, which enter into the aggregate capital accumulation process, and push up the *ACAR*, by having high 'own' rates of surplus production and accumulation. But the *ultimate destination* of such accumulated non-basics, their *raison d'être*, is the expanded production of 'pure' non-basics, or final ('luxury') consumer goods, which are consumed without any feedback augmenting the rate of capital accumulation. Consequently, the *ACAR can* indeed rise above *R* for a while in a partially decomposable model, but it must eventually become less than *R* of the system, if the process of capital accumulation is to continue.

Proposition

4 In a partially decomposable system, there is a problem of 'under-accumulation' in the sense that, although the *ACAR* might rise above or be equal to *R* for a time, *eventually* it must fall below *R*.

As noted at the beginning of this section, the existence of this 'under-accumulation' problem makes a partially decomposable capitalist model (definition 5) distinctly inferior to an indecomposable capitalist economic model (definition 1) which has no such problem.

'Demand–supply disproportionality' problems

The second problem faced by a partially decomposable capitalist economic model is the 'demand–supply disproportions' problem which also arises in an indecomposable capitalist model, as noted in proposition 2.

Indeed, in the general case of the partially decomposable capitalist model, which admits 'ordinary' joint production, non-homogeneous labour and non-constant returns, the problem is essentially the same as in an indecomposable capitalist model. The difficulty common to both is that it may not be possible to eliminate 'demand–supply disproportions' by adapting the aggregate output pattern without a change in technology, R, $ACAR$, all prices etc. (This is merely a repetition of the proposition in chapter 6, section 5, that if labour is heterogeneous, and/or 'ordinary' joint products are *not* ignorable, only semipositive sets of multipliers adapting the aggregate output pattern to the aggregate demand pattern may be available. Such multipliers are unusable, because they refer to 'negative' industries, which are devoid of any meaning.)

As we shall see in chapter 10, nineteenth-century 'imperialist' policies adopted by capitalist societies may be partly explained as attempts to use methods more sophisticated than 'colonialist' methods to adapt demands to outputs to eliminate 'demand–supply disproportions' arising in partially decomposable models.

A declining ACAR problem

A third problem which arises in a partially decomposable capitalist model is the problem of a declining $ACAR$, associated with fluctuating growth of aggregate consumption, on the basis of a given technology, a given income-distribution and given prices.

The problem originates in the variability of consumption,

which is excluded, by definition, in an indecomposable capitalist model. This is the *necessary* condition for the problem to arise. The *sufficient* condition for a partially decomposable capitalist model is not clear, and awaits further investigation.

Thus, exactly why fluctuating growth of aggregate consumption in a partially decomposable capitalist model should make the $ACAR$ decline is not clear. But equation **9** is a numerical example which shows that such a thing is *possible*. This is sufficient reason to recognize it as a third problem arising with partially decomposable capitalist models, and to examine its implications in the next chapter.

In **9**, the technological skeleton of a partially decomposable capitalist economy (with A as the basic and B as the non-basic commodity) growing over time, with given technology and income distribution (and prices) is shown for the initial period t, and subsequent periods t_1, t_2 etc.

The entries in each line to the left of the arrow indicate the commodity inputs (including direct labour written as a fraction of the social labour force); to the right of the arrow is the 'industry' output. The proportions in which inputs are combined in each industry to produce outputs remain fixed throughout (i.e. technological change – or 'non-constant returns' – taken into account in the previous section is abstracted from in this section). This is what makes prices fixed, on the assumption that the income distribution is also fixed from t_0 to t_4. The prices can be worked out by casting the data of t_0 in the form of value equations, assigning a value to r or w and applying the prices thus determined to later versions of the model in t_1, t_2 etc. to work out the $ACAR$ etc. in each period. (The omission of the direct labour terms from t_1 onwards is justified, because the terms are assumed to change in such a manner as to preserve the input proportions in each industry, so as to leave prices unchanged.) Since, as already stated, 'demand–supply disproportions' are being abstracted from, the fluctuating growth of aggregate consumption is represented in **9** by the fluctuating growth of the *output* (with which demand is assumed to be always in balance) of the single non-basic *B*-good:

$$t_0 \quad 8A + \tfrac{2}{3}L \to 12A, \qquad t_1 \quad 10A + \ldots \to 15A, \qquad \mathbf{9}$$
$$ \quad 1A + \tfrac{1}{3}L \to 1B. \qquad \quad 2A + \ldots \to 2B.$$
$$t_2 \quad 12A + \ldots \to 18A, \qquad t_3 \quad 14A + \ldots \to 21A,$$
$$ \quad 3A + \ldots \to 3B. \qquad \quad 4A + \ldots \to 4B.$$
$$t_4 \quad 15A + \ldots \to 22\tfrac{1}{2}A,$$
$$ \quad 6A + \ldots \to 6B.$$

For this technology, it is easy to see that $r = 4A/8A = \tfrac{1}{2}$. If $r = \tfrac{1}{4}$, then, by the formula $r = R(1-w)$, we have $w = \tfrac{1}{2}$. Casting the t_o version of the model in the form of value equations (see **5**), we derive $p_a = \tfrac{1}{6}$, $p_b = \tfrac{3}{8}$.

The calculations for the aggregate rate of surplus value $ARSV$ and the $ACAR$ are shown in Table 1.

Table 1 Rate values over time (in per cent)

	t_0	t_1	t_2	t_3	t_4
$ARSV$	58·3	63·3	65	66·6	71·4
$ACAR$	33·3	25	20	16·6	7·2
growth rate of non-basic B output		100	50	33·3	50
growth rate of basic A output		25	20	16·6	7·2

Thus the third type of problem which may arise in a partially decomposable capitalist model is that of a declining $ACAR$, associated with a fluctuating (falling or rising) rate of growth of aggregate consumption.

We shall see in the next chapter that imperialistic and neo-imperialistic policies, and policies of monopolistic sales-promotion of non-basics are explainable as alternative methods of dealing with the problem.

10 Capitalist Colonialism, Imperialism and Neo-Imperialism

1 Introduction

In this chapter, indecomposable and partially decomposable analytical models, whose properties and problems were examined in the previous chapter, are used in an attempt to trace the geneses of strategies of capitalist colonialism, imperialism and neo-imperialism, as well as the (strictly *non*-imperialistic) strategy of monopolistic sales promotion of non-basics.

These terms are not always precisely defined, at least with respect to their economic attributes, and are often used interchangeably in Marxian and neo-Marxian literature (which alone pay serious attention to these phenomena). However, in this chapter a sharp distinction will be drawn, for analytical purposes, between these strategies which will be treated as potential *alternatives*. (In practice, of course, it will be convenient, and necessary, to try to explain historical phenomena in terms of 'mixed' strategies involving, say, a combination of an imperialistic and a neo-imperialistic strategy, or of an imperialistic and monopolistic sales promotion strategy etc.)

Thus, colonialism and imperialism will be treated as alternative ways of dealing with the accumulation problems of a capitalist society. The essential distinction between the two is that with the former strategy there is annihilation or assimilation of the populations of pre-capitalist societies, so as to *create* 'empty spaces' available for settlement of the excess population of the colonizing country. With the latter, however, the populations of pre-capitalist societies are preserved, but their consumption patterns and production structures are drastically altered to solve the capital accumulation problems of the imperialist country.

A common feature of the colonialist and imperialist strategies must be noted. In no case can they involve a systematic transfer of economic resources from the colonizing and imperialist countries to the colonized and dependent countries. (If any colony or dependency actually does 'bleed' the colonialist or imperialist country in this manner, it will be abandoned, to write off losses. On the other hand, colonialist and imperialist strategies will generally involve outright plunder and 'tribute', i.e. a gross or net extraction of economic resources – which may also take the form of extraction of captured slaves or 'indentured labourers' – from the colonized or dependent country. These features of colonialist or imperialist strategies have been much emphasized in the Marxian literature, and are perfectly compatible with the analyses of this chapter.)

Neo-imperialist strategies are also designed to solve the capital accumulation problems of advanced capitalist societies. But it is an essential, distinguishing feature of a neo-imperialist strategy that it involves some *free* transfer of resources from the neo-imperialist country to the neo-colonial country (which, as we have just noted, is *excluded* by a colonialist or imperialist strategy), in the form of foreign economic-aid programmes. If a foreign aid programme involved *only* a free gift of economic resources which were also freely convertible, such a programme could hardly be called neo-imperialist. But we shall assume that the whole of a foreign aid programme does *not* involve this, that it is mostly on a loan basis, whether interest-free or not, and that the gift component of the foreign aid programme also consists of commodity-tied and/or country-tied transfer of resources. Foreign aid programmes on such terms are neo-imperialistic programmes because they prevent the recipient countries from adopting rapid accumulation strategies (an aspect which will be explored in chapter 11).

Imperialistic, and still more the neo-imperialistic strategies require the use of 'state-capitalist' instruments of policy. (These involve the use of partial or selective physical and monetary controls, as well as a 'functional' approach to public finance, by which government resource-mobilization and expenditure programmes are specifically designed to solve long-run capital accumulation problems in the collective interest of the capitalist class as a whole.)

By contrast, monopolistic sales-promotion of non-basics is a strictly private enterprise strategy. It is also, in principle, capable of being used as a *non*-imperialistic strategy, i.e. an 'internal' or domestic strategy which does not necessarily conflict with the interests of other capitalist societies. (Of course, this strategy is perfectly compatible with the use of state-capitalist policy instruments as a part of a short-run contra-cyclical strategy, or a long-run imperialistic or neo-imperialistic strategy.)

As we shall see in section 2, a colonialist strategy may be adopted either by a capitalist economy with an indecomposable structure of production and consumption, or by one with a partially decomposable structure, to deal with the demand–supply disproportions problem which, as we saw in chapter 9, section 2, is common to both.

Imperialistic (section 3), neo-imperialistic (section 4) or monopolistic sales-promotion strategies (section 5) are, however, more likely to be the dominant strategies adopted by capitalist societies with partially decomposable production structures to deal with the demand–supply disproportions problem. This is chiefly because they are also suitable for dealing with the *third* problem that arises in such societies, discussed in chapter 9, section 2, viz. the problem of a declining aggregate capital accumulation rate associated with fluctuating growth of aggregate consumption.

On the other hand, imperialistic, neo-imperialistic and monopolistic sales-promotion strategies are powerless to solve the *first* problem which arises in partially decomposable capitalist economic models – the problem of 'under-accumulation' (chapter 9, section 2). The *absence* of such a problem makes an indecomposable capitalist economic-model the ideal one, even though it breeds colonialism from the viewpoint of the 'historical mission' of capitalism.

2 Colonialism

As already noted in definition 1 (chapter 9, section 2), an indecomposable capitalist economic-model has no non-basics because consumption is in fixed proportions, and consumer goods enter all production processes on the same footing as feed for cattle or oil for machines.

Such a capitalist economic model could exist where Puritan capitalists preach and enforce 'consumption for subsistence' on workers and practice frugality themselves, or at any rate engage in conventional 'conspicuous consumption' in fixed proportions, along with capitalist landlords, some of whom may run large plantations on the basis of modern slave labour.

An indecomposable capitalist economic model would function (see statement 1, chapter 9, section 1) as an 'ideal' capitalist economy, in which the aggregate capital accumulation rate $ACAR$ is equal to the maximum rate of profit R. But it would face demand–supply adjustment problems originating in periodic changes in the fixed proportions involved in capitalists', landlords' or workers' consumption, or in technological progress represented by the use of new products and in the adoption of new methods of production. Such once-over changes in the fixed proportions may result from changes of fashions in consumption, the rise of new religious sects or major advances in technical knowledge (each of which may be promoted by foreign contacts through wars, trade, etc.).

In principle, an indecomposable capitalist economic model has three alternative ways of adjusting to such shifts in consumption and production patterns. The first is a purely 'internal' autarkic adaptation of input–output proportions (including those that are required to introduce new producer or consumer products), which would change R for the system, and all prices. (Assuming that demand shifts are independent of prices and incomes, i.e. that they are caused by a pure change in tastes, there would be a stable outcome in the adjustment process.) The second is an adaptation via free world trade, which could, ideally, require minimal adjustments, since the world market would have a more diversified consumption and resource-endowment pattern than any single capitalist economy.

It is clear that the second alternative would be preferred to the first, if it were available. But opportunities for free world trade might be restricted by mercantilist policies dominated by a fear of imports and a stress on exports, adopted by all nascent capitalist societies.

On the other hand, the balance of *global* economic, political and military power may be very uneven 'when the division of the world between the major capitalist powers has not yet been completed' (Lenin), or at least the balance of *regional* economic, political and military power may be uneven. This would make a third, 'colonialist' solution the most preferred alternative. Outright plunder of goods (and treasure) in foreign territory (especially of pre-capitalist societies) or imports on dictated 'concessional' terms, could be combined with missions to find 'vents' for domestic surplus production in foreign lands, to offset domestic demand–supply disproportions. (Except in so far as new goods are involved, this could also be achieved with minimal adjustment in input–output proportions, the general profit-rate, prices etc.)

Consider now a capitalist economy in which capitalists have recoiled from a Puritan ethos to adopt a Cavalier or Epicurean ethos, and have begun to recognize the 'economy of high wages', so that consumption by capitalists, capitalist landlords and by a 'labour aristocracy' is in variable proportions. (This implies not only that there are heterogeneous consumption patterns, but that they cannot be anticipated sufficiently well in advance to be taken into account as fixed inputs in the production process.)

Such a capitalist economy will have a partially decomposable production structure, in which consumer goods, and producer goods which are used to produce only final consumer goods, appear as non-basics, as in definition 1 (chapter 9, section 2).

As we saw in chapter 9, section 2, a capitalist economy with a partially decomposable structure of production and consumption, would face *three* basic problems of capitalist accumulation – the 'under-accumulation' problem, the 'demand–supply disproportions' problem, and the declining aggregate capital accumulation rate problem.

In so far as a capitalist economy with a partially decomposable production structure also functions in the context of an uneven regional balance of global power, it could adopt 'colonialist' methods to solve its 'demand–supply disproportions' problem, or the problem of declining capital-accumulation rate associated with a fluctuating growth in aggregate consumption.

3 Imperialism

However, a 'mature' capitalist economy with a partially decomposable physical structure is more likely to function in the framework of a more evenly matched balance of global economic, political and military power. In such a context, each colonialist initiative is likely to be frustrated by powerful rival capitalist powers who did not take this particular initiative, and who may 'defend' the 'victims of colonialist aggression'.

The 'mature' capitalist power could then adopt more sophisticated 'imperialist' palliatives, e.g. 'open door' policies imposed on independent pre-capitalist countries (e.g. Japan and China in the nineteenth century), 'free trade' policies plus railway development programmes to 'open up' populous, conquered territories (e.g. India after 1857), enlargement of domestic 'free trade' areas by the formation of 'common markets' (e.g. the German *Zollverein* established on Prussian initiative in 1818), the US economic penetration of Latin America which went under the cover of the Monroe Doctrine etc.

Imperialist palliatives could, of course, provide a solution for the 'demand–supply disproportions' problem. But they could also bring under control the adverse consequences for capitalist accumulation of a fluctuating growth in aggregate consumption.

What imperialist palliatives could achieve to eliminate

fluctuating growth of aggregate consumption is illustrated by
1, which is an extreme case of a near-perfect solution (which
is always available for a two-commodity model).

Equation 1 represents the same technology as the one shown
in equation 9 in chapter 9 (where the notation is explained)
in a process of 'equilibrium growth' without technological
change, with the difference that an imperialist solution is
adopted from t_2 onwards, which makes demand for the *B*-good
(which is the proxy for aggregate consumption) and *a fortiori*
the output of the *B*-good, grow at the steady rate of 25 per
cent. The imperialist solution arrested the decline in the
aggregate capital accumulation rate *ACAR*, and makes it
equal to and constant over time and equal to the rate of growth
of aggregate consumption.

$$
\begin{aligned}
&t_0 \quad 8A + \tfrac{2}{3}L \to 12A, &\qquad &t_1 \quad 10A + \ldots \to 15A, &\qquad 1\\
& 1A + \tfrac{1}{3}L \to 1B. & & 2A + \ldots \to 2B.\\
&t_2 \quad 12\tfrac{1}{2}A + \ldots \to 18\tfrac{3}{4}A, & &t_3 \quad 15\tfrac{5}{8}A + \ldots \to 23\tfrac{7}{16}A,\\
& 2\tfrac{1}{2}A + \ldots \to 2\tfrac{1}{2}B. & & 3\tfrac{1}{8}A + \ldots \to 3\tfrac{1}{8}B.\\
&t_4 \quad 19\tfrac{17}{32}A + \ldots \to 29\tfrac{19}{64}A,\\
& 3\tfrac{29}{32}A + \ldots \to \; 3\tfrac{29}{32}B.
\end{aligned}
$$

In this technology, as in equation 9, chapter 9, $R = 4A/8A = \tfrac{1}{2}$. If $r = \tfrac{1}{4}$, then $w = \tfrac{1}{2}$, $p_a = \tfrac{1}{6}$, $p_b = \tfrac{3}{8}$, and the values for the
ACAR etc. are as shown in Table 2.

Table 2 Rate values over time (per cent)

	t_0	t_1	t_2	t_3	t_4
ARSV	58·3	63·3	62·5	62·5	62·5
ACAR	33·3	25	25	25	25
growth rate of non-basic *B* output	—	100	25	25	25
growth rate of basic *A* output	—	25	25	25	25

4 Neo-Imperialism

A contemporary capitalist economy with a partially decomposable production structure exists in a world with other
state capitalist or socialist economies, in which all national

markets and investment outlets and sources of raw materials like petroleum are strongly protected against outside intervention. Attempts by even the most powerful capitalist powers to 'force open' such protective barriers by colonialist wars or imperialist penetration are blocked by the international balance of nuclear superpower.

However, foreign economic (and military) aid programmes can be used as a device to jump over these protective barriers and provide an adequate substitute for an imperialistic strategy which is no longer available, on a global scale, as the dominant strategy for solving advanced accumulation problems of capitalist economies.

As we have noted already in section 1, in general, foreign aid programmes do not consist wholly of unilateral, free transfer of convertible resources from the aid-giving to the recipient economy. Foreign aid is generally on a loan basis, and is commodity-tied and/or country-tied. Of course, in general, foreign aid programmes are not drawn up with the 'aid-tying' done purely in the interest of disposal of commodity surpluses of the aid-giving country: the requirements of the recipient economies have also to be taken into account, for aid programmes to be acceptable on a stable basis. However, the 'double-coincidence of wants' involved seems to start with the drawing up of the bill of goods which the aid-giving economy can 'spare'. The aid-receiving economy then picks and chooses out of the available assortment. Pure economic altruism by the aid-giving economy is not politically feasible unless the *quid pro quo* is in terms of clear political gain by the aid-giving economy.

In short, neo-imperialistic foreign aid programmes are *tailor-made*, like imperialistic 'open door' or foreign investment strategies, to solve demand-supply disproportions problems and the declining accumulation rate problem of advanced capitalist economies.

When massive foreign aid programmes are in operation, in the partially decomposable capitalist economic model, there is a 'sub-system' or giant foreign aid sector, which procures the bill of goods which are to be channelled through foreign aid programmes. The products of the foreign aid sector are non-basic, on the same footing as final consumer goods, which pass out of the system once they are consumed as 'luxury' products.

It is easy enough to visualize how the foreign aid sub-system can eliminate the demand–supply disproportions problem by buying up current commodity surpluses, and using the inflow of funds on account of foreign debt-servicing to eliminate shortages in the domestic market.

How a foreign aid programme can serve to offset the fluctuating growth in aggregate consumption and so arrest the decline in the aggregate capital accumulation rate is illustrated by model **2**. (In model **2**, we use the same notation as in model **1** to show the technological skeleton of a partially decomposable capitalist model which promotes growth of output without technical change, or a change in the profit rate, prices etc., from t_0 to t_4. As in model **1**, we abstract from demand–supply disproportions by making product A the proxy for all basic products in the system, and product B the proxy for all non-basic product quantities (other than those that are procured by the foreign aid sector producing product C) and product C the proxy for the bill of goods channelled out of the domestic market as foreign aid. Purely for simplicity, it is assumed that only non-basic products are siphoned off as foreign aid, so that the foreign-aid sector has only B goods as input.)

$$
\begin{aligned}
t_0 \quad & 20A + \tfrac{1}{3}L \rightarrow 60A, \\
& 15A + \tfrac{1}{3}L \rightarrow 10B, \\
& 5A + \tfrac{1}{3}L \rightarrow 5C.
\end{aligned}
\qquad
\begin{aligned}
t_1 \quad & 24A + \ldots \rightarrow 72A, \\
& 18A + \ldots \rightarrow 12B, \\
& 18A + \ldots \rightarrow 18C.
\end{aligned}
\qquad \mathbf{2}
$$

$$
\begin{aligned}
t_2 \quad & 28\tfrac{4}{5}A + \ldots \rightarrow 86\tfrac{2}{5}A, \\
& 22\tfrac{1}{2}A + \ldots \rightarrow 15B, \\
& 20\tfrac{7}{10}A + \ldots \rightarrow 20\tfrac{7}{10}C.
\end{aligned}
\qquad
\begin{aligned}
t_3 \quad & 34\tfrac{14}{25}A + \ldots \rightarrow 103\tfrac{17}{25}A, \\
& 24A + \ldots \rightarrow 16B, \\
& 27\tfrac{21}{25}A + \ldots \rightarrow 22\tfrac{21}{25}C.
\end{aligned}
$$

$$
\begin{aligned}
t_4 \quad & 41\tfrac{177}{375}A + \ldots \rightarrow 124\tfrac{52}{125}A, \\
& 28\tfrac{1}{2}A + \ldots \rightarrow 19B, \\
& 33\tfrac{531}{750}A + \ldots \rightarrow 33\tfrac{531}{750}C.
\end{aligned}
$$

In this technology, $R = 2$. If we make $r = \tfrac{1}{2}$, $w = \tfrac{3}{4}$, we get $p_a = \tfrac{1}{120}$, $p_b = \tfrac{7}{160}$, $p_c = \tfrac{1}{16}$, by writing out the value equations corresponding to the technology in t_0, and solving for r or w, p_a, p_b, p_c. $ARSV$ and $ACAR$ as before, give the values shown in Table 3.

The outcome shows how the aggregate capital accumulation rate steadies down at a constant 20 per cent, in spite of fluctuating growth of the non-basic B output, because there is

Table 3 Rate values over time (per cent)

	t_0	t_1	t_2	t_3	t_4
$ARSV$	275	350	256·4	351·6	255·5
$ACAR$	50	260	20	20	20
growth rate of non-basic B output	—	20	25	6·6	18·7
growth rate of non-basic C output	—	260	15	34·5	21·8
growth rate of basic A output	—	20	20	20	20

an *offsetting* (fluctuating) growth of the product of the foreign aid sector – the non-basic product C.

In the above illustration of a neo-imperialistic strategy, foreign aid has been assumed to be the instrument of this strategy because, as already emphasized, it is tailor-made for the purpose. (There is hardly any empirical evidence that it is instead tailor-made to serve the needs of rapid capital accumulation in the less developed economies.)

However, massive military expenditure, space programmes, or 'urban renewal' programmes in advanced capitalist societies could also serve the purpose. They are *not*, of course, tailor-made to serve as an adequate substitute for an imperialistic strategy for eliminating demand–supply disproportions or arresting declining capital accumulation rates. Their overriding objectives are to ·fulfil specific targets in military strategy, town surgery, housing construction and other such programmes. However, once these programmes attain massive dimensions, the commodity-composition of these programmes (which could embrace, indirectly, a large assortment of goods in the system) or their resource-mobiliz-

ation programmes could be suitably adjusted to give indirect
results which are similar to the more direct results of foreign-
aid programmes as illustrated by **2**.

5 Monopolistic sales-promotion of non-basics

Private monopoly-capitalist sales-promotion of non-basics
is a strictly *non* neo-imperialistic method of solving the
demand–supply disproportions problem or the declining
aggregate consumption-rate problem of a capitalist economy
with a partially decomposable physical structure. (It must be
emphasized that in a partially decomposable model of interdependent production, monopoly-capitalist sales-promotion of
basics is formally indistinguishable from technical progress,
and is not considered here.)

Model **3** illustrates a partially decomposable economic
model of private monopolistic capitalism, with one basic
product A, and a non-basic consumer good B (serving as a
proxy for all non-basics except non-basic D, which designates
the product of advertising or sales promotion of non-basic
B). Of the product of advertising activity, designated by the
non-basic D, naturally no surplus is produced (since it is
hard to see why a surplus should be produced, or how it will
be stored). However, since the product D enters into the
production of the non-basic product B as an input, and there
are fixed coefficients of production throughout the given
time-sequence in all industries, the output of product D has to
increase in the same proportion as the output of product B.

$$t_0 \quad 20A+\dots+\tfrac{1}{3}L \to 50A, \qquad t_1 \quad 25A+\dots+\dots \to 62\tfrac{1}{2}A, \qquad \textbf{3}$$
$$15A+1D+\tfrac{1}{3}L \to 20B, \qquad 18\tfrac{3}{4}A+1\tfrac{1}{4}D+\dots \to 25B,$$
$$5A+\dots+\tfrac{1}{3}L \to 1D. \qquad 6\tfrac{1}{4}A+\dots+\dots \to 1\tfrac{1}{4}D.$$

$$t_2 \quad 31\tfrac{1}{4}A+\dots+\dots \to 78\tfrac{1}{8}A,$$
$$23\tfrac{7}{16}A+1\tfrac{9}{16}D+\dots \to 31\tfrac{1}{4}B,$$
$$7\tfrac{13}{16}A+\dots+\dots \to 1\tfrac{9}{16}D.$$

In this technology, $R = 30A/20A = \tfrac{3}{2}$. If $r = \tfrac{1}{4}$, we have
$w = \tfrac{5}{6}$, $p_a = \tfrac{1}{90}$, $p_b = \tfrac{53}{1152}$, $p_d = \tfrac{25}{72}$, and the outcome is like
the values in Table 4.

Model **3** thus illustrates how, in a three-commodity partially decomposable capitalist model, in which non-basic D, the product of advertising activity, is tied to the output of non-basic B in the particular way indicated above, there is a near-perfect solution of the problem of declining capital

Table 4 Rate values over time (per cent)

	t_0	t_1	t_2
ARSV	310·1	310·1	310·1
ACAR	25	25	25
growth rate of non-basic B output	25	25	25
growth rate of non-basic D output	25	25	25
growth rate of basic A output	25	25	25

accumulation rate originating in fluctuating growth of aggregate consumption. The fluctuations in the growth-rate of aggregate consumption are eliminated, the aggregate capital accumulation rate is steady at 25 per cent, which is also the constant rate of growth of output of basic product A, non-basic product B, as well as the non-basic product of advertising activity D.

6 Concluding remarks

In sections 3–5, when discussing imperialist and neo-imperialistic strategies, nothing was said about the very first problem of partially decomposable capitalist models. As we saw in chapter 9, section 2, this is the problem of 'under-accumulation', i.e. the aggregate capital accumulation rate being lower than the maximum profit-rate, a problem which is nonexistent in *in*decomposable capitalist economic models. Nothing short of a *reversion* to an indecomposable model, it seems, will eliminate this problem. Unsuccessful attempts in the twentieth century to introduce Spartan rigidity in (consumption patterns), which is a part of the ideology of modern fascism, could be interpreted in this light, although the evidence that the ideologues of fascism in fact thought along these lines is fragmentary. The more recent stress on institutionalized technological progress through stepped-up research and development (R and D) expenditure is probably the more permanent method adopted by modern capitalist societies with a partially decomposable physical structure and an 'underaccumulation' problem to compensate for this by a continuous drive to raise the maximum profit-rate of the system through organized technological progress.

Hints have been dropped in the analyses of this chapter that West European colonialism of the sixteenth to eighteenth centuries can be explained in terms of the indecomposable capitalist economic model, while British imperialism in the nineteenth century and US neo-imperialism in the mid-twentieth century can be explained in terms of the problems of partially decomposable capitalist economic models. But the analytical models used in this chapter are versatile enough to explain other phenomena which do not quite fit into the historical stereotypes of European colonialism dominant in the sixteenth to eighteenth centuries, of British imperialism dominant in the nineteenth century, and of American neo-imperialism dominant in the mid-twentieth century. They can give an explanation of both the rise and atrophy of German fascist colonialism in Europe in the interregnum when British imperialism was no longer dominant and American neo-imperialism had not established its dominance. These models could also be used to explain a possible long-term decline in the neo-imperialistic strategy of foreign aid in the coming decades, and a switch to a mixed strategy of state-capitalist 'conquest-of-space' programmes with high-pressure sales promotion of consumer durables by private monopolies.

11 Geneses of Alternative Political–Economic Models in Former Semicolonies:

Neocolonial–Capitalist, Radical–Capitalist and Socialist

1 Introduction

In this chapter, indecomposable and partially decomposable economic models are employed to work out hypotheses about the geneses of alternative (institutional) political–economic models in former semicolonies.

The term semicolony in the present context refers to economically dependent societies, which were the objects (victims) of the imperialistic strategies of advanced capitalist societies (already discussed in chapter 10, section 3). Semicolonies are to be distinguished from colonies proper, established through policies of colonialist annexation, discussed in chapter 10, section 2. A few of these, e.g. Wales in the United Kingdom, pockets inhabited by ethnic minorities such as the American Indians or Blacks in the US, have been absorbed as regions inhabited by self-conscious, underprivileged minorities. Recognition of their special problems is sometimes responsible for a partial switch from a neo-imperialistic *foreign* economic-aid strategy to substitute neo-imperialistic strategy of *internal* economic aid to these regions. Thus, there are no special problems of a 'colonial economy' which cannot be analysed within the framework of analysis of chapter 10. But the problems of former semicolonies do deserve special attention.

From the late 1940s, most semicolonies have become, more or less abruptly, *former* semi-colonies, or, to use a slightly grotesque, but completely accurate descriptive term, post-semicolonial economies. They have suddenly found themselves living in a post-imperialistic world of strongly state-controlled capitalist or socialist economies. They have the advantage of having strongly-sheltered domestic commodity and capital markets, which no former imperialist power, singly or in combination, dares to, or is willing to, force open. This symbolizes the end of the era of domination of capitalist imperialism (as defined in chapter 10, section 3) on a global scale. But, in this post-imperialist world, the post-semi-colonial economies also face an acute disadvantage. New restrictions are placed on the access of the former semi-colonies to the commodity and capital markets of the former imperialist economies on which they were previously dependent.

In any case, for a number of specific reasons, which may differ from one semicolony to another, and some of which will be referred to in section 2 below, the former semicolonies are likely to run into a problem of potential long-term stagnation, portending an eventual capitalist doomsday in which the aggregate capital accumulation rate has sunk to zero.

Foreign economic (and/or military) aid is the most likely stop-gap remedy for such a crisis of potential long-term capitalist stagnation. (It has been accepted not only by non-revolutionary former semicolonies like Pakistan, Ceylon, South Korea and South Vietnam, or by semirevolutionary former semicolonies like India and Burma in the 1950s, but also by revolutionary Algeria in the 1960s, and Bangladesh in the 1970s.)

However, the bulk of the foreign aid originates in the former imperialist (now mostly turned neo-imperialist) capitalist countries. Moreover, it is well-known that foreign economic aid to any semicolony is never wholly in the form of outright grants (Bhagwati, 1967; Pincus, 1963).

Proposition

1 It is inherent in the logic of foreign economic aid that a period of unilateral net inflow of resources from a donor to a recipient country is inevitably followed by a period of unilateral net outflow of resources from the recipient to the donor country.

In other words, whether or not a spell of foreign economic aid inflow is followed by an *ultimate* condition of 'self-reliance' (i.e. doing without foreign economic aid received or being repaid, while maintaining a desired rate of aggregate capital accumulation, growth of output etc.), there is always an intermediate period of 'over self-reliance', when the recipient country has to arrange for a net outflow of resources without a *quid pro quo* in the current period (Hayter, 1971, pp. 174–5, quotes evidence from Latin America 1960–66, from published UN and IMF statistics; Enos and Griffin, 1971, p. 158 for their stress on this aspect of the problem created by foreign economic aid). As we shall see in section 3 below, this can easily make a neocolonial capitalist economy (i.e. a former semicolony which is dependent on neo-imperialistic foreign economic aid) relapse into potential long-term stagnation.

A radical state-capitalist political–economic model is then likely to be adopted to liquidate the problem of long-term capitalist stagnation, at least temporarily (section 4).

If the radical-capitalist model also fails in the end, a political revolution may usher in a socialist economy in a backward society (whose precise features are defined and discussed more fully in chapter 12), which adopts a strategy of socialist self-reliance.

The rough sketch outlined above is expanded in the sections below. The notation, concepts and properties of interdependent commodity-production models on which we rely are mostly the same as used in chapters 9 and 10. One additional property of partially decomposable models is identified by the notion of potential long-term capitalist stagnation.

2 A former semicolony's potential long-term stagnation problem
Assumptions

1 The economy is a *capitalist* economy in the sense that:

The bulk of its wealth is privately-owned;
The major resource flows in all branches of the economy are directed through market relations (free or government-

controlled) by capitalist enterprise, whose motivation is the accumulation of private capital;

The function of the apparatus of state-controls is to (a) control short-term departures from the long-run goals of capitalist production; (b) to harmonize the conflicting interests of different sections of the capitalist class; (c) to strengthen the social and political base of the capitalist class, by introducing new blood by political intervention and by subsidizing the numerous weaker sections of capitalists at the expense of the fewer stronger ones; (d) to pacify the workers, the poorer peasants and the middle classes, who are the victims of capitalism (including capitalist-landlord exploitation).

2 Large disparities in personal income (and wealth) exert strong pressure, compounded by a desire to imitate the consumption patterns of the rich in advanced capitalist societies, for allocation of resources for increase in *present* as against *future* consumption.

3 The economy is covered by a network of state controls – over production, trade, income, consumption, savings etc. – which impose *partial* controls over the production or consumption of some basics and non-basics, while exempting others, such that, in the context of assumption 2, there is *actual* diversion of resources from the production of basics to the production of non-basics.

4 Foreign economic aid from advanced capitalist countries is available to the post-semicolonial economy as government-to-government aid, doubly-tied (i.e. country-tied, as well as project or commodity-tied) to solve the 'disproportionality' and 'fluctuating growth of aggregate consumption' problems of advanced capitalism, as hypothesized in chapter 10, section 4 (see Bhagwati, 1970, pp. 15–16; Eckaus, 1969, pp. 145–6; Schultz, 1960, pp. 305–18). This would imply that such neo-imperialistic foreign aid would generally be available in the form of inflow of *non*-basic resources, rather than basic resources.

The apparatus of state controls has to act as a safety valve, and perform the function in assumption 1 in so far as the uncontrolled market, and the voting system (at joint-stock companies, chambers of commerce, political lobbies at the party and legislative systems) fail to establish an identity of public and private capitalist self-interest.

Anyone who strongly believes that in these countries there are precapitalist ('semifeudal') or 'post-capitalist' or 'noncapitalist' sub-economies functioning on the basis of regulated relations, after the pattern of international trade, with the capitalist sub-economy, will have to work with more complicated models. However, the model of a former semicolony employed in this chapter could then be regarded as one of the interacting models in this wider study, provided, only, that it is agreed that the capitalist 'sub-economy' contains that part of agriculture which is subject to capitalist production relations.

In a commodity-production model, assumption 2 can be given a *precise* meaning. The pressure for *present* consumption is expressed as a pressure for allocation of resources for the production of non-basics (as in definition 7, chapter 9, section 2), i.e. luxury goods, as against basics. As we shall see in a moment, allocation of resources for the expanded production of non-basic producer goods are qualitatively in the same class as allocation of resources for the expanded production of non-basic final consumer goods. Both create, ultimately, or immediately, the same problem, that of potential long-run stagnation.

Foreign aid inflow in the form of inflow of basic resources is more likely from advanced socialist countries, whose foreign economic aid programmes have, as we shall see in section 6, no recognizable economic or even political rationale. However, a foreign aid programme at its best, i.e. one which provides mainly for the inflow of basic resources, will be considered in section 3, in recognition of the fact that competitive capitalist-socialist economic aid to former semicolonies can make available such an 'optimum' foreign aid programme to a semicolony. As we shall see, this would still produce a problem of potential long-term stagnation. A typical neo-imperialistic foreign aid programme would steer the former semicolony into a condition of long-term stagnation more quickly.

Consistently with assumptions 1–4, the post-semicolonial capitalist economy which is our starting point can be formalized as a partially decomposable economic model of production and consumption represented by model **1**. This represents a post-semicolonial economy which produces a basic good A (which is a proxy for all basics in the system, as in the models of chapter 10, and for the same reasons), a non-basic producer good B (which is a proxy for all such non-basics in the system), and a non-basic final consumer good, the 'luxury' good C (serving as a proxy for all such non-basic goods in the system). (An assumption made throughout in the partially decomposable models discussed in chapters 9 and 10 of this book will be retained. This is the assumption that composite wage-goods are counted among the basics produced by the system.)

$$\begin{aligned}
t_0 \quad & 20A + \ldots + \tfrac{1}{3}L \to 26A, & t_1 \quad & 20A + \ldots + \tfrac{1}{3}L \to 26A, \qquad \mathbf{1} \\
& 3A + \ldots + \tfrac{1}{3}L \to 3B, & & 4B + \ldots + \tfrac{1}{3}L \to 4B, \\
& 3A + 2B + \tfrac{1}{3}L \to 6C. & & 2A + 3B + \tfrac{1}{3}L \to 7C.
\end{aligned}$$

In this technology, $R = \tfrac{3}{10}$, and if we assume $r = 15$ per cent, so that $w = \tfrac{1}{2}$, we derive $p_a = \tfrac{1}{18}, p_b = \tfrac{43}{360}, p_c = \tfrac{2279}{21600}$, in t_0, and $p_c = \tfrac{5087}{50400}$.

(The changing price of C reflects an 'improvement' in technology in so far as the input–output proportions in the production of the non-basic C is changed in t_1. But, since the input–output proportions in the production of the basic A and the non-basic B are unchanged, there is no change in the profit-rate or p_a or p_b. Technical progress concentrated in the 'luxury' goods industries is a likely feature of post-semicolonial economies described by assumptions 1–4.

The important performance-indicators of this post-semicolonial economy could be tabulated as shown in Table 5.

On the surface, everything about this economy is normal, from the viewpoint of the functioning of a capitalist economy. The rate of profit, as we have seen, is 15 per cent, the aggregate capital accumulation rate is declining slightly, but is still at a respectable 6–7 per cent. Market forces and government intervention are combining to act with foresight, to 'sacrifice' present consumption for the sake of increased consumption in the future, to promote an 'industrialization' drive which

Table 5 Rate values over time (per cent)

	t_0	t_1
aggregate capital accumulation rate	7·09	6·6
aggregate rate of surplus production of basic A output	0	0
rate of growth of basic A output	—	0
rate of growth of non-basic B output	—	33
rate of growth of non-basic C output	—	16·6

makes the output of the non-basic producer good B increase at a faster rate than the increased production of the 'luxury' consumer good C.

But the economy is under a cloud because the aggregate rate of surplus production of the basic good A is at 0 per cent at t_0, when $20A$ is required to produce $26A$, but the extra output of $6A$ by the basic A-industry is entirely distributed to produce non-basics B and C, so that the aggregate rate of surplus production of A in the economy as a whole is 0. Once the economy is in this state, it cannot (in the absence of technical progress in the A industry, or foreign economic aid in the form of inflow of A) attain a positive aggregate rate of surplus production of the basic good A in t_1, or in any later period.

Moreover, since, by definition (definitions 5–7, chapter 9, section 2) basics are needed to produce non-basics, but non-basics are *not* needed to produce basics, the following additional proposition (over and above propositions 1–4, chapter 9, section 2) about a partially decomposable capitalist economic model holds.

Proposition

1 If, in a partially decomposable capitalist economic model, the aggregate rate of surplus production of basics is zero, sooner

or later the aggregate capital accumulation rate must sink to zero and growth of output must come to a stop.

Thus, the post-semicolonial economy (1) is faced with a problem of potential long-run stagnation, which calls for urgent remedial measures.

3 Foreign aid inflow establishes a neocolonial capitalist economy and breaks potential long-run stagnation

A post-semicolonial economy can, in principle, adopt three types of remedial measures to avert long-run stagnation. The *first* is technological innovation in the production of basics, e.g. in iron and steel production, non-ferrous metals, electricity generation. But 'disembodied' technological progress in the production of basics is most unlikely. 'Embodied' technological progress will be easiest with the import of new basic goods required for the purpose, which may be impossible in the absence of foreign economic aid, because advanced capitalist economies will not buy traditional 'luxury' goods exported from former semicolonies. The *second* remedy is to reduce real wages of workers. In a commodity-production model of the type we are considering in this book, this would also involve a kind of 'technical change' in the proportions in which inputs are combined in the production of basics (as well as non-basics). In a post-semicolonial economy, this remedy may not work out due to trade union resistance, which may be strong, or, if there is no such resistance, because a cut in real wages would reduce labour productivity so that the problem of zero-aggregate surplus production of basics would remain unsolved.

As already indicated in section 1, the easiest, and the most likely remedy is acceptance of foreign economic aid, if only because former imperialist countries are likely to be waiting in the wings to offer foreign aid in order to solve their problems of demand–supply 'disproportions' or of declining capital accumulation rates originating in fluctuating demand for non-basics in the markets of advanced capitalist economies.

This would convert the post-semicolonial capitalist economy into a neo-colonial capitalist economy.

The *immediate* impact of acceptance of foreign economic aid, available on the best possible terms, i.e. as interest-free loans expendable for the purchase of basics, is illustrated by **2**. This represents the same technology as that for t_1 in **1** (section 2) for producing the basic good A and the non-basic B, with further improvement in the technique for producing the luxury non-basic good C. However, in **2**, unlike **1**, there is a positive aggregate surplus production of the basic good A, contrived with the help of an inflow of $4A+1B$ as additional resources made available through foreign economic aid.

$$t_2 \quad 23\tfrac{11}{13}A+\ldots+\ldots \rightarrow 31A, \qquad t_3 \quad 24A+\ldots+\ldots \rightarrow 31\tfrac{1}{5}A, \quad \textbf{2}$$
$$4A+\ldots+\ldots \rightarrow 4B, \qquad\qquad 4A+\ldots+\ldots \rightarrow 4B,$$
$$2\tfrac{2}{13}A+4B+\ldots \rightarrow 8C \qquad\quad 3A+4B+\ldots \rightarrow 9C$$

The inflow of foreign aid is assumed to cease in t_3 (when repayment in instalments begins). But the positive aggregate surplus production of the basic good A is maintained in t_3, along with a further increase in production and consumption of the luxury non-basic good C.

The performance indicators of **2** are as shown in Table 6.

Table 6 Rate values over time (per cent)

Performance indicators	t_2	t_3
aggregate capital accumulation rate	2·59	0·5
aggregate rate of surplus production of A	3·3	0·64
rate of growth of basic A output	19·2	0·64
rate of growth of non-basic B output	0	0
rate of growth of non-basic C output	14·3	12·5

Relapse into long-run stagnation in an 'over self-reliant' neocolonial capitalist economy

It turns out, however, that foreign economic aid provides only an *uncertain* respite, with the wolf remaining close to the door. Consider model **3**, which portrays what could happen to the economy (in model **2** at t_4), when the second instalment of foreign-debt payment is due.

The assumptions that foreign-aid inflow is only for one year, with repayment by instalment beginning in the very next year, has been made only to simplify the discussion. To make sure that such a construction of the problem does not pre-determine an anti-foreign aid conclusion, other simplifying assumptions have been introduced to tilt the balance as far as possible in favour of foreign economic aid. These are:

Foreign aid is repayable over three or four years, the first year's instalment of repayment being only 4% of the annual output of the basic-A, the commodity in which repayment has to be made even though it is only received for one year;

Foreign aid is entirely in the form of interest-free loans, so that the problem of compounding of interest charges is completely abstracted from;

It is assumed that in t_4 compared with t_3, policy-makers, in an effort to stave off a crisis induced by the burden of foreign-debt repayment, have cut production and consumption of luxury non-basic good C by 3·7 per cent, as an austerity measure. In actual fact, the evidence, though hard to quantify, is that the euphoria created by foreign aid makes for *increased* and not diminished conspicuous consumption. This possibility has been seriously discussed in the literature on the so-called 'two-gap approach' to foreign aid and development (see, in particular, Bruton, 1962, pp. 439–46; Chenery, 1969, pp. 446–9).

$$t_4 \quad 23\tfrac{1}{13}A + \ldots + \ldots \rightarrow 300A, \qquad\qquad \textbf{3}$$
$$4A + \ldots + \ldots \rightarrow 4B,$$
$$2\tfrac{12}{13}A + 4B + \ldots \rightarrow 8\tfrac{2}{3}C.$$

The performance indicators of this economy are shown in Table 7.

These performance indicators dramatize the fact that a neo-colonial capitalist economy may have the unique misfortune (almost impossible for any other capitalist economy) of running into a bizarre catastrophe. Thus, while the post-semicolonial economy, portrayed by model **1**, was only *heading* towards an inevitable zero rate of aggregate capital accumulation, the neocolonial capitalist economy represented by model **1** has not only reached the capitalists'

Table 7 Rate values over time (per cent)

Performance indicators	t_4
aggregate capital accumulation rate	0
aggregate rate of surplus production of A	0
rate of growth of basic A output (on t_3)	−3·84
rate of growth of non-basic B output (on t_3)	0
rate of growth of non-basic C output (on t_3)	−3·70

doomsday, but has already started to atrophy, with negative rates of growth of output. Furthermore, with the position of aggregate rate of surplus production of the basic good A, in which all foreign-debt must strictly be repaid, the economy is in no position to repay the second year's instalment of the foreign loan, and must default.

The reason for such a bizarre outcome is that, in a neo-colonial capitalist economy, the aggregate capital accumulation rate is a function of three parameters:

The annual burden of repayment of foreign loans;
Consumption in fixed proportions of basic goods by workers and salary-earners (if this is lowered, the aggregate rate of surplus production of the basic good A can be raised);
The pressure for increased allocation of basic resources for the expanded production of the 'luxury' non-basics like C.

Now, it is clear in the sequence from t_0 in **1** to t_4 in **3** that the crisis has not originated in the second parameter since there is no change in the input–output proportions in the basic A-industry. Nor has it originated in the third parameter, since there is actually a precautionary *cut* in non-basic C output, and no change in B output.

So it is clear that in **3**, the crisis has obviously originated in the first parameter, i.e. because the commodity-composition of the annual repayment burden (that it must be paid by shipments of the commodity A), and its size (unadjusted by rescheduling arrangements), have been rigidly fixed on the basis of a unilateral overall political-economic (and military) assessment of its consequences made by the aid-giving country. (In this particular example, if the donor country was willing to accept repayment through shipments of the 'luxury' good C produced by the aid-receiving country, instead of insisting on payment in shipments of the basic good A, a marginally heavier cut in domestic consumption of C, to the level of $7\frac{5}{9}C$ in t_4, would have left the neo-colonial capitalist economy with a *positive* aggregate capital accumulation rate of 0·8 per cent.)

Once the position portrayed by **3** has been reached, a capitalist economy can survive only if a 'consortium' of aid-giving countries makes fresh loans to ease its burden of foreign-loan repayment, or if the neo-colonial capitalist economy is converted into a radical-capitalist economy. The first palliative provides another uncertain respite. The second is discussed in the next section.

4 A radical-capitalist strategy to overcome long-run stagnation

A radical-capitalist strategy, designed to eliminate the long-run stagnation-atrophy problem discussed in the previous section, could be based on the following propositions.[1]

Propositions

1 No foreign economic aid is available or acceptable. (Alternatively, the first step towards a position of zero gross aid is taken by adopting a policy of zero net aid; see proposals in Government of India, Planning Commission, 1973, ch. 6, p. 12).

2 Wealth-and-income or wealth-and-consumption expenditure measures to reduce disparities would achieve a drastic cut

1. Outlines of such a strategy, with variations, are visible in recent policy proposals in India and Bangladesh and in Chile before the military coup.

in the production of non-basics, and set free basic resource for increased production of basics.

These measures could be:

Nationalization of large-scale banking and redirection of credit to weaker sections of the capitalist class;
Ceilings on the ownership of agricultural land and urban house-property;
Increased state trading to strengthen a permanent public distribution system for mass consumption goods;
Conversion of government investment into equity-holdings and formation of enterprises jointly owned and managed by private capitalists and government representatives for tighter control over allocation of resources by the government (see Government of India, Planning Commission, 1973, chapters 2 and 6, pp. 1–3, 16–22).

3 A reduced profit-rate, and a consequent rise in the share of wages (and salaries) in the net national income, would reinforce disparity-reducing measures listed in proposition 2. (No similar proposal is incorporated in the Government of India's Planning Commission's *Approach to the Fifth Plan*, which has, as just noted, several other proposals for a radical state-capitalist economy.)

What a radical-capitalist strategy could achieve is illustrated by **4**, which represents the same techniques for producing the basic A and the non-basic B as in **3**. This starts in t_5 by investing resources inherited from the neo-colonial capitalist economy in t_4, and repays $1\frac{1}{2}A$ of the foreign loan in t_5, the balance outstanding of $1\frac{3}{10}A + 1B$ in t_6, so as to achieve 'self-reliance' in t_7.

t_5 $25\frac{1}{2}A + \ldots + \ldots \rightarrow 33\frac{3}{20}A$,   **4**
     $4A + \ldots + \ldots \rightarrow 4B$,
     $\frac{1}{2}A + 4B + \ldots \rightarrow 6C$.

t_6 $25\frac{3}{20}A + \ldots + \ldots \rightarrow 32\frac{139}{200}A$,
     $5A + \ldots + \ldots \rightarrow 5B$,
     $1\frac{1}{2}A + 4B + \ldots \rightarrow 11C$.

Calculating the performance indicators for 4, and making comparisons with 3, we see that, by cutting down non-basic production (and consumption) drastically by 26·9 per cent between t_4 and t_5, the aggregate capital accumulation rate is raised from 0 per cent to 5·6 per cent, and the repayment of the second instalment of the outstanding foreign debt is made, equivalent to $1\frac{1}{2}A$.

However, in t_6, there is a spectacular 83·3 per cent rise in the production (for domestic consumption) of the 'luxury' non-basic C, even though, with repayment of $1\frac{3}{10}A+1B$ on the foreign-debt account, the foreign debt is finally liquidated, to make the radical-capitalist economy a strictly 'self-reliant' one (i.e. an economy which neither receives, nor repays, nor pays interest on, foreign government loans).

The consequence of this spectacular increase in the output of the 'luxury' non-basic C is that the aggregate capital accumulation rate sinks to a 3·3 per cent level. The cause of this increased pressure for the production of the non-basic 'luxury' consumption good could be increased consumption-disparities once the economy is restored to health. Not only the increased wealth, income and conspicuous consumption expenditure of the *nouveau riche* among the capitalists, including peasant beneficiaries of agrarian reforms, but also competitive feather-bedding, often at each others expense, by sectional pressure-groups among workers, peasants, ex-landlords and the salaried middle-class, could be the reason for this.

If this trend continues, the radical-capitalist economy may re-enter the *cul-de-sac* of a condition of long-run stagnation, to which it was supposed to be an antidote. Re-acceptance of foreign economic aid, even if it is done with the padding of loans from advanced socialist economies, will then earn once more an uncertain respite, and discredit the radical-capitalist strategy.

Either because this happens, or because the radical-capitalist managers of the economy, under heavy pressure to accelerate production of 'luxury' C goods, postpone the attainment of self-reliance in the first place by accepting rescheduled debt-repayment arrangements, a socialist model of a backward economy may emerge, as a successor, by political revolution, of the discredited radical-capitalist economy. However, sectional, competitive attritional feather-bedding by potentially revolutionary anti-capitalist forces may produce fragmentation and a sterilization of revolutionary politics, which could block a socialist outcome. The conditions for a breakdown or non-breakdown of capitalism are discussed further in the next chapter.

5 A radical state-capitalist strategy in oil-rich backward economies

With the explosion of a world-wide petroleum crisis in the early 1970s, it is possible to identify a group of oil-rich backward economies in the Middle East, whose 'self-reliance' (as defined above) is imminent.

The external setting of this curious phenomenon arises from (a) the concentration of most of the world's known petroleum reserves in these economies, and current non-availability of substitute fuels (nuclear or other), partly because of an excessive desire in the advanced capitalist societies to avoid pollution hazards, and (b) the balance of world power which debars foreign intervention in these countries to prevent a price-hike in their petroleum exports (with or without a cut-back in production).

The internal setting is defined by the radical state-capitalist measures adopted by governments of these countries. These measures extend from effective nationalization of the petroleum-producing enterprises located in these economies, in the sense that petroleum prices are now fixed with the prime aim of speeding-up the achievement of 'self-reliance', to the adoption of industrialization programmes on the basis of state-controlled (and partially state-managed) enterprises, land reforms which undermine near-feudal production-relations which have dominated agriculture etc.

These countries' self-reliance has been all but achieved, though the achievement may be temporary. It is theoretically conceivable that some at least of this small minority of contemporary resource-rich but manpower-poor backward capitalist-societies will repeat the performance of resource-poor but manpower-rich Japan in accomplishing a transition from a backward to an advanced capitalist society. On the other hand, the basis of their sudden (imminent) self-reliance, a favourable turn in their international terms of trade may be slowed down, or even be reversed. This may be caused by spiralling export prices of their petroleum exports and import prices of their capital-goods and luxury goods imports. Moreover, their industrialization programmes may be de-formed by the familiar pressure for accelerated import and domestic production of luxury consumer-goods in a highly inegalitarian backward capitalist society. The problem may be further aggravated by excessive allocation of resources for procurement of armaments to fulfil 'great power' ambitions.

6 A post radical-capitalist socialist model

A hypothetical post radical-capitalist socialist economy could be distinguished from a radical-capitalist one by features described by the following propositions.

Propositions

1 Production of all basics (without exception) is reserved for the public sector (i.e. all existing private capitalist enterprises are nationalized, and all new enterprises producing basics are public sector enterprises).

2 Public-sector enterprises producing basics are *socialized*, i.e. there are no privately-owned shares in public-sector enterprises producing basics, and sub-contracting to private capitalist firms producing basics is prohibited.

3 The socialized public sector incorporates all projects and enterprises which are involved in the supply of basic resources (e.g. electricity, water by irrigation, fertilizer, steel, cement etc.) to agriculture, so that the production of grain, as well as other agricultural basics, is firmly under the control of the socialized sector.

4 The basic motivation of capitalist economies – the passion to accumulate capital – is replaced by the socialist motivation of the maximization of the rate of growth of the output of basics (including in this, as everywhere else in this book, composite consumer goods).

The reasons for inserting propositions 1 and 3 in this list will be further discussed in the next chapter. Briefly, they are needed to ensure the irreversibility, for purely economic reasons, of the transition to socialism, so that if capitalism can be restored at all, it will be only by an 'irrational' (to a Marxist), purely political counter-revolution, which lacks an economic basis. A backward economy which is *not* described by these propositions is *not* identifiable as a socialist economy, is indistinguishable from a radical-capitalist economy, and requires no new model for analysis.

The inclusion of proposition 2 in the list is necessary, to eliminate the possibility, which must be excluded in a socialist model, of the use of the apparatus of public-sector enterprises and public controls, inherited from the predecessor radical-capitalist model, for private capitalist accumulation.

Proposition 4 follows directly from the economic back-wardness – in terms of consumption levels and technology – inherited by societies represented by the hypothetical socialist political-economic model. This proposition holds, even if the existence of elite groups in such socialist societies is a (perhaps ineluctable) fact of life. In such societies, parsimony and labour productivity may be emphasized, collective incentives and *homogeneity* in consumption may be enforced, in periods of 'cultural revolution' (or during revolutionary wars). In their absence, *heterogeneous* consumption patterns may prevail. But in *both* cases, aggregate consumption is mostly in *fixed proportion*, even though these proportions themselves are subject to periodic planned change. This means that the basic motivation of a backward socialist society can unambiguously be formulated as above, viz. the maximization of the growth-rate of output of basics.

A partially decomposable economic model of socialist production–consumption

Proposition 4 seems to imply that a backward socialist economy should be portrayed by an *indecomposable* production–consumption model consisting only of basic products (including among these, of course, basic consumer goods which are consumed in fixed proportions).

However, this is unlikely, if only because when a socialist economy starts functioning by stopping all non-basic production, it may throw more producers out of employment than can be absorbed in the basic industries (or be expected to emigrate like the refugees from Tibet after its land was socialized under Chinese hegemony, who, helpfully for socialist Tibet, emigrated to India). Thus, a typical economic model of a backward socialist economy is likely to be a *partially decomposable* one, with the specific feature that non-basic output-levels are kept *constant*. (The non-basic output may be converted via foreign trade, if possible, into basic resources for increased production of basics. Alternatively, a limited production of non-basics may be continued to allow limited consumer choice (variability in consumption) by the socialist elite.)

Model 5 represents the socialist economy which is the successor to the radical-capitalist economy of 4, which, it will be remembered, has liquidated its foreign debt, but may be running into a fresh long-run stagnation crisis induced by a reckless increase in domestic non-basic production. (As in previous models in this chapter, technical change is confined to the production of the non-basic C at a constant level, after being cut back by 45·4 per cent compared to the level of output in t_6 in the radical-capitalist model 4.

t_7 $26\frac{1}{2}A + \ldots + \ldots \rightarrow 34\frac{9}{20}A,$ **5**
     $4A + \ldots + \ldots \rightarrow 4B,$
     $\frac{1}{2}A + 4B + \ldots \rightarrow 6C.$

t_8 $29A\frac{19}{20} + \ldots \rightarrow 38\frac{187}{200}A,$
     $4A + \ldots + \ldots 4B,$
     $\frac{1}{2}A + 4B + \ldots 6C.$

In the first year of the functioning of the socialist model, in t_7, growth of basic A output (compared to the pre-socialist output level in t_6) is 7·4 per cent, which is lower than the aggregate surplus production rate of A in t_7 at 9·7 per cent. (The difference is due to the repayment of the remaining balance of foreign debt in t_6.) But, because the socialist economy has no foreign debt to repay, and holds constant the output-levels of non-basic products B and C in t_8, the rate of growth of A output (with t_7 as base year), and the aggregate rate of surplus production of A are both equal at a higher level of 12·01 per cent (in t_9, on the stated assumptions, this common rate would rise above 13 per cent, and so on).[2]

Indeed, in a socialist economic model, on these assumptions, the rate of growth of basic A-output and the aggregate rate of surplus production of the basic product would always be equal, and the common rate would rise steadily as long as the growth of population, and/or its changing age-structure, and/or rising consumption needs of the population require this.

Socialism and self-reliance

In the foregoing model, it has simply been assumed that the backward socialist economy has no burden of foreign aid repayment to carry, and is also doing without fresh foreign aid. This section offers an interpretation of a possible concept of 'socialist self-reliance'.

As a preliminary, since the question of aid cannot be divorced from the question of trade, it should be recognized that any socialist economic model has to be basically autarkic, al-

2. As repeatedly stated earlier, the single products A, B and C are proxies for many products in each case, as they are in earlier chapters. However, in this particular (socialist) case, where aggregate capital accumulation rates are not relevant and are not considered, it has been possible to assess the performance of the socialist economy *without* reducing the technological skeleton of the economy into value equations and deriving the profit-rate, prices etc. This is an advantage, because the entire question of the method of allocation of resources, of the enforcement of a socially-desired (planned) allocation of resources in a socialist economy is a major one, which is discussed separately in chapter 14 of this book.

though this may mean that a viable socialist economic model must comprise not one, but several political-economic entities. (This must hold, if only because socialist planning must be distinguished, as we shall see in chapter 13, from a 'free market' planning, at least in a backward socialist economy. Such socialist planning is practically impossible in a truly 'open' economic model. The uncertainties in such a model are too many to be taken into account by planners by any known method.)

At the same time, as we have recognized above, periodic shifts in the fixed consumption patterns, and some scope for consumer choice are likely even in an 'ideal', near-homo-geneous socialist community. Thus, commodity-wise 'demand–supply disproportions' may arise and go counter to the socialist objective of maximizing the growth-rate of output of basics. (Furthermore, given consumer choice, there is a partially decomposable economic model. In such a model, whether it represents a capitalist or a socialist economy, the problem of fluctuating growth in the demand and supply of non-basics may arise. As confirmed in model **9** (chapter 9) to describe a capitalist economy, but which also can be used to represent a socialist economy, this leads to a decline in the rate of growth of output of basics, which goes counter to the basic motivation of a socialist society.)

Of course, a socialist economy *can* deal with these problems by adopting purely 'internal' remedies. A socialist anti-consumerist drive could do just as well as a capitalist sales-promotion (the latter is the polar *opposite* of the former). But, since the world's demand pattern is likely to be more diversi-fied (even in a world of restricted world trade) than the demand-pattern in any one country, foreign trade agreements may be helpful as (economically cheaper) substitutes or supplements.

Propositions

1 Although a socialist economic model must be basically autarkic, it gains by limited foreign trade.

2 Foreign economic aid from advanced to backward socialist economies in the form of loans from the former to the latter is justified on 'international socialist principles' if there is a coordination of the national economic plans of the countries concerned so as to ensure a desired pattern of growth of output in the backward socialist economy, throughout the period of acceptance and liquidation of the foreign debt.

Now, it is obvious that, unlike capitalist neo-imperialistic foreign aid, international socialist aid described by proposition 2 has a built-in safeguard against 'socialist stagnation' as a possible outcome of aid to a backward economy.

Foreign economic aid on these terms is essentially on the same footing as international exchange, via foreign trade, on the basis of international specialization, optionally undertaken only if the terms are mutually advantagous to both the aid-giving advanced and the aid-receiving backward socialist economy. Its only distinctive feature is that it promotes an intertemporal international exchange of products, instead of a unitemporal exchange on a current-payment basis. (Whether such loans are interest-free or not is a minor matter connected with the accounting methods in vogue in the socialist economies concerned. Incidentally, in a socialist economy represented by a partially decomposable model, and assuming there is insurance against insurable risks, there is no role for the interest-rate as a premium for time-preference. The time-preference pattern is already incorporated in the structure of interdependent commodity production. Time-preference premiums, if any, are already reflected in the accounting prices which can always be worked out, though not necessarily charged, in any Marxian socialist economic model.)

There is, however, an uncovered gap in proposition 2. What, exactly, are the 'international socialist principles' which should regulate foreign economic aid, and *a fortiori* foreign trade, between socialist economies? The least controversial of such principles is, of course, incorporated in proposition 2. It may be called the principle of 'non neo-imperialism' in relations between socialist countries. But what is one to do if the proposed scheme of coordinated national economic planning results in an enforcement of the condition of 'non neo-imperialism', i.e. it gives the desired rate of growth of output in the *backward* socialist economy, but not the desired rate of growth of output in the *advanced* socialist economy? To accept it would be to invoke a principle of socialist altruism by the advanced socialist economies *vis-à-vis* the backward ones. But such a principle is in contradiction to the fundamental principle applicable in some (albeit restricted) form in all socialist economies – the principle of 'from each according to his powers, to each according to his work'. Moreover, if there is, formally or *de facto*, multi-national coordinated economic planning involving several backward and several advanced socialist economies, enforcement of even the apparently simple principle of 'non neo-imperialism' may prove difficult. A highly controversial way out of the impasse could be:

Proposition

3 Each socialist economy accepts a foreign trade-*cum*-economic aid agreement with another socialist economy if the terms of the agreement are better than any other available (including the terms available from capitalist economies).

Given proposition 1, i.e. that autarky tempered with limited foreign trade is in the interests of a socialist economy, the way out of the impasse just mentioned would solve the problem (proposition 2 would also be subsumed under it). (If this involves 'arbitrary' terms of international exchange of commodities between socialist economies, the arbitrariness seems ineluctable. There seems to exist no other way of determining the terms of international exchange of products between socialist economies.)

It goes without saying that a programme of socialist self-reliance must exclude acceptance of:

Neo-imperialistic economic aid from foreign capitalist governments (because they impose the danger of 'socialist stagnation');

Foreign economic aid in the form of outright grants or gifts.

Acceptance of such aid even from advanced *socialist* economies is ruled out on the socialist ideological principle: 'from each according to his powers, to each according to his work', which has already been referred to above.

Socialist economic aid and radical capitalist economies

It is worth exploring, at the end of this chapter, how far the economic aid of advanced socialist countries to backward radical-capitalist countries can be justified. The economic rationale of such foreign economic aid is by no means clear, and can only be justified by proposition 3 in the previous section.

A radical-capitalist economy is likely to have some sort of national economic planning system in operation, and acceptance of foreign economic aid from advanced socialist economies can be justified from *its* point of view, if there is co-ordinated planning to prevent the onset of capitalist stagnation òr atrophy via mounting repayment obligations. Such coordinated planning with the aim of avoiding capitalist stagnation imposed by repayment obligations to a socialist economy will also be justified from the viewpoint of the socialist economy, on the principle that a socialist economy must not adopt a neo-imperialistic strategy.

But what if, as noted in section 4 above, the plan targets go awry due to the ever-present pressure for greater allocation of resources for the production of non-basics?

The aid-giving advanced socialist economy would then be condemned to make an existentialist choice between two evils from the socialist ideological standpoint. The first is to insist on repayment 'according to plan' (why should a socialist economy go to the rescue of a capitalist economy, albeit one which is radical-capitalist?). But then the behaviour of the socialist aid-giver would be identical with the behaviour of a neo-imperialist, capitalist aid-giver. The second is to write off loans which cannot be repaid, i.e. to convert some loans into outright gifts. But to this there are strong objections, if the socialist principle 'from each according to his powers, to each according to his work' is to be observed. This principle forbids gifts by socialist communities, not only to capitalists (including the radical-capitalists), even if they are justified as being in the interests of workers belonging to the radical-capitalist economy. And the offence would be all the greater if the radical-capitalist economy accepted such write-offs from socialist aid-givers, but also entered into fresh foreign economic-aid agreements with neo-imperialist capitalist governments, because it cannot impose the necessary cuts on resources allocated for the production of 'luxury' non-basics. The socialist aid-giver would then be instrumental in keeping the capitalist neo-imperialistic machine going.

All this underlines what should be apparent from a similarly inconclusive discussion in the previous section. Despite what most sincere socialists believe (Hayter, 1971, p. 192), there does *not* seem to be available an economic rationale justifying international socialist economic aid. International socialist economic aid can be justified, in the end, if at all, only on purely political grounds. But even with a concept of politically-motivated socialist foreign economic aid, there are difficulties. It may be possible, in theory at least, to calculate the precise quantum of socialist foreign economic aid to a third (radical-capitalist, post-semicolonial or backward socialist) country to ward off a potential imperialist attack. But how can an advanced socialist economy adopt a stop–go foreign economic aid strategy to help *promote* a friendly socialist revolution in a backward country? Once a socialist political revolution has initiated an 'irreversible' transition from a capitalist to a socialist economy (with the fulfilment of conditions to be discussed in the next chapter), there is no doubt that a policy of foreign economic aid from a friendly socialist country can make the transition easier. But it is doubtful whether a stop–go strategy with socialist foreign economic aid can prevent a radical-capitalist regime from sterilizing potentially revolutionary socialist forces and thus promoting a successful socialist revolution. Socialist economies have always been able to recognize, and support with economic and/or military aid 'irreversible' transitions to socialism which have started. They have almost never been able to use foreign economic aid on a stop–go basis to promote such transitions *before* they have begun.

12 Conditions of 'Capitalist Breakdown'

1 Introduction

Analytical Marxian (or neo-Marxian) models of 'capitalist breakdown' have not been very successful. Neither the falling profit-rate, nor a simultaneous decline in profits and wages, nor increasing severity of the periodic crises of capitalism, nor 'insoluble' 'realization crises', can be proved and be used to construct such models. However, several political-economic 'breakdowns' *have* occurred in the twentieth century (even if they are restricted to the less developed capitalist societies). It ought to be possible to define precisely the conditions of such breakdowns in analytical models.

In this chapter, the techniques of modern game-theory analysis are used for the purpose. The framework constructed strongly resembles an adaptation of the well-known 'prisoners' dilemma' problem (Luce and Raiffa, 1957, pp. 94–7; Samuelson, 1970, pp. 482–3). The adaptation (by Samuelson) discusses the social problem of pollution.[1]

In the prisoners' dilemma problem, a judge, acting on the basis of insufficient evidence on minor offences, will sentence two partners to a major crime to one year each in jail, if neither confesses. If one confesses, but the other does not, then the confessing criminal will be let off with three months, but the one who does not, gets ten years. If both confess, each will be given five years in jail. In fact, *both* will confess,

1. Unlike the original 'prisoners' dilemma', which is cast in the form of a two-person game, the adapted 'pollution problem', as well as the models of this chapter, refer to *n*-person games. This adaptation to handle *n*-persons games is valid (Sen, 1969a, pp. 12–15). The results of the two-person games carry over, except that in the *n*-person case, collective solutions are not unique.

because (a) each thinks the other is a fool and will not confess, so that he who does confess will strike it lucky with a three-month sentence (when the other one, who does not, will get ten years), *or* (b) each thinks the other will outsmart him and confess (hoping to get three months and foist a ten-year term on the other).

In the pollution problem, it is assumed that each individual (a) detests pollution which harms him as well as others by reducing longevity, but (b) each prefers to pollute when others do not, rather than not pollute, while others do. The result is that all pollute, though there would be a unanimous vote for a strictly enforced law against pollution.

In this chapter, we construct a problem which resembles the pollution problem model more than the original 'prisoners' dilemma' problem, to get an 'impossibility result', i.e. a proof of the *non*-breakdown of capitalism. We then explore the conditions of an 'escape' from this impossibility result.

Definitions

1 Socialism implies public ownership of the means of production (no distinction is made between an 'elitist' or an 'egalitarian' socialist society).

2 A worker engages in 'selfish political action' when he 'makes the best out of capitalism' and gains, as a part of a group, *at the expense* of other workers. Such action may involve 'feather-bedding' by trade unions (or cooperatives) at the expense of non-capitalist consumers, or non-capitalist tax-payers (whose taxes subsidize wage-gains by workers in state-owned enterprises) or workers organized in weaker trade unions (other examples will be discussed in section 5 below).

3 A worker engages in '*un*selfish political action' when he engages in none of the activities associated with 'selfish political action'. (This is not entirely illuminating. More will be said on this in sections 6 and 7.)

Assumptions about the environment

1 Socialism is a feasible alternative to capitalism.

2 Workers' preferences are unaffected by capitalists' preferences.

3 There is a (revolutionary) transition to socialism when all workers unite to establish a decisive majority (or minority) for socialism.

Assumption 1 implies that there is no 'technological barrier' to the establishment of socialism, in the sense that the Marxian 'productive forces' are fully 'ripe' for the establishment of socialist 'production relations'. (The socialist revolutions of the twentieth century seem to demonstrate that this assumption is true almost everywhere.) It also implies, of course, that modern technology has *not* rendered capitalist production relations 'obsolete', and that it is compatible with either capitalist or socialist production relations.

Assumption 2 is a very 'strong' assumption inserted to underline the paradoxical nature of the 'impossibility' (of capitalist breakdown) result discussed in section 2, which says that capitalist breakdown may be impossible even if all workers want socialism.

Assumption 3 identifies the workers as the main instruments of revolutionary political action for socialism, and is so worded as to make the model applicable to contemporary backward as well as advanced capitalist countries. (The actual experience, at least in West Bengal (India), in the second half of the 1960s, shows that workers' unity, represented by the united front of parties committed to Marxism, is a good index of the unity of the 'revolutionary classes' (workers, peasants etc.). Conversely, the disunity of workers (and their parties) is an exact reflection also of divisions among the revolutionary classes. The problem of a *united* working-class which is unable to exercise hegemony over its potential revolutionary allies was never faced in West Bengal. So assumption 3 represents a useful simplification for analysing such cases.)

Workers' preference ordering

4 Each worker prefers socialism to capitalism.

5 Each worker prefers to act 'selfishly' unless other workers act 'unselfishly' (in which case, he too will act 'unselfishly').

Assumption 4 is another 'strong' assumption, made in order to sharpen the paradox in the 'impossibility' result. Assumption 5 is also a strong assumption made for the same reason. But it can also be justified on grounds of realism as suggested in section 3.

2 An impossibility result

It is easy to see from assumption 5 that all workers will act 'selfishly' because no one can trust any other to act 'unselfishly'. But 'selfish' action by each worker will not only *justify* a paranoid attitude of other workers towards him (and of his attitude towards other workers etc.). Considering the specification of 'selfish political action' by workers in definition 2, 'selfish' action by all workers would also consolidate and develop *capitalism*, though (by assumption 4) we know that *every* worker wants socialism!

It should be emphasized that, although in the illustration given for definition 2 defining 'selfish action', the reference was to trade-union 'feather-bedding', there are exact counterparts to trade-union 'feather-bedding' in any kind of parliamentary political activity, or in urban (or rural) armed guerilla activity by socialist workers (or, more generally, 'proletarians'). Moreover, voting in some form, including vote-buying and vote-selling, is by no means a special feature of parliamentary or 'electoral' politics. Voting in some form is essential in *any* trade-union or armed-guerilla activity (any absolute personal dictatorship is an impossibility); and voting in any set-up (and not only in the discredited parliamentary one) *can* involve the corruption of vote-buying and vote-selling. On the other hand, intimidation, violence and terror are widely used political instruments in all three types of political activity. In short, a strict adherence to boycott of elections, opposition to 'economism' by trade unions, or an exclusive dedication to armed guerilla activity is no guarantee against 'selfish' political action by workers and the 'impossibility' result.

How very different revolutionary roads may still lead warring communist parties to engage in 'selfish' political action whose end-result is the same 'impossibility' (of capitalist breakdown) result, is a hypothesis supported by political opinions and actions recorded in the legal and underground press in West Bengal in the late 1960s. (We overlook, in saying this, a curious doctrinal inertia which made them adopt as their strategic objective the elimination of imperialism and feudalism, but not of capitalism.)

The self-proclaimed communists (Marxist) wanted tradeunion and political feather-bedding 'today', to strengthen their hegemony as a prelude to revolution 'tomorrow'. Their programme for 'today' was very nearly implemented successfully when they seized control over the portfolios of internal security, labour and land revenue (through which agrarian reforms could be proposed and land distributed to their own supporters) in a 'united front' regional ministry (of parties of the left and centre). The decisive levers of statepower (viz. control over the armed forces, power to levy taxes on imports, exports, non-agricultural incomes, to collect excise duties on industrial products) were retained by the federal Indian government, formed by a bloc of the centre and the right, represented by the Congress party. But the communist-led regional government benefited from infighting within the federal Congress government, which more or less ensured federal non-intervention for a time.

The self-proclaimed communists (Marxist–Leninist), the so-called 'Naxalites', on the other hand, wanted revolution 'today', when, according to them, 'an excellent revolutionary situation existed'. They tried to spark it off by forcible occupation of government-owned land in the Naxalbari area of north-west Bengal.

Each party wanted to make a revolution in the interest of all, provided the other party fell in line. When the other party did not, each tried to annihilate the other at first by polemics and terrorism, and then by 'allying with the devil' where possible, to strengthen its own hegemony at all costs, at the other's expense. In the end, both very nearly atrophied as revolutionary parties, and ensured the non-breakdown of capitalism, which neither desired.

Occasional attempts by both sides to break the vicious circle of inter-communist attrition by striking at the 'common enemy' failed. (The communists (Marxist) tried to do so by organizing region-wide political *bandhs*, i.e. total work-stoppage except in exempted essential services, in industry, trade and transport, directed against federal government policies. The communists (Marxist–Leninist) tried with village *jacquerie*, led by urban youth, against landlords, iconoclastic statue-smashing in towns etc.) The upshot was:

1 Effective decimation of revolutionary communist cadres as much through mutual attrition as through military counter-insurgency operations by the federal reserve police. (The regional police, imperfectly semipoliticized by the communists (Marxist), and subjected to annihilatory attacks by communists (Marxist–Leninist), had ceased to be a disciplined force capable of purposive action.)

2 Discredit of communist electioneering, rather than of parliamentary electioneering as such, was the main outcome of a Naxalite attempt to impose a 'revolutionary boycott' of elections. This, buttressed by selective, occasionally neo-fascist rigging of trade-union and parliamentary elections by a dead-centre (rather than left-of-centre) renovated Congress party, finally dethroned the communists (Marxist) as the biggest single electoral force in West Bengal.

3 The strengthening of capitalism in West Bengal, more through a Malthusian 'natural check' type of remedy for the growth of revolutionary forces, than through a revival of the investment climate to raise the rate of capitalist accumulation (up to 1973, there has been no such revival, except, perhaps, to a limited extent in agriculture before the 1972–3 drought,

despite a step-up in federal expenditure for urban renewal in the Calcutta metropolitan region. For this, the imitation by the warring factions within the centrist Congress party, of some of the tactics employed in the inter-communist warfare of the 1960s, seems to have been chiefly responsible.)

Overall, the results of this aborted revolution are two. First, West Bengal, which *could* have survived, along with kindred Bangladesh, as a composite revolutionary base for a protracted constitutional-revolutionary struggle for the establishment of socialism in the Indian sub-continent has become more like a desert where the more things change, the more they remain the same, as in Anatole France's novel *Penguin Island*, and in which only radical political bourbons of the centre and left operate.

Second, the wider spin-off in the 1970s is the result that political trade-union feather-bedding is a major political-economic fact of life all over the Indian sub-continent, not excepting residual Pakistan, with its newly constructed parliamentary-state structure. But the technique is more successfully employed by, and benefits more, those who, unlike the communists of Bengal (or of Kerala), have no interest in the achievement of an egalitarian socialism. These are highly-placed technocrats and bureaucrats (including members of competing trade-union bureaucracies), engaged in an intensely 'selfish' Darwinian struggle for the survival of the fittest in a state-capitalist spoils system. (The struggle is made more intense by an inflation which is partly caused by it.) They have an overt vested interest in the preservation and extension of a radical state-capitalist system. Indeed, in such a system, political and trade-union feather-bedding is more or less indistinguishable from, and is a complement to, capitalist profit-maximizing activity. This is so, even if it involves lightning work-stoppages in power stations, steel plants, transport and banking to redress managerial grievances or the grievances of competing trade-union bureaucracies. Such stoppages are likely to reduce industrial wage-earners' earnings through increased lay-offs more than they reduce industrial profits. Even politicians and economists who are right of centre have little reason to be allergic to such activities, which are not very different from frequent, short-notice price-hikes in the midst of the inflationary spiral. The bourgeois ethics of radical state-capitalist enterprise could impartially sanction both.

Thus, a political-economic documentation of events in the Indian sub-continent in the 1960s and 1970s could provide good empirical support to the hypothesis that 'selfish' political action by dedicated communist revolutionaries can make a capitalist breakdown impossible. An alternative hypothesis, as to what *could* have happened, is discussed in section 5.

3 Conditions for a breakdown of capitalism

A logical deduction is no stronger than its assumptions (and the strength of its logic, if correct).

An obvious way to establish the possibility of capitalist breakdown is to replace assumption 5 in section 1.

Assumption

6 Each worker acts 'unselfishly' *unconditionally*, i.e. regardless of what other workers do (leaving the other assumptions of the model unchanged).

Given the other assumptions in section 1, assumption 6 is both a necessary and sufficient condition for workers uniting to establish socialism. (However, if assumption 3 does not hold, assumption 6 will remain as a necessary condition, but not as a sufficient condition, assuming that the other assumptions hold. On the other hand, if assumptions 4 and 5 do not hold, with or without assumption 2, but other assumptions hold, then assumption 6 is a necessary as well as a sufficient condition for capitalist breakdown.)

4 Alternative conditions of capitalist breakdown

The analysis of the conditions of capitalist breakdown attempted in earlier sections of this book is not the only game-theory analysis of the problem available.

The 'battle of the sexes' problem, also studied in game theory (Luce and Raiffa, 1957, pp. 90–92) supplies one alternative. In the original version of the problem, the husband prefers to go to a boxing match and the wife to a ballet, but both prefer an evening together to enjoying the preferred entertainment alone. If the husband can convince the wife that he *will* go to the boxing match, come what may, *he* wins; if the wife can convince the husband that *she* will have her way, *she* wins. In the present setting, the problem is that if the workers are *determined* to seize power to establish socialism, they may rally a decisive majority (or minority) for socialism. The capitalists may give in, rather than face a permanent break-up of the country. *If* capitalist Taiwan is peacefully reintegrated with socialist China, the 'battle of the sexes' type of problem may represent a simple rationalization of the event. But no such case has yet occurred. (On the other hand, there *have* been cases of capitalist breakdown in the twentieth century, so that one can hardly say, in a 'battle of the sexes' setting of the problem, that because capitalists are *always* more determined than workers, *all* socialist revolutions are abortive.)

A better, more illuminating alternative is to formulate the problem strictly in terms of the original 'prisoners' dilemma' (converted into an *n*-person game), which has been suggested to the author by Pattanaik. We assume that every worker wants socialism, but to fight for socialism involves a cost, simply of overcoming a natural inertia, or, better, fear of repression if the effort is unsuccessful. Each worker prefers socialism to capitalism. But each worker prefers all others to act for socialism, rather than act himself, *both* because, (a) no one will be victimized, and (b) the inaction of one will make no difference, as there will be socialism in any case, and all will benefit, including the worker who did not act.

The 'cost–benefit' approach just sketched has the merit of focussing attention on represssion, or fear of repression, which certainly deters workers' action in promoting a capitalist breakdown. This aspect of the problem was ignored in earlier sections, but not because it is unimportant.

The difficulty with the cost–benefit analysis of the problem is that it suggests, immediately, that 'unconditional action for socialism' by each worker is both a necessary and a sufficient condition of the breakdown of capitalism. However, as noted in earlier sections, such 'unconditional political action by workers for socialism,' after they have rid themselves of the 'fear complex' of repression, may be either 'unselfish' or 'selfless' (or, it may even be 'selfish'), with the different consequences which have already been discussed. If this is recognized, the cost–benefit formulation of the problems remains (only) as a useful prelude to a fuller discussion of the problem along the lines attempted earlier.

5 The meaning of 'unselfish political action by workers'

But what, exactly, is 'unselfish political action' by workers? So far, it has been defined negatively as political action by workers which is *not* 'selfish' (definition 2, section 1). But something more can be said about it. We ignore so-called 'selfless' action by workers which is transparently hypocritical, such as reduced work during normal hours, in order to earn extra pay at over-time rates. (This may be justified in the 'sweated' trades, but *not* as examples of socially-motivated 'selfless', altruistic action. It is as spurious as bourgeois altruism symbolized by the little boy in John Galsworthy's *Forsyte Saga* giving a bad penny to a beggar, or the upper-class Bengali school girls in Mrinal Sen's film 'Calcutta 1971', who demanded an ice-cream each as a reward for a half-hour's work in aid of refugees fleeing from Pakistani persecution in Bangladesh.) Such action by workers is obviously indistinguishable from 'selfish' action and deserves no further attention.

Workers' political action which is genuinely *not* selfish can be either (a) action which serves each worker's self-interest *without* harming the interest of other workers, or (b) action which involves 'self-sacrifice' or 'selfless' action by workers (without being a hypocritical subterfuge for 'selfish' action). The nature of (a) has been discussed in sections 1 and 2. But what is the nature of (b)?

Within the framework of the basic model used in earlier sections, 'unselfish' political action *cannot* mean action which involves neglect of each worker's individual self-interest. For in the model, if one worker acts against his individual self-interest, e.g. by forgoing a wage-claim at a time of inflation, so will all. Capitalists will gain at the expense of the collective interest of all the workers and add to their profits. This would sow mutual distrust among workers, and hinder workers' unity to achieve a capitalist breakdown. In the context of intercommunist warfare (essentially a quarrel over the timing of the revolutionary overthrow of capitalism) discussed in section 2, 'selfless' action would have involved a *unilateral* surrender by one side. This is against a primordial right of survival. It would probably (in view of total mutual distrust) only have played into the hands of the other side (and/or third party anti-communist coercive forces), and stabilized, if not strengthened, capitalism. In other words, 'selfless' or 'self-sacrificing' action by a worker, in disregard of his individual self-interest, motivated by a concern for the interests of others (which is the dictionary meaning of the word 'altruism'), produces exactly the same result as 'selfish' action by the worker, viz. the *non*-breakdown of capitalism.

We can now add a definition of 'selfless political action' by a worker, an additional assumption involving such action, and sum up the results of different kinds of action by a worker.

Definition

4 A worker acts 'selflessly' (or 'self-sacrificingly') when he acts against his individual self-interest.

Assumption

7 Each worker acts 'selflessly' unconditionally (selfless action *must* be unconditional, since it is inspired by concern for others).

Ceteris paribus, adoption of assumptions 5, 6 and 7, produces the following results:

Rules

1 If assumption 5 (each worker acts 'selfishly' unless all others act 'unselfishly') holds, then there is a *second-best* result. Some workers may gain more at the expense of other workers, but there will be an assured *non*-breakdown of capitalism, although *all* workers want this breakdown.

2 If assumption 7 (each worker acts 'selflessly' unconditionally) holds, the result is the *worst* possible. There is an intensification of the capitalist exploitation of all workers, as well as the non-breakdown of capitalism.

3 If assumption 6 (each worker acts 'unselfishly' unconditionally) holds, there is the *best* possible result. There is a reduction in the capitalist exploitation of workers (since workers' individual and collective self-interest is protected under capitalism), as well as a breakdown of capitalism.

It is worth noting that in the 'pollution model' referred to in section 1, if a non-pollution result is obtained by each individual deciding to non-pollute unconditionally, the individual is acting 'unselfishly' and *not* 'selflessly'. This is because non-pollution serves each individual's self-interest, as well as the collective interest of society, since the result is that all live longer (it being implied that all desire to live longer). On the other hand, if each individual pollutes, because he prefers to pollute when others do not, rather than let others pollute when he does not, he is then acting 'selfishly'. But, unless in defining his individual 'self-interest' *more* weight is given to the kick he gets out of polluting when others do not, than to his desire for a longer life, by being 'selfish', each individual harms his individual self-interest, as well as the public interest by acting 'selfishly'.

6 The operational distinction between 'selfish' and 'unselfish' political action by workers

The distinction between 'selfish' and 'unselfish' political action by workers in terms of pursuit of workers' self-interest, made in the previous section, is not the only one of interest. There is an operational distinction, which must now be discussed.

Every political action in pursuit of workers' self-interest is not guaranteed to be successful 'unselfish' action, which promotes workers' immediate self-interest (under capitalism) and also a breakdown of capitalism. It could easily degenerate into 'selfish' political action, which, as we have seen in the previous section, goes against workers' self-interest at least in so far as it promotes the *non*-breakdown of capitalism.

What actually happens depends on the factual context, and the nature of the programme of political action in pursuit of workers' self-interest adopted.

Thus, trade-union action to secure wage-gains would serve workers' (individual and collective) self-interest, if there is minimal shiftability of the initial burden on capitalists (through adjustment of other wage-rates, of consumer-good prices, tax-structures etc.) on to the shoulders of other workers, or the shifting of the burden is explicitly disallowed by the programme of action adopted (which must then be an integrated policy-mix covering the relevant wage–price–tax structure).

Selections of industries to be nationalized, and their administration after nationalization (or the choice and administration of a system of controls imposed on private enterprise) could also form an integral part of a programme of either 'selfish' or 'unselfish' political action by workers. It works out as a programme of 'selfish' political action by workers, if it involves political 'feather-bedding', to which there was a reference in section 1 above. Such political 'feather-bedding' has all the features of 'trade-union feather-bedding', except that its gains are collected by members and fresh recruits to the political party holding the ministry concerned, who may or may not also be strongly organized in trade unions which are politically aligned with the party holding the ministry.

It should be noted that armed guerilla action by the urban or rural poor can also be based on either 'selfish' or 'unselfish' political action by workers. It works out as a programme of 'unselfish' political action if a principle of non-coercion of supporters and the winning of voluntary support is strictly adhered to. Action on this principle would involve collection of arms from defeated (but won over), fraternizing or deserting military units, collection of taxes (in money or kind) only on a *quid pro quo* basis, when economic and social reforms have been effectively enforced by armed guerilla power to give benefits to the exploited whether they were in favour of guerilla action or not. In the context of inter-communist partisan warfare, referred to in sections 2 and 4, 'unselfish' political action by communist workers would involve effective stoppage, by invoking discipline, or, if this fails, by political excommunication of those on one's own side who engage, of aggresive armed action (compared with armed action in self-defence) against rival communist commando units. (This is by no means militarily or politically impossible. De-escalation of armed partisan warfare through declared or undeclared bilateral disengagement agreements *have*, in practice, been achieved, e.g. currently in South Vietnam. This could set the stage for renovated communist politics geared to political action in the interest of all workers, regardless of party loyalties.)

7 Realism of the stated conditions of capitalist breakdown

Doubts about the realism of the 'conditions of capitalist breakdown' specified in this chapter, are likely to arise over the interpretation of assumption 5 about workers' preference-ordering.

According to this assumption, each worker will act 'selfishly' unless all others act 'unselfishly', in which case, he too will act 'unselfishly'.

Objections may be raised on two counts. *First*, is it realistic to imply that in politics (including revolutionary politics) *each* worker acts 'atomistically', i.e. that he takes an independent, individual decision whether to act 'selfishly' or 'unselfishly' (or 'selflessly')? *Second*, is it realistic to suggest that workers always decide *unanimously* whether to act in one way or another (as is definitely implied by the wording of assumption 5)?

Actually, in response to these objections, the assumption could easily be reworded (without loss) to read: each worker will act 'selfishly' unless *a sufficient number* of other workers act 'unselfishly', in which case he too will act 'unselfishly'. But there is some point in retaining the assumption as it is. In revolutionary times, it is observed that there are no 'individualistic' workers left. Each worker is involved in *group action* under the guidance of political parties. Moreover, there are, very much as in Eugene Ionesco's play *Rhinoceros*, landslide gains by a particular workers' party, which dominates, and imposes more or less 'unanimous' decisions in the name of the working class (which no worker dares to oppose). So, it is a matter of indifference whether the reference in assumption 5 is to 'each worker', or to 'each worker's party'; and the suggestion that decisions are unanimous is not unrealistic. (For further reference to game theory see Luce and Raiffa, 1957; Samuelson, 1970, Sen, 1969a.)

13 Transitions to Socialism: An Economic Interpretation of a Paradox in Theory and History

1 Introduction

From the *Communist Manifesto* (Marx and Engels, 1950, pp. 21–61, section 2), to the programmatic writings of Lenin (1964a, b, c, d) and Mao (1956, pp. 275–6), revolutionary-socialist blueprints have proposed a strategy based on *three* fundamental propositions.

Proposition

1 The socialist *political* revolution could be more or less 'one-stroke',[1] i.e. more or less instantaneous (as it was, historically, in Russia), or 'protracted',[2] (as it was, historically, in China).

2 A socialist *economic* revolution must accompany a socialist political revolution, and eliminate all vestiges of private property in the means of production and 'socialize'[3] all the principal means of production. In other words, there is no scope for an indefinite 'coexistence' of capitalism and socialism within the political boundaries of the country in which the socialist revolution has taken place.

3 But the economic (institutional) counterpart of the political socialist revolution, i.e. the socialization of all the principal means of production, must proceed by a revolutionary step-by-step transition, and not by 'one-stroke'.

1. The term has been used by Lenin (1964c, p. 90) and Lange (1956, section 6, especially p. 124). It has also been referred to by Mao (1956, p. 276).
2. The term is used by Mao (1956, p. 276).
3. See, particularly, Lenin (1964e, especially p. 241).

In this chapter, we shall not be concerned with the speculative question as to how far proposition 1 is relevant in the present epoch.

We shall also accept proposition 2 as a historically tested Marxian dictum, which is probably not in dispute among modern revolutionary socialists (including those who represent post-Marxian or anarchist trends). (However, the rationale of this proposition does not seem to have been discussed or clarified adequately in the literature. A direct attempt to do so, by Preobrazhensky (1972, pp. 145–6) is based on the *assertion* that if, in Marx, the self-expansion of capital represents 'capitalism in (perpetual) motion', 'socialism is still more rapid motion', from which he deduces his special theory of 'socialist accumulation'. It would probably be more convincing to argue that a strategy of eliminating capitalism, i.e. proposition 2, is *forced on* revolutionary socialists, as it were, for sheer survival against capitalism, which is expansionist, *sui generis*.)

In this chapter, we shall concentrate on proposition 3, for several reasons.

First of all, the rationale of the proposition has hardly been discussed in orthodox Marxian literature, except in only one of its aspects, viz. the question of relations between the proletariat and the peasantry (see, for example, excerpts from the writings of Engels, Marx and Lenin in Progress Publishers, 1967, chapter 5, pp. 327–52).

But the proposition is quite general, and was made explicit in the *Communist Manifesto*: 'The proletariat will use its political supremacy to wrest, by degrees, all capital from the bourgeoisie, to centralize all instruments of production in the hands of the State, i.e. of the proletariat organized as the ruling class.' (Point four of the ten-point programme in the Communist Manifesto proposes confiscation of the property of rebels and émigrés, and point five, centralization of all credit in the State bank, which will have exclusive monopoly rights. Point seven speaks of 'extension of factories and instruments of production owned by the State' (Marx and Engels, 1950, vol. 1, pp. 21–61, section 2).)

For a strategy of revolutionary transition to socialism formulated in this *general* form, in which a step-by-step strategy is proposed not only as between industry and agriculture, but also as regards different branches of industry to be socialized, the orthodox Marxian rationale is given in Lenin's numerous comments (1964a, b, c, e). It is simply an argument against spreading *thinly* over all branches of the economy, the numerically small revolutionary-socialist elite in existence on the morrow of the revolution.

The trouble with the argument just noted is that the priority list on the basis of which the revolutionary strategists are to pick and choose the branches of the economy for their step-by-step socialization programme is by no means clear.

Historical transitions, in *all* socialist countries, without exception, but notably in China, have in fact been based on some 'step-by-step' strategy. Moreover, in almost all cases (the Paris Commune of 1871 and the Hungarian Soviet Revolution at the end of the First World War seem to be the only important exceptions), the strategy has not only been successful, but apparently *irreversibly* so. Facile explanations often given, in terms of a series of mainly 'political' accidents favouring socialism, are obviously unconvincing, and leave us with a historical paradox.

We get no ready help from either standard neo-classical economic theory or from orthodox Marxian economic theory in finding a rationale for these historically 'over-successful' step-by-step economic transitions to socialism.

Indeed, if we make 'The reproduction schemes' of Marx's *Capital*, volume two (1957, Part 3, pp. 351–523; Lange, 1959, ch. 3, pp. 218–29) the starting-point of a capitalist economy in transition to socialism, a step-by-step transition for 'economizing' in the deployment of scarce revolutionary cadre is justified, but not uniquely determined. Furthermore, while some versions of the strategy could satisfy the conditions laid down in propositions 2 and 3, and guarantee 'irreversible' transitions, others could only initiate abortive or 'reversible' transitions. Thus, if only the Marxian 'Department A' enterprises and industries are socialized, the attempted transition may prove abortive because of the *mutual* inter-dependence of Department A (producing all capital goods) and Department B (producing all wage-goods). On the other hand, if *both* Departments A and B are *wholly* socialized, a more-or-less cast-iron basis for an 'irreversible' transition is established. (The transition is then 'irreversible' in the sense that for reversal to take place, adverse, counter-revolutionary, 'political' factors must be strong enough to subvert the economic basis favourable for the transition.) An intermediate strategy, in which *some* enterprises (or sectors) belonging to both the Marxian 'Departments' is socialized, ensures indefinite survival and growth of both the socialized and the exempted (capitalist) sectors, unless this outcome is ended by a political decision, at some stage, to enforce proposition 2.

On the other hand, with the Lange–Lerner economic models of socialism, built on neo-classical foundations (Lange and Taylor, 1956, section 2, p. 68; section 3, pp. 73–4), only the intermediate version of the step-by-step strategy is conceivable, or a 'one-stroke' strategy, in which the once-over socialization of only some (unspecified) selected sectors is recommended (and proposition 2 violated). This follows from the basic assumption made in these models that there are 'ultimate productive resources' (labour, capital and natural resources) (Lange and Taylor, 1956, p. 68), which produce commodities which may be classifiable as intermediate and consumer goods. Although Lange rejected the possibility of *any* step-by-step strategy of transition to socialism with an unconvincing argument[4] such a strategy *is* conceivable on these neo-classical assumptions (subject to the limitation, of course,

4. Lange's argument was that if some branches of the economy are socialized today, with others earmarked for socialization in the future, all investment by capitalists in the exempted branches would come to a stop, and they would face certain ruin (1956 pp. 122–4). But if the socialist state uses fiscal instruments and political pressure to bar export of capital, and to impose curbs on luxury consumption, what alternatives would capitalists have to investment in the temporarily exempted branches of the economy (except emigration as destitutes)?

that proposition 2 is likely to be violated). The socialist state and private capitalists may each own a portion of the 'ultimate productive resources' available, on the basis of some arbitrary, political decision. But Lange himself categorically recommended 'one-stroke' socialization of all the sectors to be socialized, along with a 'guarantee of absolute security' (from socialization) for the exempted sectors (Lange and Taylor, 1956, section 6, pp. 123–6). In other words, Lange, in his 1936 article, advocated a politically-decided *indefinite* coexistence of socialism and capitalism, and rejected proposition 2.

Thus, Marxian capitalist-reproduction schemes seem to be more versatile in historical step-by-step revolutionary transitions to socialism, the majority of which have been historically 'irreversible', than the rival neo-classical economic models of competitive capitalism, which have no economic rationale for 'irreversible' transitions. However, as we saw in chapters 5 and 8, the Marxian model of competitive-capitalist equilibrium is formally defective, and, at best, its 'simple labour theory' version is acceptable as an 'economic parable'. Since Marxian capitalist-reproduction schemes represent precisely such models, we cannot rely on them to explain historical strategies of revolutionary step-by-step transitions to socialism.

Fortunately, post-Marxian commodity-production models of capitalism and socialism are also more versatile than their neo-classical counterparts, and can be used to interpret various strategies of revolutionary step-by-step transitions to socialism, including the 'irreversible' ones.

The purpose of the present chapter is to show how this can be done. Definitions and propositions about the production–consumption models required, and about capitalist and socialist political-economic models required are mostly those that have already been used in chapters 9–11, or earlier in the present section. These are recalled for convenience, in the next section, where a few additional definitions and propositions are also introduced, along with a new type of commodity-production model, viz. the completely decomposable type, which has not been discussed so far. Later sections of the chapter sketch, in outline, alternative strategies of step-by-step transition to socialism, illustrated with the help of the partially decomposable, and completely decomposable production–consumption models presented in section 2.

2 Definitions, models and their properties

In this chapter, two types of production–consumption models are used – the partially decomposable type and the completely decomposable type.

However, in defining *both* types of models, and to distinguish between the two, we introduce, explicitly, 'semibasic' commodities, along with the basic and non-basic commodities (as definitions 2 and 3, chapter 9, section 2) which are to be found together in all models which are not indecomposable.

Definitions

1 Semibasics are *necessary* (or essential) consumer goods or wage-goods, which are consumed in variable proportions. (According to the two-commodity taxonomy of commodities used so far in this book, semibasics are non-basics, since they do not enter, as producer goods or consumer goods, in fixed proportions in the production processes.)

To illustrate, using the notation of chapters 9–11, model **1** represents a partially decomposable technology, in which L represents quantities of direct labour, A and B are basic commodities, C is a semibasic, and D is an ordinary non-basic ('luxury') commodity:

$$1A+2B+0C+0D+\tfrac{1}{8}L_a \to 8A,$$
$$2A+1B+0C+0D+\tfrac{3}{8}L_b \to 8B,$$
$$3A+1B+0C+0D+\tfrac{1}{4}L_c \to 2C,$$
$$1A+3B+0C+0D+\tfrac{1}{4}L_d \to 3D.$$

1

On the other hand, model **2** represents a national economy whose production–consumption structure is *completely* decomposable, in the sense that production processes for A and B belong to one (indecomposable) production–consumption model, and those producing C and D belong to another (partially decomposable) model. However, C being assumed to be a semibasic, consumed in variable proportions by labour employed in *all* the processes, it is meaningful to speak of all four processes together as belonging to a completely decomposable economic model:

$$1A+2B+0C+0D+\tfrac{1}{6}L_a \to 8A,$$
$$2A+1B+0C+0D+\tfrac{2}{3}L_b \to 8B,$$
$$0A+0B+0C+1D+\tfrac{1}{12}L_c \to 6C,$$
$$0A+0B+0C+2D+\tfrac{1}{12}L_c \to 8D.$$

2

2 A collection of production processes (or technology) is completely decomposable if it contains semi-basics which alone bind together sub-sets of processes, each of which contain (separate) basics and are indecomposable or partially decomposable.

Whether the economic model with which we start is partially decomposable or completely decomposable, any strategy of revolutionary step-by-step transition from capitalism to socialism involves the conversion of a capitalist political-economic model into interdependent socialist and capitalist 'sub-economies', each of which contains fragments or integral parts of each process in the technology, and is governed by the basic motivations of socialist and capitalist societies respectively.

The following propositions about socialist and capitalist sub-economies involved in the process of revolutionary step-by-step transition from capitalism to socialism may be helpful for understanding later sections of the present chapter.

Proposition

1 The basic motivation of a socialist sub-economy is the maximization of the rate of growth of output of basics (including in this consumer goods consumed in fixed proportions). (This is merely an application of proposition 4 chapter 11, section 6.)

2 The basic motivation of a capitalist sub-economy is capitalist accumulation for expanded reproduction. (This is an application of proposition 1, chapter 6, section 6.)

3 A capitalist sub-economy functions, on the basis of its basic motivation referred to in proposition 2, subject at least to minimal restrictions on money supply and foreign trade imposed by the socialist government in charge of the economy, which issues currency and controls all foreign transactions. (Other restrictions could be (a) inflationary purchases from the capitalist sub-economy for manipulated transfer of resources to the socialist sub-economy, (b) taxes, notably turnover taxes, taxes in kind or compulsory 'delivery quotas' on production in the capitalist sub-economy, (c) manipulated prices of products originating in the socialist sub-economy which enter into trade between the two sub-economies, so as to turn the terms of trade against the capitalist sub-economy. These are essentially instruments of 'primitive socialist accumulation' first studied by Preobrazhensky (1972, pp. 130–48).)

In keeping with what has just been said in proposition 3, and with the discussion of alternative Marxian economic models of a socialist economy in chapter 14, it is *not* assumed, in what follows in later sections of this chapter, that the exchange of commodities between the socialist and capitalist sub-economies takes place on the basis of payment of transactions prices in all cases.

However, the use of such transactions prices is not excluded, and their nature is specified by the following propositions.

Propositions

4 Enterprises belonging to the capitalist sub-economy charge profit-maximizing prices for their mutual transactions, as well as for their dealings with the socialized enterprises.

5 Enterprises belonging to the socialist sub-economy base their dealings with capitalist enterprises, though not necessarily for internal transactions within the socialist sub-economy, on 'shadow prices' which are worked out on the basis of the investment–production plan of the socialist sub-economy (which includes targets for their transactions with the capitalist sub-economy).

6 In working out the profit-maximizing, actual transactions prices and the planned 'shadow prices' in the two sub-economies, the profit-rate may be assumed to be equal in all processes *within* each sub-economy, though (possibly) un-equal to each other, or unequal also *within* each sub-economy.

The profit-rate within the capitalist sub-economy may be equalized by conditions approximating to perfect com-petition (or by the policy of the socialist government in imposing a ceiling on profits in the capitalist sub-economy). The profit-rate within the socialist sub-economy may also be equalized, but purely for the sake of administrative (and accounting) convenience. In general, in the absence of the conditions just specified, there will be a pattern of unequal profit-rates prevailing in both the sub-economies. (Since commodity-production models with such unequal profit rates have not been discussed so far in this book, the Appendix to chapter 13 is devoted to a brief discussion of such economic models.)

Finally, in discussing alternative strategies of step-by-step transitions in the following sections, changes in technology involving changes in production methods of basics, semi-basics and non-basics are *not* abstracted from. The only restriction on technical progress assumed is that changes in technology should not be so drastic as to alter the (partially or completely decomposable) nature of technology repre-senting the economy.

The propositions written down above about the use or non-use of transactions prices as economic instruments and about the nature of technological progress make it unnecessary to spell out the time-sequence of the economy in transition in discussing alternative strategies of transition in later sections, as was done in chapters 10 and 11, or to derive the profit-rates and prices on the basis of which transactions *may* take place.

Consequently, reference will be made to a single partially decomposable economic model with semi-basics (model 1) in sections 3, 4 and 5, and to a single completely decomposable economic model (model 2) in section 6. As in chapters 9–11, and for the same reasons, the two basics A and B, the single semibasic C and single 'luxury' non-basic D, in these models stand proxy for any number of basics, semibasics and 'luxury' non-basics in any actual economic model of an economy in transition.

3 Socialization of monopoly-capitalist enterprise networks

The socialization[5] of monopoly-capitalist networks was proposed in Lenin's *The Impending Catastrophe and How to Combat It* (1917), published on the eve of the socialist revolution (Lenin, 1964b, p. 329).

As typical monopoly-capitalist networks are likely to extend over basic, semibasic and non-basic industries, this strategy would establish socialist and capitalist sub-economies *each* of which produces *all three* types of products. (However, since some industries are likely to be completely monopolized, it is likely that the socialist sub-economy would have exclusive control over the supply of some commodities, including some 'monopolized' basics.)

Now, this strategy, like others which are discussed later, is worth studying only on the assumption that it is adopted as a 'pure' strategy, i.e. only on the assumption that politically decided 'switches' in strategy, involving further doses of socialization will not interfere with the *denouement*, nor will major technological change convert basics into non-basics or vice versa so as to alter the 'balance' between the two sub-economies. (In history, as we shall note in section 7, 'switches' in strategy *have* occurred. But the only way to analyse such historically adopted 'mixed' strategies is to sort out the 'pure' strategies which are 'mixed' by political decision in this way.)

The likely outcome of this strategy, adhered to as a 'pure' strategy, is an indefinite survival of both the socialist and

5. Lenin used the term 'nationalization', but clearly wanted 'revolutionary-democratic' workers' control over enterprises which were nationalized, and rudimentary central planning through a state-owned banking monopoly. So there is no harm in using the term 'socialization' in this context.

capitalist sub-economies. In other words, it ensures an 'irreversible' *partial* socialization of the national economy, with the fulfilment of the supreme objective of the socialist revolution, viz. the socialization of *all* the principal means of production (specified in proposition 2 in section 1) put off to an infinitely remote future.

The outcome follows from the hard fact that in a partially decomposable economic model like model **2**, if each sub-economy monopolizes the production of some basics, e.g. if the socialist sub-economy monopolizes the basic A, and the capitalist sub-economy monopolizes the basic B, neither sub-economy can maintain or expand its output, without *ipso facto* assuring the survival (and perhaps also the expansion) of the other.

This outcome is guaranteed, regardless of whether products are exchanged between industries belonging to the two sub-economies through the use of the price mechanism, or through administratively controlled allocations. If the price mechanism is used, effective 'service competition' by capitalist enterprises may help them to displace non-basics or semibasics produced in the socialist sub-economy in the entire consumer-goods market (serving both sub-economies). Defensive retaliation by the socialist sub-economy in the shape of quota restrictions on the sale of its basic products to the capitalist sub-economy will be counter-productive. (Growth of production and employment in the capitalist sub-economy will then be retarded, *if* the quota restrictions are effective, but so will the growth of output and employment in the socialist sub-economy be retarded. For this reason, the quota restrictions are *not* likely to be effective, and the black-market will by-pass the restrictions.) The alternative would be to retain the price mechanism, and for the socialist sub-economy to improve its efficiency in service-competition with the capitalist sub-economy by moral or monetary incentives (on an individual or group basis) offered to both producers and buyers of its non-basic or semibasic products. But in all these cases, *every* success of either the capitalist or the socialist sub-economy in its 'competitive coexistence' with the other will ensure the survival of its rival. (An exception to this rule is conceivable, *only* if, by the initial historical 'accident', or by technological progress later, both the sub-economies contain fragments of *all* basics and semibasics and non-basics in the system. If this is so, the success of each sub-economy will become independent of the success or survival of the other, and, in principle, *either* sub-economy could 'wither away' and atrophy as the result of 'economic competition'.)

4 Socialization of all basic industries

Socialization of *all* basic industries, leaving the capitalist sub-economy with branches of the economy producing semi-basics and non-basics, is an obvious alternative to the strategy considered in the previous section.

A draft decree proposed by Lenin in December 1917, calling for the conversion of all joint stock companies into (socialist) state property (Lenin, 1964, vol. 26, pp. 391–94), amounted to a programmatic re-orientation towards such a strategy. (With staple wage-goods, which are consumed in fixed proportions, counted as basics, as in the commodity-production models used in this book, socialization of all joint stock companies would socialize all basic production, and leave semi-basics to peasant agriculture, and 'luxury' non-basics to the petty commodity-production sector.)

At first glance, this might seem to be a 'stronger' socialist strategy, perhaps a decisive one, which would assure the *completion* of a step-by-step revolutionary transition, which, as we saw in the previous section, the first strategy does not.

However, if there is a post-revolution increase in variable consumption by workers, or, with restricted export markets, semibasic (agricultural) exports by the socialist economy were required to ensure expansion of capacity and production in the socialist sub-economy, the socialist sub-economy's control over basics would be matched by the capitalist sub-economy's control over semi-basics.

In such an event, the overall situation would not be qualitatively different from the situation arising from the socialization of capitalist monopolies, except that with the two sub-economies operating in two different markets, there would be no scope for 'service competition' between them.

By this strategy, too, the survival of the socialist (and the capitalist) sub-economies would be assured for an indefinite future, regardless of the expansion of the capitalist sub-economy selling semi-basics and non-basics.

However, in this case, *any* growth of output in the capitalist sub-economy would induce a *growth* (and not merely maintenance) of output in the socialist sub-economy (on the reasonable assumptions that technological progress is of the 'embodied' kind, involving the use of new assortments of inputs of basic commodities).

Nevertheless, such assured growth of output in the socialist sub-economy does not guarantee the increasing absorption of the growing labour force of the economy.

5 Socialization of all basic and semi-basic branches of the economy

By elimination, the only alternative left to be considered is the strategy of socialization of all basics and semibasics, leaving (strictly) non-basic 'luxury' commodities to the capitalist sub-economy. (This would *not* be tantamount to a one-step socialization strategy, as against a step-by-step transitional one. The economy inherited by the socialist revolution may be a very undeveloped one, with the socialized branches of the economy being unable to absorb, initially, more than a small fraction of the total labour force. On the other hand, imitative conspicuous consumption by workers in both sub-economies, imitating the consumption patterns of the dispossessed landlords and capitalists, may maintain high levels of production and employment in the capitalist sub-economy producing non-basics for a long time.)

As with the strategy of socialization of all basics, but only basics, any growth of output of non-basics in the capitalist sub-economy would induce growth of output in the socialist sub-economy of semibasics as well as basics.

This is the only strategy of step-by-step revolutionary

transition to socialism in which the growth of output of the capitalist sub-economy is completely *independent* of the growth of output of the capitalist sub-economy. (This will be so, at any rate, as long as the growth of demand for semibasics (and consumer basics) is sufficient to ensure growing production at full-capacity in the socialist sub-economy.)

Thus, this is the only strategy which accomplishes an economically 'irreversible' step-by-step revolutionary transition to socialism, i.e. the eventual socialization of the whole economy. (The socialist government can allow the capitalist sub-economy to die out by absorbing the entire labour force in the socialist branches of the economy and eliminating imitative conspicuous consumption requiring the production of non-basics.)

6 Strategies with completely decomposable economic models

If the economic structure of the country where the socialist revolution occurs is represented by an economic model like model **2**, the strategies of step-by-step transitions to socialism are all, strictly speaking, irrelevant. (Completely decomposable economic models may be found if there is coexistence of technological pre-modern agriculture represented, for example, by production processes for commodities C and D in **2** side by side with advanced industry, represented by processes producing A and B. Backward agriculture may do without electric power and chemical fertilizers, and make do with animal power and animal manure. Advanced industry may be more or less self-contained, with synthetics and man-made fibres having substituted agricultural raw materials.)

Attempts to adopt socialization of monopoly capitalist networks or to socialize all joint stock companies may establish a socialist sub-economy which contains processes producing A and B in **2**, while the capitalist sub-economy monopolizes the production of C and D, of which C is the semibasic, which is consumed in variable proportions by the labour force employed in all branches of the economy.

In this case, the attempted step-by-step transition would be economically 'reversible', were it not for the socialist government's control over the foreign trade of the semibasic-producing capitalist sub-economy (provided for by proposition 3 in section 2 above). Given the socialist government's control over the capitalist sub-economy's foreign trade, the capitalist sub-economy would have to depend upon the *demand* for its surplus production of semibasics in the socialist sub-economy, just as the socialist sub-economy would have to depend on *supplies* of semibasics from the capitalist sub-economy. The likely outcome, therefore, is an indefinite mutually complementary growth of output in both the socialist and capitalist sub-economies.

The outcome will be fundamentally the same if, on the morrow of the socialist revolution, processes producing semibasics are fragmented between the socialist and capitalist sub-economies.

Only if there is socialization of the branch of the economy producing the semibasic C, as well as the one which produces D, which is essential for producing C, is the capitalist sub-economy at the mercy of the socialist sub-economy, as it were, with the eventual completion of the socialist economic revolution assured.

7 Concluding remarks

The alternative strategies of step-by-step revolutionary transitions from capitalism to socialism discussed in this chapter throw some light on actual, historical transitions, most of which, as already noted in section 1 above, have been 'irreversible' in the sense that repeated, determined attempts to reverse them by military–political–economic foreign intervention have ended in failure.

Once it adopted socialist objectives, the contemporary Cuban Revolution obviously followed the strategy of socializing all basics and semibasics (Baran, 1969, pp. 404–12). Both the Soviet and Chinese Revolutions seem to have started out by trying to use the strategy of confiscating 'monopoly capital' or 'bureaucratic capital' and of the feudal *latifundia*. But both these revolutions seem to have run into the kind of problems which arise with completely decomposable economic models discussed in section 6. They solved them, and completed their revolutionary transitions to socialism, by switches in strategy which involved experiments with alternative institutions, mainly for integrating semibasic-producing agriculture into the socialist sub-economies (e.g. different types of collective farms in the Soviet Union, different types of people's communes in the People's Republic of China). At the same time, continuous attempts have been made, by technological modernization of all branches of the economy, to convert these economies from loosely integrated, completely decomposable structures, into closely integrated, partially decomposable ones.

Appendix: Socialist Pricing

1 Introduction

As stated in section 2 of chapter 13, the allocation of goods and resources within a socialist sub-economy does not necessarily require the use of transaction prices fixed for the purpose. We shall see in the next chapter, however, that there is a case for using transaction prices for socialized commodities as instruments for the *implementation* of centralized socialist plans (though the plans themselves may be drawn up without reference to these prices used as determinants of socialist planning).

In this Appendix, we use highly simplified commodity-production models to examine the implications of alternative methods of socialist pricing, viz. arbitrary pricing, fixing prices which are proportionate to labour-embodied quantities, and fixing shadow prices with unequal process-wise profit-rates (which permit investment and reproduction according to socialist plan targets).

2 Arbitrary socialist pricing

As the first step in discussing the feasibility of arbitrary socialist pricing, let us consider **1** as a portrait of the technological skeleton of a socialist economy (or sub-economy). (The notation is the same as the notation used in chapters 9–13.)

$$2A + 2B \rightarrow 8A,$$
$$2A + 5B \rightarrow 8B.$$
1

It is an indecomposable economic model, in which the labour terms are not shown explicitly, because producers' consumption is in fixed proportions, so that wage-goods enter the picture as basics.

Suppose the prices are fixed arbitrarily (at random, or by taking historical prices as the starting-point), at $p_a = \frac{1}{4}$, $p_b = \frac{1}{8}$.

The industry-wise accounts of the system will then read as follows:

	Capital outlay	Profit margin	Profit rate	Value of gross product
A-industry	$\frac{3}{4}$	$\frac{5}{4}$	$\frac{5}{3}$	2
B-industry	$\frac{9}{8}$	$-\frac{1}{8}$	$-\frac{1}{8}$	1

Now, it is clear that with this arbitrary set of prices, the B-industry cannot even recover its capital. The A-industry's nominal profit-margin is $\frac{5}{4}$ (nominal, because its actual sales will be reduced by the shortfall in the deficit of B-industry's purchase of the A-good); its actual profit-margin (or realized profit-margin) will be slightly lower at $\frac{19}{16}$. With the net product of the system $(4A+1B)$ valued at $\frac{18}{6}$, this means the A-industry will be able to expand, but the B-industry will be forced to contract.

There are two ways of avoiding such an outcome, which is not likely to be acceptable (because it gives a *contracting* B-industry):

1 The price-fixing socialist authority may refuse to change the prices, but pool the system's social profit and re-allocate it (by using fiscal or credit instruments) in such a manner as to avoid any contraction. For instance, if each industry is to expand by investing $2A+\frac{1}{2}B$ in the next period, their expansion plans will go through if each gets a half-share of the aggregate social profit, and the profit-rate (after re-allocation) is 75 per cent in the A-industry and 50 per cent in the B-industry.

2 Alternatively, by a process of trial computations, it may be discovered that by reducing the price of A and raising the price of B, till *both* are equal to $\frac{1}{6}$, the A-industry's profit-margin is cut to $\frac{2}{3}$ (and its profit-rate to 100 per cent), the B-

industry's profit-margin is raised to $\frac{1}{6}$ (and the profit-rate to a little over 14 per cent). If the A-industry is required (by the plan) to invest $4A$ more in the next period, and the B-industry is to invest $1B$ more, these adjusted prices will put through the investment plans without the need for any fiscal intervention.

Thus, arbitrary methods of socialist pricing can be made to work, at least in principle, to prevent undesired contractions and 'economic chaos' resulting from them.

However, the first method examined above involves a rather draconian tax-subsidy (or credit control) system. This will be especially the case if advance information concerning future expansion possibilities are not made available in time to the fiscal (or credit-control) authorities, so that tax and subsidy rates will have to be recomputed and revised repeatedly.

Besides, there seems to be something inherently irrational about a method according to which the planners first create a problem, as it were, by fixing prices arbitrarily, and then try to solve it by fiscal interference.

On the other hand, the chief defect of the second method is that it involves time-consuming and costly trial computations involving a large number of commodities whose prices have to be fixed.

3 Socialist prices which are proportionate to labour-embodied quantities

Now, it turns out that fixing prices of socialized commodities which are proportionate to their labour-embodied quantities involves a much simpler procedure compared to arbitrary-pricing procedures examined in the previous section.

To check this, let us write out the technology represented by **1** in its expanded form **2**, in which the direct labour terms have been filled in, as L_a and L_b:

$$2A+2B+\tfrac{3}{4}L_a \rightarrow 8A, \qquad\qquad 2$$
$$2A+5B+\tfrac{1}{4}L_b \rightarrow 8B.$$

Now, we have noted in chapter 3, section 3 that, if a technological skeleton of this kind is converted into a set of value equations in which the profit-rate is made equal to 0, so that the entire national income is paid out as wages, we have a formal system of prices which are equal to quantities of labour embodied in these commodities. We also noted there that such a set of prices is of purely formal interest, since it is *unusable* for discussing any real-life economic model of capitalism, in which the profit-rate must be positive. Now, this holds *also* for a socialist economy (or sub-economy), where prices *cannot* be made equal to the labour-contents of commodities, simply because out of the revenue earned in each industry, there must be contribution to the social insurance (and accumulation) funds etc., of the socialist economy, as Marx made clear in *The Critique of the Gotha Programme* (Marx, 1949a, pp. 20–21).

Fortunately, the contributions to various social funds, including the investment-accumulation fund, which every socialized industry *must* make, can very well take the form of a proportional wage-tax collected from each industry (which is also what Marx (1949a, p. 22) suggested). This would make the prices of socialized commodities proportional to their (total) labour-contents.

Thus, in **2**, if we visualize a 10 per cent tax on the unskilled-labour wage-fund in each industry, in the value equations, we can put $w = \frac{9}{10}$ (since the national income is equal to one in models of this kind). We would then get the price-ratio $p_a/p_b = \frac{11}{12}$ – which is exactly what we would get, if we made $w = 1$ (i.e. if unskilled labourers' wages claim the whole of the net national income, and prices are equal to labour-embodied quantities).

This method of socialist-pricing is particularly suitable also because, as noted in chapter 6, section 4, once the input–output proportions are fixed by the central socialist plan, the 'reduction method' of solving simultaneous equations (or, where joint products are involved, the 'sub-systems' method) can always be used for 'decentralized' derivation of these prices which are proportional to labour-contents by the producers in each socialized enterprise.

However, one strong reason for looking for better alternatives to prices which are proportional to the total labour contents of socialized commodities is that, like the arbitrary pricing procedures discussed in the previous section, the present procedure will not, generally, leave the socialized enterprises and industries with profit margins or investment funds which coincide with the targets set by the socialist plan. Thus, in this case, too, 'corrective' fiscal measures (taxes and subsidies, or plan-enforcing buffer-stock operations) or credit-control measures, will have to be adopted to enforce plan targets.

It is shown in the next section that it is possible, with com-modity-production models, to work out a solution of the socialist-pricing problem which also ensures an automatic fulfilment of the planned investment-targets. Before we pass on to this alternative solution, however, two powerful argu-ments in favour of the method discussed in the present section should be noted.

First, in spite of its awkwardness, the two-step method of first making prices proportional to total labour-contents of socialized commodities, and then using fiscal or credit-control instruments to implement plan-targets, is the only 'sure-fire' method available, as long as there is a time-lag between estimating in the initial period t_0 the production requirements in the next period t_1, and estimating subsequent investment requirements in t_2, the period after next. As long as, for practical reasons, the two pieces of information cannot be sent to the centralized price-fixing authority together, i.e. in t_0, *before* the prices for t_1 are computed, there is no pos-sibility whatever of employing the method indicated in the next section, as will become clear in a moment.

Secondly, even if the time-lag-in-estimations hurdle is somehow overcome, the method of fixing prices which are linked with unequal industry-wise profit-rates (which conform to target requirements of the plan) sets a large (centralized) computational task compared to the modest (decentralized) computation of labour-content prices (at the industry or enterprise level) and tax-subsidy estimates. (Centralized price-computation with unequal profit-rates not only requires a solution at the centre for all prices, but also of a different profit-rate for each industry, as will be seen in the illustration considered in the next section.)

4 Socialist plan-enforcing prices with unequal industry profit-rates

Let us suppose that the economy or sub-economy represented by **3** – which is the same technological skeleton as **2** – is one about which the price-fixing centre has received in advance, in the initial 'price-setting period' t_0, information concerning the period t_1 for which the prices are to be set, and about the investment plan for each industry fixed for t_2 the next period. (It is also assumed that a social decision has also been taken concerning the residual surplus product in t_1 to be made over as the 'bonus' income paid out of the surplus of the period t_1, to wage and salary-earners employed in t_1.)

These items of information available to the socialist price-fixing authority are summarized below:

$$2A+2B+\tfrac{3}{4}L_a \to 8A, \qquad\qquad\qquad\qquad\qquad 3$$
$$2A+5B+\tfrac{1}{4}L_b \to 8B.$$

Standard income[1] $\tfrac{8}{5}A+\tfrac{16}{5}B.$ $\qquad\qquad\qquad\qquad\qquad$ **4**

Expansion demand of A-industry in t_2 $3A.$ $\qquad\qquad\qquad$ **5**

Expansion demand of B-industry in t_2 $\tfrac{1}{2}B.$ $\qquad\qquad\qquad$ **6**

Bonus income in t_1 $1A+\tfrac{1}{2}B.$ $\qquad\qquad\qquad\qquad\qquad$ **7**

Out of the information summarized, we choose **3–5** – we could just as well have chosen **6** in place of **5** – and **7**, and cast them into the value equations **8**, which is a system of five independent equations with five unknowns – p_a, p_b, r_a, r_b and w – to be determined. (p_a and p_b represent unit prices of A and B respectively, r_a and r_b represent the profit-rates in

---

1. The method of converting any nonstandard system like **3** into a system in 'standard proportions' and working out the 'standard income' or net product of the 'standard system' corresponding to the actual system is explained in Sraffa (1960, chapters 4–5).

the A-industry and the B-industry respectively, w is the 'bonus income' of the wage-and-salary earners in t_1).

$$(2p_a+2p_b)(1+r_a)+\tfrac{3}{4}w = 8p_a, \tag{8}$$
$$(2p_a+5p_b)(1+r_b)+\tfrac{1}{4}w = 8p_b,$$
$$\tfrac{8}{5}p_a+\tfrac{16}{5}p_b = 1,$$
$$(2p_a+2p_b)r_a = 3p_a,$$
$$w = 1p_a+\tfrac{1}{2}p_b.$$

Solving these equations, we get:

$$p_a = \tfrac{19}{88}, \quad p_b = \tfrac{18}{88}, \quad r_a = \tfrac{57}{74}, \quad r_b = \tfrac{9}{128}, \quad w = \tfrac{28}{88}.$$

Industry-wise accounts are:

	Capital outlay	Profit margin	Profit rate	'Bonus income'	Value of gross product
A-industry	$\tfrac{74}{88}$	$\tfrac{57}{88}$	$\tfrac{57}{74}$	$\tfrac{21}{88}$	$\tfrac{152}{88}$
B-industry	$\tfrac{128}{88}$	$\tfrac{9}{88}$	$\tfrac{9}{128}$	$\tfrac{7}{88}$	$\tfrac{144}{88}$

The net product of the actual system represented by **8** is:

$4A+1B$ (in physical terms) $= \tfrac{76}{88}+\tfrac{18}{88} = \tfrac{94}{88}$ (in value terms).

These accounts show that provided the bonus-income receivers spend their bonus income equal to $\tfrac{28}{88}$ in buying the $A+\tfrac{1}{2}B$, valued at $\tfrac{28}{88}$ allotted for the purpose, the A-industry would be able to spend its $\tfrac{57}{88}$ profit-margin in making the desired extra investment of $3A$ or $\tfrac{57}{88}$, and the B-industry would be able to make an extra investment of $\tfrac{1}{2}B$ (valued at $\tfrac{9}{88}$), as desired in the socialist plan.

Thus, 'shadow prices' linked to unequal, industry-wise profit-rates to enforce socialist plans can work, but their limitations have been pointed out in the previous section of this Appendix.

14 The Outline of a Post-Marxian Political Economy of Socialism

1 Introduction

This chapter is devoted to an analysis of certain problems of a socialist society which must be discussed in a formulation of the elements of an elementary political economy of socialism. They have been referred to in Marxian, non-Marxian or neo-Marxian literature on socialism under various names, and may be identified as the problems of:

(a) Bureaucratic wastes;
(b) The functioning of 'democratic centralism' (with which socialist personality cults seem to be invariably associated);
(c) Parasitism;
(d) Alienation;
(e) Elitist inegalitarianism – in socialist societies.

Marxian doctrine identifies (a), and to some extent (c) and (d). What it has to say about (d) scarcely satisfies the curiosity of scientific investigators. It ignores, underplays or explains away the existence of (e), which has received recognition only in very recent neo-Marxian writing (e.g. Nove and Nuti, 1972, p. 9).

However, while these problems are by now well-established as the hard facts of life in socialist societies, the references to them in the literature are often imprecise and obscure. For example, socialist 'democratic centralism' is a mystique, rather than a precise concept, which has never been subjected to a scientific investigation. Similarly in so far as modern Marxian critical (or polemical) literature, e.g. Chinese communist literature, recognizes the problem of inegalitarianism in modern (Soviet-type) socialist societies, it is identified as a species of exploitation of man by man belonging to the same genus as capitalist exploitation. However, the notion was lacking in analytical precision, until this was supplied very recently (von Weizsacker, 1972, section 11, pp. 35–8), to which further reference will be made in section 6.

The beginning of an attempt to fill this gap in the literature is made in this chapter. The tools of analysis employed are: modern commodity-production models already used in chapter 13, and the Appendix to chapter 13, to discuss problems of socialist economies; some results of the modern theory of collective social choice referred to in discussing capitalist exploitation in the Appendix to chapter 6, or in discussing a socialist 'non-breakdown thesis' in the next chapter (chapter 15).

2 Commodity (market) relations and socialist planning

For reasons which are somewhat obscure, Marxian doctrine is irreconcilably opposed to a full 'market-socialist' model (such as the 'decentralized' version of the Lange–Lerner model of socialism, where the preference scales of individual consumers determine the 'planned' allocation of resources (Lange and Taylor, 1956, section 3, pp. 72–90)). However, as we shall see in the next section, this *caveat* leaves the door open for alternative Marxian political-economic models of socialism, including a pure 'anti-market' ('war communism') model, as well as several others which utilize market relations, without being governed by them.

Neo-physiocratic (anti-mercantilist) notions about the 'sterility' of mercantile and trading activity could, perhaps, account for this Marxian verdict against the 'rule of the market', though the argument does not seem to have been spelt out in the Marxian 'classics'.[1] On the other hand, the Marxian doctrine that *any* commodity production (which, in Marxian terminology means production for the market, as opposed to production for self-consumption by producers)

1. In modern commodity-production theory, used as one of the foundations for the post-Marxian political economy developed in this book, there is *no* support for any such physiocratic notion.

'generates capitalists constantly and continuously' (Stalin, 1947, pp. 257–8; Spulber, 1964, pp. 266–78) as the basis for this verdict against market rule is not very convincing in the context of 'full socialism', i.e. in a society where the transition to socialism (discussed in chapter 13) has been completed, and all the principal means of production are publicly owned.

The Marxian verdict against market rule in a socialist society makes better sense in the context of the Marxian theory of alienation of man in any society based on commodity (market) relations, which will be discussed in section 6. However, as we shall see in these later sections, avoidance of market rule by adopting political consultative procedures (overtly or covertly involving voting) outside the market framework for plan-making is at best a necessary, but not by itself a sufficient, condition for the eradication of the problem of alienation inherited by a socialist society from its capitalist past.

Actually, the really cogent argument in favour of this Marxian 'institutional datum' about socialist economies is to be found in the modern (non-Marxian) general critiques of the efficacy of the Walrasian *tatonnement* procedure and analyses of causes of 'market failure'. Developed in the context of theories of a capitalist economy (Bator, 1958, pp. 351–79), the argument has recently been extended to cover socialist economies as well (Bliss, 1972, pp. 90–92, 99–100).

But whether we are impressed by any of these arguments or not, a strict separation in time of plan-making, or plan-formulation by some political (non-market) procedure, and plan-implementation with or without use of the market-mechanism, is an 'institutional datum' for all socialist economies extant, from 1917 to date. Surprisingly, this hard fact of socialist reality has been ignored in almost all 'stylized' models of socialist planning available in the literature, from the Lange–Lerner model (Lange and Taylor, 1956) to the more recent Marglin–Weitzman models (Marglin, 1969; Weitzman, 1970).[2]

2. This is also true of the more general literature on planning not restricted to socialist economies. An exception, which explicitly

To redress the balance a little, in the present chapter the focus is exclusively on alternative political-economic models of socialism, all of which provide for allocative (planning) decision-making outside the market mechanism, completed *before* plan-implementation begins. But some of them provide for plan-implementation through the market mechanism (i.e. by using price indices and inter-enterprise market contracts, as in the Soviet Union and most East European countries after the recent 'economic reforms' (Ellman, 1972, chapters 4, 8–10; Wilczynski, 1972, ch. 3)).

The essentials of the planning process in such Marxian models of socialism involve three kinds of functions:

1 The 'associated producers' at the enterprises 'send up' messages to the planning centre, conveying (a) their draft production plans, and (b) reports on alternative production possibilities rejected by them, through signals other than market 'signals'. These messages specify the quantities of commodities and of direct labour required. It is a matter of indifference whether the quantities specified are expressed in their respective natural physical units (e.g. tons of high-speed steel) or conventional physical units (e.g. tons of steel, with no distinction made between different types and qualities of steel), or in terms of their historical prices (Kyn, Sekerka and Heijl, 1967, p. 104). However, if historical prices are used, the temptation to 'aggregate' is strong, and this may create complications (Ellman, 1972, ch. 6, Appendix 1, pp. 95–100).

2 The planning centre (a) collates the information received from the enterprises, (b) tests the feasibility of the collated national economic plan, (c) considers technological reports on alternatives not considered (or considered and rejected) at the enterprise level, and market forecasts based on surveys and projections including foreign trade forecasts, to construct an alternative, feasible plan, which meets politically approved overall social objectives, such as full employment, and/or a

allows for plan-formulation by a political voting procedure which is separated from plan-implementation, is a recent contribution by Sen (1969a, section 3, pp. 204–206).

desired rate of growth and/or a desired pattern of personal income-distribution.

3 The planning centre then 'sends down' messages ('directives') for implementing the approved plan in the form of physical or financial 'quotas' and/or 'price indices', depending on the type of model of socialist planning in vogue.

The above account of the common essential features of socialist planning processes in which plan formulation (by a political consultative procedure) is separated from plan implementation is highly idealized. In practice, the functions enumerated are very imperfectly fulfilled (Ellman, 1972, ch. 6, pp. 60–93, ch. 7, pp. 113–27). But this is immaterial for the present discussion.

The two parts of the planning process just described – the plan formulation and the plan implementation – deserve equal attention. However, for convenience of exposition, discussion of the various problems encountered when plan-formulation is done through a political-consultative procedure is postponed to sections 5 and 6. In the next section we concentrate on a comparison of four stylized Marxian models of socialist plan-implementation, in terms of the bureaucratic waste of economic resources involved.

3 Bureaucratic (economic) wastes in Marxian models of socialist plan-implementation

Alternative Marxian models of socialist plan-implementation

A sketch is given below of some essential features, in terms of *ideology* in the sense of Lange – 'a system of social . . . ideas, on the basis of which men evaluate social relations' (Lange, 1963, p. 24) – and the *practice of plan-implementation*, corresponding to four highly stylized prototypes of Marxian models, which have the common feature that they are associated with plan-formulation through political-consultative procedures. The nomenclature is purely suggestive, not historically exact.

War Communism

Ideology: any use of the market-mechanism or commodity relations 'generates capitalists constantly and continuously'[3] and is anathema in a socialist state fighting for survival. *Corollary:* planned disparities in personal incomes should also not be used as instruments of plan-implementation, because a socialist society should undermine and not preserve bourgeois inequality, even if it cannot immediately adopt the principle of 'to each according to his needs'.

Practice of plan-implementation: resource allocation strictly and only through quantitative quotas, including in this statutory, egalitarian rationing of *all* consumer goods (including housing), payment of wages and incomes in the form of 'meal tickets' or consumer coupons, so that allocation of consumer goods to enterprises *ipso facto* (though indirectly) allocates labour. (Arbitrarily fixed and enforced prices and money-incomes subject to egalitarian ceilings are used as the financial counterpart of the planned material flows, and to eliminate black-market interconsumer transactions.)

The classical Soviet socialist model

Ideology: prices and incomes determined by free market forces indeed generate capitalism and perpetuate bourgeois inequalities. But a structure of controlled prices and unequal personal incomes is helpful in (a) consolidating 'socialism in one country' against 'capitalist encirclement', and (b) to establish the material-technological foundations of a full communist society, where commodity production and circulation, i.e. market relations, will be completely abolished, and personal income-distribution will be on the principle of 'to each according to his needs'.

Practice of plan-implementation: quantitative input–output quotas, reinforced by directives regarding 'technological

3. Most clearly expressed in Stalin's polemics against Bukharin over the New Economic Policy which followed war communism in the Soviet Union (Stalin, 1947, pp. 257–78).

norms' should be the basic instruments of socialist plan-implementation. But these should be complemented by socially-manipulated (socialist) prices of consumer goods (and imputed prices of producer goods), unequal personal incomes and taxes (especially the turnover tax), so as to frustrate individualistic counter-manipulation of prices, personal incomes and resource allocation through the black-market mechanism.

The post-classical Soviet-type socialist model

Ideology: Decentralized price-fixing at the enterprise level (including both material input–output and wage-rates) would indeed undermine socialist planned development and generate capitalist relations. But *centralized* socially-manipulated planned prices and incomes are perfectly reliable as the basic instruments of socialist plan-implementation. They could be made more effective by (a) legal enforcements of the inviolability of plan targets and inter-enterprise contracts, (b) simplifying plan-implementation procedures by *reducing* the number of instruments of centralized control (maximization of the number of instruments of control does *not* maximize efficiency in plan-implementation), (c) pressing into service the instruments of credit control through the socialized banking system (which had fallen into disuse since the early period of the socialist revolution), (d) introducing a new system of collective (enterprise-wide) as well as individual 'material incentives' based on bonus incomes, better working conditions, shorter working hours etc. as rewards for fulfilment of planned output and income targets.

Practice of plan-implementation: abolition of quantitative input–output quotas, and the use of price–income and tax-subsidy-credit 'directives' as the principal instruments of plan-implementation (along with legal enforcement of planned targets, contracts, changed working conditions etc.).

A possible 'Hungarian' model of socialist plan-implementation[4]

Ideology: socially-manipulated prices and incomes *can* be entirely enforced through the market mechanism, i.e. through utilization of commodity relations, subject to overall fiscal and credit controls, in a socialist economy, based on public ownership of the principal means of production. They do *not* generate capitalism or capitalists, at least not after a revolutionary transition from capitalism to socialism has been completed, with the 'collectivization' (or 'communization') of agriculture.

Practice of plan implementation: improve upon the post-classical Soviet-type model by (a) perfecting consumer-demand forecasting, so that allocation of resources for production of consumer goods indirectly allocates labour, as in the war communism model (even though in this case, there is 'variability' in consumption, in the sense defined in chapter 9), (b) 'decentralizing' the functions of price-fixing of non-basics, and of allocation of basics made available by central planners for non-basics' production, at a sub-central level. ('Pure' non-basics, which do not enter into the production of *any* product, have their prices fully determined as soon as their basic prices are fixed at the planning centre. 'Interconnected' non-basics, which enter into each other's production (only), have their prices calculated and announced at sub-central price-fixing centres manned by representatives of producers of interconnected non-basics, who work with the basic prices fixed by the planning centre taken as data. Thus, these plan-

4. So named because interdependent production models play an essential role here. Such production models, which may be contrasted to 'Austrian' production models, have received more attention in Hungary, the home of the von Neumann model of economic equilibrium, though in the present context the interdependence in production is assumed to be partially decomposable, unlike the von Neumann model, which is an indecomposable model. Also, the 'Hungarian model' in this chapter provides for sub-centralized plan-implementation in certain specified sectors, which to some extent resembles 'two-step' planning advocated by Kornai and Liptak (1965) in Hungary.

ning sub-centres are firmly guided by the 'invisible hand' of the central planning council, and *not* to any extent by the 'invisible hand of the market'. Hence, no 'compromise' between the socialist 'plan' and the 'free' market is involved. The extent of 'sub-centralization' has *nothing* to do with ideology; it is dictated purely by technology, i.e. the nature of interdependence in production and the importance of non-basics in the economy.)

As already indicated, the four models of socialist plan-implementation sketched above are 'suggestive', rather than historically exact. But each of them resembles Marxian plan-implementation models which have been proposed, discussed or used. Together, they exhaust the range of prototypes which have actually been used (or, very nearly, since not enough is yet known about some of them, e.g. the Chinese prototypes).

A problem of assessment

In the theoretical literature (including theoretical models which formalize the actual practice in socialist economies), alternative economic models of socialism are assessed in terms of criteria which are hardly appropriate in an assessment of the four prototypes considered above.

One such criterion is the 'maximization of the growth rate' of the socialist economy. On this criterion, the classical Soviet-type model sketched above (which resembles the soviet plan-implementation techniques of the first three five-year plans) would probably outclass all others, if we go by statistically measured growth-rates. But it is easy to see that this has to do with the planning strategy (i.e. the physical pattern of resource allocation) adopted through political-consultative procedures of *plan-formulation*, which is *independent* of the institutional pattern of *plan-implementation* adopted (in principle, each of the four prototypes is compatible with high or low rates of growth).

Another criterion often invoked is the scope for 'de-centralized' incentive-payments to optimize resource-allo-cation (or the rate of growth, rate of technical progress etc.) (Liberman, 1972, pp. 309–18; Marglin, 1969, pp. 76–7).

The multiplicity of incentive systems in force in the classical Soviet-type model is thought to be responsible for avoidable economic wastes (Ellman, 1972, pp. 60–94). But no way seems to have been found yet of reducing such wastes in models which resemble the post-classical Soviet-type prototype (Ellman, 1972, pp. 113–27). This is not surprising. It is a feature of real-life socialist planning models, as of the four prototypes, that consumption–investment decisions are taken *independently* of the functioning of the incentive-payment system connected with plan-implementation – by a *prior* political-consultative process. Consequently, the incentives structure is *centralized* in these models, where the planning process is *disintegrated* into a plan-formulation process which *precedes* the plan-implementation process. (This is in sharp contrast to *integral* socialist planning models (e.g. Marglin, 1969; Lange, 1967; Weitzman, 1970) where there is an integrated process of plan formulation and plan implementation.) With such a centralized incentive-structure, 'decentralized' incentive-payments or 'bonus incomes' will be limited to gains by one set of individuals or enterprises at the expense of others which leave unaffected the socially-determined centralized structure of consumption, investment and resource-allocation.

A third criterion often invoked is the minimization of the difficulties connected with the so-called 'convergence problem' involved in iteration (*tatonnement*) planning procedure assumed in the usual 'integral' type of planning process discussed in academic literature (e.g. Marglin, 1969; Lange, 1967; Weitzman, 1970). It is argued that if importance is attached to increasing returns to scale, or in the absence of institutional factors like perfect futures markets covering all goods – quantitative allocation or rationing of inputs is to be preferred (Bliss, 1972, p. 100). There is also an argument that because the market is a (cheaper) sociological substitute for the mechanical computer (pointed out by Lange in 1957 (Nove and Nuti, 1972, pp. 402–4)), the planning centre should send down quantitative directives while the enterprises send up price-type directives. But the most compelling argument in favour of the planning centre handing down quantitative directives, while the enterprises send up price-type directives, has to do with their greater efficiency in solving the fundamental problem of collecting the required information for plan formulation and implementation analysed recently (Weitzman 1970, p. 50–65). This is formally stated in terms of the proposition that there is no presumption that convergence will always be achieved, and that quantitative directives by the planning centre do better than any alternative, in this context.

Thus, the intractable 'convergence' problem seems to make some of the recently proposed *integrated* plan-formulation–plan-implementation procedure more efficient from the informational point of view than the alternative Marxian planning models, which *separate* plan making from plan implementation, of which four prototypes have been listed above.

However, the institutional structure of the informationally efficient integrated planning procedures require an extended discussion, which will not be attempted here. Instead, we shall make a comparative assessment of the four Marxian institutional prototypes, in which the problem of information gathering is simply ignored, but there is no presumption that 'convergence' is always achieved.

The criterion of minimization of bureaucratic (economic) wastes

A suitable criterion for assessing alternative Marxian models of socialist planning could be the criterion of the minimization of the communications load carried by each model. Since *some* procedure of political consultation for making the plan is attached to each of the four prototypes of plan implementation, the 'size' of the communications-load carried with each type of overall planning model will be measured by the total number of 'messages' exchanged back-and-forth between the enterprises 'below' and the central planning council 'above'. (The 'size' of the communications load carried in each case will depend partly on the plan-implementation prototype in vogue, and partly on the number of products and processes, the nature of the 'structure of production' (i.e. the one-way and two-way relations of interdependence in the production processes) and the number of alternative 'technologies' (i.e. methods of interdependent production of all products of the system) available about which information is exchanged.)

Since resources have to be allocated for transmission of these 'messages' through the communications system, and, *ceteris paribus*, the larger the total communications-load the greater is the cost, in terms of time lost in formulating and implementing a socialist plan, the 'communications-load minimization' criterion is equivalent to the criterion of minimization of bureaucratic (economic) wastes in the planning process. (These economic wastes are very similar to those referred to in *Parkinson's Law* (Parkinson, 1958, pp. 9–21), and are undoubtedly classifiable as 'bureaucratic'.)

This criterion permits an exact ranking of the four prototypes of socialist plan-implementation as shown below.

Notation, definitions and assumptions for alternative Marxian models of socialist planning

Notation: n represents the number of processes, equal to the number of products (including in this 'produced' skilled labour-power) of the technology selected through the political-consultative process of socialist plan formulation incorporated in each Marxian model of socialist planning.

k represents, for the selected technology, the number of commodities (i.e. the non-basics) whch do *not* enter, directly or indirectly, into the production of all the n processes of production. Thus, the n commodities of the selected technology consist of k non-basics, plus $n-k$ basics, which *do* enter, directly or indirectly, into the production of all n commodities.

m represents the total number of 'entries' with reference to commodities entering into processes, in all available technologies about which information is collected in the process of plan-formulation and 'sent up' to the planning centre. Thus, if two 3×3 production matrices are available as alternatives, two consisting of two basics and one non-basic each, the third consisting of one basic and two non-basics, then $n = 3$, $m = 19$, 18 or 17. i.e. m is not uniquely determined. But as we shall see, this does not affect the ranking of alternative Marxian models compared.

l represents the total number of entries of direct, unskilled labour, into the processes in all available technologies. Thus, if direct labour enters into both processes in two available technologies consisting of 2×2 matrices, $l = 4$.

q represents the number of quantitative quotas, or 'directives' used in some of the models considered, by which the planning centre fixes targets for commodity inputs and outputs for plan implementation. Thus, if a 2×2 production matrix is selected, and absolute quantitative 'quota directives' are used by the planning centre, $q = 3$ if there is one basic and one non-basic.

w represents the wage-rate of unskilled labour, which, by definition, is of one kind, so that $w \equiv 1$.

Assumptions

1 There is at least one technology available.

2 For each available technology, the production matrix is partially decomposable, with at least one basic and one non-basic (so that $1 \leqslant k < n$).

3 In each available technology, while all basics enter by definition directly or indirectly into all processes, *all* or *none* of them may enter *directly* into all processes.

4 Primary, unskilled labour is homogeneous (see chapter 6, section 3 for explanation), and enters into at least some processes in each technology, and heterogeneous skilled labour is 'produced' as joint products (or single products) of the processes incorporated in any technology (see chapter 6, section 3 for explanation).

5 There is one wage-rate for homogeneous unskilled labour in each technology.

Corollaries

1 Assumptions 1–3 together imply that $2n \leqslant m$ (i.e. m has a minimum value when there is only one technology available, and the only (partially decomposable) technology available has the property that all except one commodity is basic, but all basics enter only indirectly into the production of other commodities).

2 Assumptions 4 and 5 together imply that $1 = w < n$.

3 Assumption 4 for primary unskilled labour implies that the minimum number of direct, unskilled labour entries into processes in the selected technology must be equal to, or less than, the number of products, or $1 \leqslant n$.

4 Assumptions 1–3 together imply that the minimum value for q is $2n$, which is reached when the production matrix selected has only one non-basic, and no non-basic enters directly into the production of any other commodity (i.e. $2n \leqslant q$).

An exact ranking of alternative Marxian political-economic models of socialist planning

The notation, assumptions etc. of the previous section are now used to tabulate the communications-load in alternative Marxian models of socialist planning.

(Where communications with respect to prices are entered, there are $n-1$ prices, because one of them is adopted as the numeraire. The profit rate is not entered separately in any model, on the assumption that, for reasons explained in the Appendix to chapter 13, section 3, prices which are proportionate to labour-embodied quantities (implying a zero profit-rate) are preferred to others. But one could just as well assume that the profit rate is uniform at a positive level, or *non*-uniform at a positive level (this case is discussed in the

Appendix to chapter 13, section 4). Messages about taxes and subsidies, which play an essential role in some of these models, are disregarded, because they do not affect the ranking on the chosen criterion. It should be noted, finally, that in the Table below the nomenclature of the alternative Marxian socialist planning models coincides with the nomenclature adopted earlier for Marxian socialist plan-implementation prototypes. This is justified, because the main difference between alternative Marxian models of socialist planning is accounted for by differences in plan-*implementation* procedures, rather than by differences in plan-*formulation* procedures (which are discussed in section 5 below.)

Table 8

Messages	War communism	Classical Soviet-type model	Post-classical Soviet-type model	Hungarian-type model
'sent up'	m	$m+l$	$m+l$	$m+l$
'sent down'	$+q$	$+q+n+l+w-1$	$+n+w-1$	$+n-k-1$
total	$m+q$	$m+q+n+2l+w-1$	$m+n+l+w-1$	$m+n+l-k-1$

It is evident from the Table that omission or inclusion of messages about direct labour quantities and the wage-rate for unskilled labour-power, of quantitative quotas or price directives, of directives about non-basic prices, account for the inter-model differences in the total communications load, and determine the ranking of each model.

Intuitively, it would seem that the classical Soviet-type model would be lowest in rank, and the Hungarian-type model the highest, if we judge exclusively by the communications-load minimization criterion.

To verify this, we have to prove that the expression measuring the *excess* of the total communications-load carried by the Soviet-type classical model is always *positive* when it is compared with every other alternative, and the *excess* of the communications-load carried by the Hungarian-type model as compared to every other alternative model is always *negative*.

Now, the excess of the communications-load carried by the classical Soviet-type model is:

$n = 2l+w-1$ over war communism, **1**

$q+l$ over the post-classical Soviet-type model, **2**

$q+l+w+k$ over the Hungarian-type model. **3**

Since n, l, q, w and k are positive, by definition, and by assumptions 1–4 above, $1 < n$, **1**, **2** and **3** always have a positive value. So the classical Soviet-type model ranks lowest by the communications-load minimization criterion.

The communications-load carried by the Hungarian-type model exceeds all alternatives by:

$n+l-q-k-1$ over war communism, **4**

$-l-q-k-w$ over the classical Soviet-type model, **5**

$-k-w$ over the post-classical Soviet-type model. **6**

As already noted, l, q, k and w are positive by definition, so that expressions **5** and **6** are always negative. As regards **4**, by corollary 3, we have $n+1 \leqslant 2n$; by corollary, 4, we have $2n < q$, so that $n+1 < q$. This makes the expression $n+1-q$ always negative, and therefore the whole expression **4** is always negative. Thus, the Hungarian-type model ranks highest if we judge only by the communications-load minimization criterion.

It can also be shown that these rankings are unaffected by the number of products and greater possibilities of technical choice, i.e. by the 'complexity' of the physical production-structures available. However 'undeveloped' the socialist economy – in the extreme case, with a few hundred as against the over 16 000 'most important commodities' in 1968 in the Soviet Union (Ellman, 1972, ch. 6, p. 68) – and with 'fixed coefficients' in production (and/or consumption), the Hungarian-type model is still better than all alternatives on the basis of the communications-load minimization criterion, which, as argued above, is equivalent to the criterion of the minimization of bureaucratic (economic) wastes.

4 Socialist institutional mutation, democratic centralism, choice-theory assurance problems and personality-cults

Recorded facts show that each socialist society has experimented with more than one model of socialist planning resembling some of the models of section 3. Moreover, such experiments have outlasted the completion of the transition to 'full socialism' (i.e. the stage where the principal means of production have been socialized, or brought under public ownership). Nor do they (as yet) seem to have much to do with the transition from 'full socialism' (the 'lower stage of communism') to 'full communism' (the 'higher stage of communism').

Such experimentation suggests the existence of a phenomenon of 'socialist institutional change', which is at least as much worth investigating as the phenomenon of 'capitalist institutional change' discussed in chapters 10 and 11.

In the present section, we concentrate on two somewhat puzzling features of this process of socialist institutional mutation, connected with the *political mechanism* by which these changes are brought about. The first feature is that the arguments which have been advanced justifying a change in the socialist institutional pattern have seldom been self-evidently justified, and yet there has never been a reversion to a discarded socialist institutional pattern (either in name or in fact). The second feature is the outstanding fact that every decision for socialist institutional change seems to have been, formally, as well as in substance, a *unanimous* decision, first by the communist party central committee and the central government, then by the entire communist party (formalized by a conference or party congress, or simply by dissidents conceding defeat) and (usually) finally by a popular vote, 'on the streets' or through the ballot-box.

Democratic centralism and choice-theory assurance problems

The official communist creed is to explain the two above-mentioned features, and their mutual compatibility, in terms of the working of the political principle of 'democratic centralism'. However, beyond stressing the obvious truth that in a socialist society (as in any society) there is participation in social decision-making by consent, abstention or veto by those at the base as well as those at the apex, the principle says very little. (It does not even have the merit of drawing attention to an unalterably 'pyramidal' structure of social decision-making as a feature of modern socialist societies, not, at any rate, after the 'direct democracy' methods of the recent Chinese cultural revolution have been legalized at least in China as being compatible with the principle of 'democratic centralism'.) Moreover, except in semi-official pronouncements (e.g. Mao Tse-tung's remarks to Edgar Snow in 1965 and 1970, quoted in Kaul, 1973, pp. 1813, 1815), there is no recognition of the role of the socialist personality-cults (positive or negative) in the successful functioning of socialist 'democratic centralism' as instruments of socialist institutional change.

In what follows, we first try to understand the problem of political decision-making leading to socialist institutional change by formulating it as a problem belonging to the same class as choice-theory 'assurance problems' used in the discussion of the optimum rate of (social) savings (Sen, 1967a, pp. 114–15; 1969a, pp. 3–6). This isolates the role played by socialist personality-cults, and possible alternatives to it, discussed next.

In the original setting of the 'assurance problem', there is a situation where each man would make a donation, *if only* others will. In later applications to the problem of optimizing the social rate of savings, or 'the minimum size of fruitful effort', it is specified that there is an agreed best outcome, so that no enforcement of the best outcome is necessary. What the outcome will be depends entirely on each having an assurance as regards what others will do. (This also means that any solution of an 'assurance problem' will be unanimous.) Finally, to secure a *unique* collective solution, it is essential to make sure that the problem is not an n-person problem, but is a two-person problem (Sen, 1969a, pp. 13–15).

In analysing the problem of socialist institutional change as an 'assurance problem', we start with the following assumptions about the environment, and the individual's preference ordering.

Assumptions

1 There is 'full socialism' (i.e. revolutionary socialization of all the principal means of production has been achieved).

2 Decisions about *socialist* institutional reforms (i.e. institutional reforms which do *not* pave the way for a capitalist restoration) are permitted, but must be taken *unanimously* by all members of the socialist community. (This is an institutional datum of a socialist society: the product of socialist ideology, or inertia, or indifference in a socialist society where a section of the population is stricken with *anomie*.)

3 Unanimous decisions about socialist institutional change must be reflected at all levels of party and state decision-making in line with the principle of socialist democratic-centralism. The pattern of unanimous decision-making will include unanimous denunciation of active dissent (by a minority or majority) at any particular point of the social decision-making apparatus by the remainder.

4 Each individual will reveal his preference (i.e. 'vote') for socialist institutional reform if all others will do so. He will vote against it, if he thinks others will vote against.

5 Each individual will prefer all voting for a socialist institutional reform to all voting against it.

Assumptions 4 and 5 together define the present problem as an 'assurance problem'. A third feature of the individual's preference-pattern in such a problem, viz. that each individual regards some voting for, and others voting against the proposed institutional reform as a second-best outcome, is in this case ruled out by the environmental assumptions 2 and 3. Assumption 5 in the individual's preference-ordering may be a reflection of a belief in *socialist* change as representing progress compared to socialist inertia, as an article of faith in a socialist ideology.

The set of assumptions 1–5 is mutually compatible, and ensures that all voting unanimously for a socialist institutional reform will be regarded as the best outcome. However, the best outcome will materialize *only if* each has the assurance that all others will vote for change.

As already indicated, several such cases of unanimous social decisions in favour of socialist institutional reform have occurred in fact. What has supplied the element of assurance which is decisive? In a search for an answer to this question, we have to discuss the socialist personality-cults.

The role of the socialist personality-cult

Widespread revolutionary hero-worship, and its conversion into socialist personality-cults are recorded facts about socialist societies, which can hardly be denied. Their association with socialist institutional reforms embodied in the classical Soviet-type model of socialist planning in the Soviet Union or elsewhere in eastern Europe (or in the *abandonment* of the classical Soviet-type model in China during and after the 'Great Leap forward' phase) are also facts of recorded history. However such an association of socialist institutional reforms with socialist personality-cults does not by itself suggest that these cults act as catalysts in an assurance-problem interpretation of socialist institutional reforms.

What *does* point in the direction of such a hypothesis is the difficulty in finding alternative rational explanations of the phenomenon of the socialist personality-cult. An explanation in terms of a particular personality-cult, e.g. Stalin, developing purely as a response to an anti-socialist, personality-cult, e.g. Hitler, or one socialist personality-cult, e.g. Mao Tse-tung, developing in response to another, e.g. Stalin, begs a chicken-and-egg question – which came first?

On the other hand, if we formulate a problem of socialist institutional change as an assurance problem, and try to find an explanation for a positive 'best' outcome in several cases, the socialist personality-cult falls into place as the element which supplies the needed assurance, and acts as a catalyst of socialist institutional reform. (It is worth noting that a socialist personality-cult like any (e.g. a fascist) personality-cult, is by nature and by definition a cult about a *single*, supreme personality, although at any one time the single positive personality-cult, e.g. Mao Tse-tung, is likely to be bracketed with a single negative personality-cult, e.g. Liu Shao Chi or Lin Piao. This ensures that the assurance-problem model of socialist institutional reform is converted into a version with strictly two possible outcomes – the 'best' and the 'worst' – which alone has the certainty of a unique best-outcome solution. In choice-theory literature on the assurance problem, a unique best-outcome solution is certain only in a two-person version (Sen, 1969a, pp. 13–15), as already indicated above. But in the present context, the socialist personality-cult converts the problem into a two possible outcomes game, by making it impossible for anyone to visualize any outcome other than all voting in favour of the personality's proposed reform, or all voting against. Assumption 5 then ensures a unique best-outcome solution.)

Alternatives to the socialist personality-cult

The problem of socialist institutional reform formulated as an assurance problem can have a unique best-outcome solution in favour of change even in the absence of a socialist personality-cult. The cult is a sufficient, but not a necessary condition for a unique solution in favour of socialist institutional change.

However, it does seem impossible to do without a substitute 'cult of the revolutionary socialist (communist) party', or, in the last analysis, of a cult of the people, which supplies the element of assurance. These supply a rationale for unanimous decisions as regards socialist institutional reform, which are an essential feature of the problem. Whoever is in charge of the party apparatus, even if he secures this position initially by a majority vote in committee, and does not develop a positive cult of his own (nor a negative anti 'top-person-in-party' cult), can rely successfully on a cult of the party, and, *a fortiori*, a cult of the people whose instrument is the party, for the promotion of socialist institutional reform in an assurance-problem setting.

If political life in socialist societies is to be freed from the influence of the cult of the infallibility of the party and the revolutionaries 'who can do no wrong', the price may have to be paid in terms of institutional conservatism or inertia.[5] How far such an outcome may be avoided by the adoption of the alternative to majority decisions (as opposed to unanimous decisions) which are taken on the merits of each proposal for socialist institutional reform, will be discussed to some extent in section 6.

5 Socialist plan-making by political-consultative procedures

We now revert to a discussion of the problems encountered in socialist plan-formulation by political-consultative procedures which was postponed at the end of section 2, where it was noted that there *is* a rationale for such 'political' plan-making outside the market-mechanism in a socialist society based on the hope that it by-passes the 'convergence problems' encountered in integrated plan-formulation-*cum*-implementation procedures working through the market processes.

But, as also noted in section 2, this may not be so. 'Political' plan-making in socialist societies may run into problems of its own: some of these may not be dissimilar to the 'convergence problems' of 'market socialism'. In fact, there are references in the literature to 'convergence'-type problems arising when the classic Soviet 'method of balances' is used in plan-making, which are *not* abolished when more refined input–output techniques are employed (Ellman, 1972, pp. 70–88).

5. Of course, a socialist personality-cult itself may become an instrument of institutional conservatism. On the other hand, the personality about whom there is a cult can 'come alive', so to speak, and lead a successful revolution to smash the fossils in the establishment run in his name. Such a denouement was previewed as fiction in an allegorical play, *Achalayatan*, by Tagore, the Bengali poet–playwright, years before the recent Chinese Cultural Revolution, which resembles it in fact. Pirandello's *Henry IV* could also be interpreted as an allegory about a personality-cult which destroys the personality who creates it.

However, one expects intuitively to handle this kind of problem better with a political-economic analytical apparatus which recognizes the essential similarity of socialist decision-making through market processes and through overtly political voting procedures, and pays special attention to the latter.

As noted in the Appendix to chapter 6, such an analytical apparatus is to be found in the fast-growing modern literature on the theory of collective social choice, which goes as far back as the works of Borda (1784) and Condorcet (1785) in the 1780s. In fact, a connection between the choice-theory discussion of 'impossibility theorems' in political-economic social decision-making models and the problems of socialist planning was seen quite early in the modern literature (e.g. Arrow, 1951, 1970, ch. 7, section 3, pp. 84–5). A direct connection between the modern choice-theory discussion and the Marxian theory of socialism was also established in an unpublished paper (Sen, 1967b, section 4, pp. 18–24). Finally, there is also a literature on 'political' plan-making in general terms (i.e. without specification of a socialist institutional framework) based on a modern choice-theory approach (e.g. Sen, 1969, sections 2–5, pp. 202–13).

Thus, a connection between the discussion of socialist 'political' plan-making and modern political-economic 'impossibility theorems' *has* been established. To strengthen this connection, and to explore its potentialities is the purpose of the present section and the section that follows.

Alternative political voting-procedures and the Arrowian 'impossibility theorem'

As already stated in the Appendix to chapter 6, the 'impossibility theorem' of Arrow consists of certain propositions (propositions 1–4 in this Appendix) which prove that if we want to relate social preferences to individual preferences, we cannot find a method which will do so and still satisfy *four* reasonable conditions, viz. the 'condition of unrestricted domain' (or the existence of a complete social ordering in the minds of individuals), the so-called 'weak Pareto principle' (which says that if everyone prefers x to y, then society must also prefer x to y), the so-called 'independence of irrelevant alternatives' (which says that social choice between x and y is unaffected by (a) individual ranking of any other alternatives *and* also (b) the intensity of preference for x and y (Sen, 1970, 89–91)), and (personal) non-dictatorship.

The theorem is extensive in its scope. It covers covert voting in economic market-structures, overt voting in political assemblies, or even social judgements which involve no voting at all, e.g. a judgement on whether the social welfare of Romans was increased or decreased when Nero fiddled while Rome burned. As regards its application to socialist 'political' plan-making, like the literature on the 'convergence problem' in market-structures, it takes into account individual, or social, preferences not only with respect to consumption but also 'producers preferences' with respect to production techniques.

In one branch of the literature on the subject, close attention has been paid to the precise ways in which some well-known overt political-voting procedures are defective or violate one or another of the conditions of Arrow's 'impossibility theorem'.

Summaries

1 Political decision-making on the basis of the principle of consensus or a 'unanimous vote' is loaded in favour of inertia or conservatism (Sen, 1970, ch. 2, section 3, pp. 24–7).

2 The simple majority-decision rule (based on the practice of direct democracy) leads to inconsistencies (Sen, 1970, pp. 38–9).

3 The multi-stage majority-decision rule (based on the practice of indirect, representative democracy) either violates the non-dictatorship condition or has a restricted domain (Pattanaik, 1971, pp. 59–61).

4 Rank-order voting violates the condition of the independence of irrelevant alternatives (in rank-order voting, alternatives in each voter's preference-ordering are ranked according to marks given in descending order, and the alternative scoring top marks in the ballot wins) (Sen, 1970, p. 39).

Escape routes from the impossibility result

The defects and 'impossibility' results connected with 'political' plan-making discussed in the previous section by no means underscore their 'unworkability'. Rather, they suggest precise 'escape routes'.

We first note that *unanimous* decision-making, with its bias in favour of the *status quo* may *not* exercise such a bias if there is a cult of worshipping 'new' projects which change the *status quo*, or any mechanized projects, perhaps in the name of 'Reason' (an illustration is found in Scene One of Brecht's *The Caucasian Chalk Circle* (1969, pp. 3–7) where members of two collective farms reach unanimous agreement on building a dam for extending an orchard). On the other hand, simple-majority decisions based on the practice of direct democracy are obviously irrelevant where the interdependence in production and consumption is complex, the number of socialist enterprises large etc.

As for the remaining two political-voting procedures, viz. the multi-stage majority-decision method, or the rank-order voting method, there are at least five 'escape routes' from the Arrowian impossibility result.

The *first*, and an obvious one, is for a socialist elite to act on the basis of the Hegelian notion of 'society' 'as an abstraction *vis-à-vis* the individual' and draw up, arbitrarily, '*socialist*' plans in the name of the socialist 'society'. The early Marx emphatically rejected this method (Marx, 1961, p. 105). But it seems to be implied in the recommendation of the 'principle of democratic centralism', interpreted to mean 'the centralization of basic decisions and the centralization of operational functions', in recent Soviet discussion of possible reform of the Soviet plan-making procedures, by an extension of the implications of the theory of linear programming (Ellman, 1972, p. 46).

The *second* 'escape route' is a reliance on 'value-restricted' individual preferences to eliminate the 'impossibility' of using multi-stage majority-voting in 'political' plan-making under socialism. A mixed bag of 'value-restricted' individual preference patterns are in fact likely to be available (or be contrivable) in socialist societies. The euphoria of revolutionary-socialist nationalism may establish more or less homogeneous, i.e. identical, preference patterns among individuals, or at least give Arrow's 'single-peaked' preference patterns (which is equivalent to a condition where any one in any triple of alternatives is accepted as 'not worst' by all voters (Sen, 1969a, p. 205)). But when individuals adopt extremist positions around any one issue of planning, with or without a socialist personality-cult being responsible, this could equally well produce these preference patterns (Sen, 1969a, p. 206). The preference pattern in this case is 'single-caved' (Inada, 1964). A watered-down 'limited leadership' by (party) leaders could also serve the purpose. It is enough if there is universal agreement with the opinion of a leader about the relative position of any *one* alternative in every triplet of alternatives (Sen, 1969a, p. 206). Also, if there are 'value-restricted' preferences, regardless of how many voters are 'indifferent', the 'impossibility' problem disappears (Sen, 1970, pp. 188–9).

Dropping the condition of the 'independence of irrelevant alternatives' allows rank-order voting to be used in socialist plan-formulation. This is a *third* escape from the 'impossibility' result.

A *fourth* method of getting round the 'impossibility' result is available, if we (a) do not insist that all concerned must be consulted when making a plan, and (b) assume that there is a 'planner' who acts on the basis of his 'impersonal' or 'ethical' preferences. (The planner's 'ethical preferences' are determined when he considers that there is an equal chance of his being in the shoes of those for whom he plans (Sen, 1969a, pp. 210–13; Pattanaik, 1971, pp. 151–66, interpreting Harsanyi, 1955, who first introduced the concept of 'impersonal', 'ethical' preferences, to be distinguished from personal 'subjective' preferences).) Condition (a) is reasonable in so far as it is *unavoidable*, since any socialist plan must decide investment patterns, whose results will affect the unborn, who cannot possibly be 'consulted' (Sen, 1961; Sen, 1969a, p. 212).

Moreover, an 'impersonal' planner might be able to be more imaginatively sympathetic to the needs of future generations, than each of the more 'selfish' members of the present generation. However, it must be emphasized that condition (b) actually prescribes completely paternalistic planning by a *single* planner, whose ethical preferences are embodied in the socialist plan. If there is more than one 'planner', each acting 'impersonally', there is a problem of non-uniqueness in the outcome of socialist plan-making, which must be avoided (Pattanaik, 1971, p. 166, interpreting Sen, 1969a, pp. 212–13). The cult of a 'supreme planner' or of a 'great socialist helms-man' (Wheelwright and McFarlane, 1973, p. 20), if not a fully fledged socialist personality-cult (discussed in section 4), might be required to make socialist planning, based on planners' 'ethical preferences', produce unique results.

There is an almost equally depressing *fifth* 'escape route'. The failure of individuals (maybe a large number) to reveal their preferences may ensure a stable outcome of a political voting system to decide the shape of the socialist plan (Hinich, Ledyard and Ordeshook, 1972, section 1). Also, if there are 'value-restricted' preferences, regardless of how many voters are 'indifferent', the 'impossibility' problem disappears (Sen, 1970, p. 188–9).

6 Social ills under socialism: how they can be avoided or counteracted

Some of the plan-making and plan-implementation methods, as well as the mechanism of socialist institutional mutation, discussed in sections 3–5, point to certain social ills under socialism, which are discussed in this section. We also consider alternative planning-methods, from the list of those surveyed in those sections, which can avoid them, or other specific measures to counteract them.

Socialist parasitism

Socialist parasitism is a necessary part of the 'bureaucratic wastes' which arise in any planning model which does *not* minimize the communications-load involved in plan implementation. (In other words, as brought out in section 3 in so far as socialist parasitism arises from an excessive communications-load, it occurs in any planning model which does not use the Hungarian method of plan-implementation.) An excess communications-load will almost certainly imply the employment of 'surplus' or 'unproductive' labour in the communications system (i.e. labour in excess of the labour required in the plan-implementation system with communications-load minimized). But there is also a 'communications-load', measured by the number of messages exchanged in back-and-forth consultations between the planning centre and the enterprises, involved in most methods of plan-making surveyed in the previous section. Each of these methods – not excluding the first method based on an Hegelian socialist despotism by planners, or the 'impersonal' planner's rule used in the fourth method – involves some 'communications-load', and, *a fortiori*, 'unproductive labour' in excess of the minimum possible.

The institutional part of the remedy is to adopt the Hungarian method of plan-implementation. This should be combined with the use of a communications technology for minimizing the size of the labour force directly or indirectly engaged in transmitting messages, and in the use of a computer employed in making the required iterative calculations needed to keep the labour force directly or indirectly employed for this purpose at a minimum.

In this way, 'socialist parasitism', measured by the extent of 'unproductive labour' employed in the planning process, can be reduced to a minimum as long as the choice is restricted to Marxian models of 'disintegrated' planning. (But 'integrated' planning models, which are informationally more efficient, referred to in section 3, may do better in reducing 'unproductive labour'.)

Socialist alienation

The Marxian critique of capitalism puts equal emphasis on the *exploitation* of workers by capitalists, originating in capitalistic property ownership (discussed in Part One of this book), and on the *alienation* of workers (and *also* of capitalists),[6] originating in capitalist commodity (market) relations. The Marxian revolutionary-socialist programme therefore proposes the eradication of both.

Though completely ignored in the long debate on the socialist economic model, dating back to Barone's early work in 1908 (Barone, 1933; and excerpts in Nove and Nuti, 1972, pp. 52–74), the Marxian theory of 'alienation' under capitalism and the emphasis on its eradication under socialism has received serious attention with the recent revival of interest in Marx's early writings, especially in the *Economic and Philosophical Manuscripts of 1844* (Marx, 1961), and the *Grundrisse* (Marx, 1973; selections (ed. McLellan), 1971). The vivid portrayal of the problem of human alienation under feudalism or capitalism in modern literature such as Kafka's *The Castle* of 1926 (Kafka, 1971), or Beckett's *Waiting for Godot* of 1952 (Beckett, 1970) shows that the problem is by no means to be dismissed as a figment of the Marxian imagination. On the other hand, in Ionesco's *The Bald Prima Donna* (Ionesco, 1965), the problem *is* portrayed as a problem of self-centred individualism in conventional living in *any* kind of society.

In a systematic exposition of the problem (to which there are scattered references in Marx's *Capital* and *Theories of Surplus Value*, and Engels's *Anti-Duhring*) in the *Economic and Philosophical Manuscripts of 1844* (Marx, 1961, pp. 72–8), Marx asserts that under capitalism, man (and this, as already mentioned, includes *both* the capitalist and the worker) is alienated from the product, from his fellow men, from his productive activity and from his 'species being', i.e. from his potentialities of the human species as distinct from other living beings (Ollman, 1971, p. 151). (The last-named of these four aspects of Marxian alienation[7] seems to have very little

---

6. Marx, 1961, p. 126. In Beckett's *Waiting for Godot*, there is a vivid, ironic portrayal of the capitalist's alienation in the bourgeois Pozzo's anguished complaint against his 'carrier' Lucky (Beckett, 1970, p. 34).

Actually, 'self-estrangement' is a *fifth* aspect of Marxian alienation.

to do, directly, with economics (or politics), and will not be discussed.)

Now, it is clear from what has been said in the preceding sections of the present chapter that a problem of alienation of the producer from his product, and from his fellow producers, can very well arise under socialism, but that it can also be avoided.

Socialist 'parasitism', which could arise in Marxian planning procedures, can also send producers in a socialist society on an endless search for messages and directives through the never-ending corridors of a labyrinthine communications system, much as is the case with the land surveyor (Maximilian Schell) in Nuelte's film version (1970) of Kafka's *The Castle*. The land surveyor's extreme isolation from other inmates of The Castle, which ultimately condemns him to death from sheer frustration – is a powerful portrayal of a problem of alienation, the outcome of socialist parasitism as we have identified it above, which *could* arise under socialism. But a remedy for socialist parasitism, of the kind discussed in the previous section, is also a remedy for this kind of alienation.

More generally, it is easy to see that some methods of socialist plan-formulation *wholly* alienate producers from their products and fellow producers, while others could be *mildly* non-alienating. Thus, 'Hegelian'-type plan-making by socialist despots who act in the name of society, could be wholly alienating (though no despot can in practice ride rough-shod over *every* individual's preferences in any society and be 'totalitarian'). Majority-voting or rank-order voting to decide the shape of the socialist plan, taking advantage of various 'value-restriction' possibilities, or a personality-cult or acceptance of 'limited leadership' in plan-making etc., can be mildly alienating. (However, insincere or 'strategic' voting by some voters who deliberately misrepresent their 'true'

It is vividly portrayed by Emil Jannings in the role of the schoolmaster in the German film classic of the twenties, *The Blue Angel*, and in Satyajit Ray's more recent film, *Debi*, in which a young girl suffers interminable agonies of self-estrangement when she is worshipped by a doting father-in-law as a goddess-incarnate.

preferences, *may* – though this is not certain, since 'honest voting' may also be the best policy – more strongly alienate the honest voters against whom they manipulate the plan (Sen, 1970, pp. 192–4).) On the other hand, 'sincere' (overt or covert) voting plus completely (i.e. perfectly) 'impersonal' planning by the 'supreme planner' may approximate to socialist planning which involves *no* alienation of producers from their products or their fellow producers.

Nothing has, however, been said *explicitly* above about the *third* aspect of the alienation problem, i.e. the alienation of the producer from the production process, or his productive activity. Formally, of course, this aspect is already covered whenever we discuss methods of going from individual to social preferences (since 'preferences' in principle should include preferences as regards the nature of the productive activity). However, a rigorous investigation seems to uncover certain specific problems requiring special attention.

One of them has been uncovered in a recent enquiry (Nell and Nell, 1972) into the implications of the adoption of a principle of 'from each according to his ability, to each according to his needs', when 'needs' are defined explicitly to take into account productive activity of the individual's own choice, i.e. on 'a denial of a distinction between *work*, need and reward'. According to the authors, such a principle, if adopted, can solve an enormous number of resource-allocation problems in a socialist society. But they concede that it cannot solve the problem of 'distribution of un-mechanized chores and of the material by-products of creative endeavour' (Nell and Nell, 1972, p. 491). Moreover, the negative edge of their conclusion on this point becomes even sharper if one takes into account the fact that any 'non-alienating' socialist productive activity (classic examples since Morris's *News from Nowhere* (1946, pp. 91, 125) are 'art products' produced under idyllic, non-polluting, conditions, involves the use of material inputs, which may have to be produced by activity which is by itself 'alienating', and inter-dependence of production is recognized as an unalterable fact of technology.

A solution has been proposed, based on *three* key ideas:

1 A socialist society eager to eradicate a producer's alienation from his productive activity must also, rationally, be interested in getting essential, uncoveted work done, for which a supplementary principle for the distribution of these chores must be accepted.

2 Such a supplementary principle could be a principle which assigns, on the basis of comparative advantage, 'to each the drudgery at which he is relatively best'.

3 There can be no serious objection to such a supplementary principle 'as long as such alienating work is only a small fraction of man's total activity, conferring no special status [or influence]' (Nell and Nell, 1972, p. 491).

The proposed solution is somewhat limited, however, because it begs the question as to whether non-alienated labour is non-alienated from the viewpoint of the individual or of society. *My* 'non-alienating labour' may consist of painting pictures (or writing a book) which alienates some others, so that supplies exceed demand. (This is a separate class of problems compared to the much-discussed problem of a musician playing a trumpet noisily, *when* another musician (next door) is playing the more gentle piano (Braithwaite, 1955, p. 37). Communist ethics would eliminate the problem. However, in the case of pictures or books, too, there *is* a social cost involved, although it is only indirectly imposed on the community by someone's labour which is 'non-alienating' from his individual viewpoint.)

Presumably, the accepted canons of rational behaviour in a communist society, where *most* labour is non-alienating, would have to tolerate such consequences of activity which is non-alienating from diverse individual points of view, and bear the social cost. (The social cost will also have to be shared, of course, by the painter who has to agree to the periodic destruction of his unwanted paintings because the cost of storage exceeds the cost of destruction.)

Socialist elitism

Somewhat inchoate references to 'elitism' in contemporary socialist societies often occur in the recent literature (e.g. Wheelwright and McFarlane, 1973, pp. 226–8). Unfortunately, a precise understanding of its nature is hampered, rather than helped, by the tendency to confuse the phenomenon with manifestations of a survival or restoration of capitalist exploitation. This is even true of a recent analytical break-through in handling the problem as a species belonging to the same genus as capitalistic exploitation, which reaches the conclusion: 'exploitation due to material incentives, including wage differentials, is a phenomenon which unites socialist and capitalist countries' (von Weizsacker, 1972, p. 38).

The powerful argument which identifies socialist elitism with a phenomenon belonging to the same genus as capitalistic exploitation (based on private property in the means of production) runs as follows. Any modern capitalistic or socialist society has an economic model in which groups are differentiated according to whether they provide enough labour to produce the consumption goods they consume (von Weizsacker, 1972, p. 7). If there are groups which consume more than is producible with the labour they supply, there must be other groups which consume less than is producible by the labour they supply. The former then 'exploit' the latter. (In a capitalistic society there are groups, viz. the capitalists, who provide *no* labour, who consume entirely the consumer goods produced by the rest.)

Now, in a socialist society, the differentiation into groups of the type sketched above can arise *either* because the extra incomes of 'produced' skilled labour (common to all socialist pricing-models discussed in the Appendix to chapter 13) are allowed to be privately appropriated, *or* because plan-formulation is deliberately manipulated by would-be 'elite' groups (maybe through the strategem of 'insincere' voting) to secure higher wages for providing homogeneous unskilled labour-power. (We disregard, for reasons already stated in chapter 6, section 3, the argument that genetic factors are responsible for the essential heterogeneity, *sui generis*, of unskilled labour treated as a primary factor in any 'final' model of capitalism *or* of socialism.)

However, 'group elitism' under socialism of the kind just noted can be easily eliminated by imposing a tax to prevent the private appropriation of the surplus income of 'produced' skilled labour, or by employing one of the 'non-alienating' methods of plan-formulation discussed in earlier sections. This last statement, however, is subject to an important proviso. A socialist personality-cult, used as a 'non-alienating' method of plan-formulation *does* alienate its *victims*,[8] so that the believers (who may constitute the overwhelming majority) *do* constitute an elite.

Actually, the bracketing of the problem of socialist 'elitist egalitarianism' with the capitalistic exploitation problem would tend to *understate* the extent of the socialist 'elitism' problem.

Firstly, it ignores other forms of socialist elitism based on individualistic, materialistic gain, which may be incorporated in manipulated socialist plans. The socialist pricing-policy adopted may make workers in different industries (or enterprises) give unequal contributions to the social-investment fund for the growth of the national income, whether this is done by fixing an equal profit-rate or by fixing unequal profit-rates (in the manner noted in the Appendix to chapter 13). Of course, this may be avoided by having 'labour-embodied' prices, and raising contributions to the social investment-fund through personal income-taxes proportionate to incomes, which themselves are made equal (pre-tax) to 'work'. But the plan may still be manipulated so as to provide unequal satisfaction

8. The facetious argument that the victim should willingly, for the cause of socialism, serve as a whipping-boy or a symbol like a Guy Fawkes effigy (Robinson, 1969, p. 65) may amuse a victim in flesh and blood less than it will an outside observer. Even an outsider may remain unconvinced unless he is persuaded that persecution of suspected enemies (who profess loyalty), and the self-degradation or self-destruction of the victims which follows, themselves constitute evidence of the socialist nature of a successful revolution.

of 'needs' for the elite and the rest (this is further complicated by the fact that 'needs' themselves are likely to be unequal).

Secondly, it completely overlooks a phenomenon of socialistic elitism arising from an unequal political and social (or cultural) *influence* in the socialist community, which may or may not coexist with the individualistic socialist elitism of material 'incentives'. (In a socialist society, a 'selfless' response to 'moral incentives' may play a positive role which, as noted in chapter 12, it almost never plays in a capitalist society. In a backward socialist society, such selfless response to moral incentives may make some or all work harder, accelerate the eradication of poverty, unemployment etc. But 'moral fervour' may also rally the dedicated to work harder, contribute more to the social investment-fund etc., while the less dedicated 'outsiders' drag their feet and work less. The 'selfless' dedicated ones would enjoy an elite status in terms of social and political influence, while the less dedicated enjoy an 'elite' status in terms of 'selfish' material gain.)

However, the specific remedies already mentioned in passing in earlier paragraphs can reduce to a minimum *both* individualistic and 'collective' (or group-based) socialist 'elitism' of material gain, as well as of gain in terms of political and social influence.

15 The Question of Socialist Breakdown

1 Introduction

In this chapter, a socialist society is defined simply as one where the principal means of production are publicly owned (possible problems of 'alienation' or 'elitism' in such societies, discussed in the previous chapter, are ignored).

Since 1917 no fully established socialist society – and their number has increased over the period – has been overthrown. There has been no 'restoration of capitalism', or a 'breakdown of socialism' by violent or other means.

All the same, it has been a universally accepted Marxian tenet that each such society has been almost constantly on the verge of violent overthrow by external capitalism. Moreover, after 1950, every one of these societies has been suspected, by Marxists living in these societies, or outside them, to be on the verge of a sudden or gradual, peaceful or violent restoration of capitalism engineered by 'capitalist roaders', 'bourgeois nationalists', 'renegade cliques', hidden agents of capitalist or 'social' (i.e. socialist) imperialism, etc., who conspire to make the ruling Communist Parties of these countries 'change colour'.

There is some kind of historical paradox here: persistent predictions of 'socialist breakdown' which never seem to materialize, even though almost all citizens of a socialist society are suspected at various times of wanting it! It is worth investigating the problem with the help of political-economic models of the modern theory of collective choice, already referred to in chapter 12. They resemble the more general models of modern mathematical game-theory which are powerful tools for investigating such widely disparate phenomena as wars, arms-limitations negotiations, the dilemma of prisoners awaiting sentence, the optimum rate of (social) savings in economics, etc. All these problems are concerned with the rationality of apparently inconsistent preferences and decisions by individuals in their individual and 'social' capacities (i.e. as members of a social collective).

Now, it turns out on investigation (undertaken in this book), that the most suitable analytical model for this purpose is the model of the so-called 'isolation paradox' (Sen, 1961, pp. 487–9; Sen, 1962, Appendix E, note to ch. 8, pp. 123–4; Sen, 1967a, pp. 112–14) identified in the literature on optimizing the (social) rate of saving. In this original setting of the problem, each isolated individual, doing his saving through the capital market-mechanism will save nothing, or save less than he would if there were an 'indivisible political decision' binding on all, for each to save a certain positive amount. The paradox consists in the fact that isolated decisions go contrary to collective social decisions, that each isolated individual has an interest in trying to violate the 'social contract', so that the social decision must be enforced, even though each individual would vote for a collective decision for each to save a certain positive amount, in a referendum.

In this book, an isolation paradox in a socialist community is held responsible for the *non*-breakdown of socialism, even on assumptions which are most favourable to a socialist breakdown, viz. a situation where *all* prefer capitalist restoration. (The element of paradox in this case is stronger than in the problem of optimizing the rate of saving. In the savings model the contradiction between what the individual does, acting in isolation, and what he does in his 'social capacity' in voting in the referendum arises from a 'subjective' phenomenon, i.e. his 'social consciousness'. In the present case, the contradiction is due to an objective problem, viz. the nature of capitalism which is conceived of as an alternative to socialism.) Possible 'escape routes' from this impossibility result are then investigated. Finally, there is a brief re-discussion in terms of the so-called 'assurance problem' model, also considered in the discussion of the 'savings' problem

(Sen, 1967a), with the negative conclusion that the model is inapplicable in the socialist breakdown case.

Environmental assumptions

1 There is a fully established socialist society (i.e. where the seizure of political power by revolutionary socialists has been followed up by establishment of public ownership of the principal means of production).

2 The choice is between all living under socialism and all living under capitalism. (Halfway houses are ignored as spurious. Possible choices between partitioning the country, so that one part is socialist, another part capitalist, or between two alternatives of socialism, are ignored for purposes of the present discussion.)

3 In a capitalist society, everyone cannot be a capitalist; some must be wage-workers who own no means of production.

4 In a socialist society, a decision to restore capitalism, i.e. to promote a 'breakdown of socialism' (in view of assumption 2), can only be taken *unanimously* (so that all members of the socialist society undergo a chameleon-like 'change of colour').

5 An individual's wanting of capitalism in place of socialism is *ipso facto* an expression of his wanting to become a capitalist, i.e. his wanting to exploit others, the wage-workers.

The individual's preference-ordering

6 Each individual living in a socialist society wants capitalism if and only if he can himself be a capitalist *Everybody* living in the socialist society has become a 'capitalist roader' or 'an internal (bourgeois) émigré'. This extreme assumption has been adopted to underline as much as possible the paradoxical nature of the conclusion.

7 Given the choice between all living under socialism and all living under capitalism, each individual prefers to live under socialism.

2 The impossibility of socialist breakdown: an isolation paradox

Given environmental assumptions 3 and 5, there is no self-contradiction in the individual's preference-ordering. Assumptions 6 and 7, which make up the individual's preference-ordering, are perfectly consistent with each other.

But assumption 4, i.e. that the decision to restore capitalism can only be taken *unanimously*, in the context of the other assumptions of the model produces an 'impossibility result': they prove that a socialist breakdown is impossible.

Moreover, no individual has an interest in breaking the social contract (in favour of socialism) because of assumptions 2 and 5. So no special enforcement (punitive) machinery is needed to preserve socialism. Also, no one has an interest in rallying others for capitalism (because of assumptions 3 and 5).

Thus, the assumptions of the model establish the following results:

1 The impossibility of a socialist breakdown.

2 The complete (political) inactivity of those who want capitalism as far as the objective of achieving the restoration of capitalism is concerned, even if this category includes *all* the citizens of a socialist society.

3 The complete harmlessness (from the point of view of a threat to the socialist social order) of freedom of thought and expression which permits pro-capitalist ideas to circulate provided they do not take the form of capitalist *apologetics*, i.e. pretend that in a capitalist society there is *only* self-employment by commodity producers, or if they do, are not taken seriously by a population consisting of hard-headed realists. (This has a corollary: even *political* dissidence in favour of capitalism of this type is harmless, at least as long as the single political power-structure represented by the Communist Party is left undisturbed in practice.)

3 Escape routes from the impossibility result

At least three 'escape routes' from the socialist *non*-breakdown result can be thought of.

1 Drop assumption 5, retaining the other assumptions of the model.

With 1, assumption 7 is reversed (to be consistent with assumption 6 in the individual's preference-ordering). The paradox disappears. Socialism is replaced by capitalism (1 may hold if individuals in a socialist society want capitalism, *even if* they know some of them will *not* be capitalists, maybe because they expect to be better off under capitalism even as wage-workers than as members of a socialist society).

2 Drop assumption 2, so as to allow for a partial restoration of capitalism, retaining the other assumptions of the model.

With 2, the outcome is uncertain in the sense that whether socialism survives or not depends on whether the partial restoration of capitalism involves capitalist production of *all* 'basic' commodities, i.e. commodities which enter directly or indirectly into the production of all commodities in a partially decomposable system of interdependent production (Sraffa, 1960, pp. 7–8, 51). The 'partial restoration of capitalism' may take the form of 'concessions' to nationals or foreign capitalists, i.e. 'licensed capitalism' in a predominantly socialist society. The matter has been fully discussed in chapter 13.

4 A re-discussion in terms of an 'assurance problem'

As already mentioned in section 1, 'the assurance problem' model which has been specified in the discussion of the optimum rate of (social) savings (Sen, 1967a, pp. 114–15) might also seem relevant in our present discussion. However, it turns out that this is not so.

In the original setting of the assurance problem, each donor would donate, if only others will (which might be used in a model of foreign aid on the basis of highly restricted and unrealistic assumptions). In the context of the savings problem, there is an 'assurance problem', in that each would save if others will, but will not save if others do not. What each will *do* depends upon his *expectation* of what others will do; and, if he decides to save, he will do so *voluntarily* (through the

market-mechanism) without any need for political enforcement. (Of course, he may also save, under protest, under
compulsion, but such conduct falls outside the framework of
the pure assurance problem.)

Now, it is easy to see that assumptions 3 and 5 in section 1
exclude a re-cast of the socialist breakdown problem in the
form of an 'assurance problem'. If these assumptions hold,
each would want capitalism only if others do not, and would
want socialism if others want capitalism – which is the exact
opposite to the individual's preference in an assurance-
problem setting, at least in the context of the donors' problem,
or the social-savings problem. (Moreover, assumption 4 rules
out a drastic adaptation of the 'assurance problem' to deal
with the present case. An 'assurance problem' is impossible
to construct where all decisions have to be unanimous.)

Marxian and Post-Marxian Theories about Economic Theories

16 Ingredients of a Theory About Economic Theories

1 Introduction

In Part One of this book, the reader was introduced to a selective survey of certain major controversies about Marxian political economy, which culminated in a sketch of a post-Marxian political economy, which re-states Marx's analyses of value, capital and exploitation under competitive capitalism, integrated in a single theoretical system.

In Part Two, the analysis was extended to interpret some historically observed phenomena of revolutionary and non-revolutionary institutional change in advanced and backward capitalist and socialist societies.

Part Three contains two concluding chapters which discuss fragments of Marxian and post-Marxian theories about economic theories. If Parts One and Two have aroused the interest of the reader, they must have posed questions about the Marxian and post-Marxian theories formulated in Part One, and applied in Part Two. What is the nature of these theories? How do they compare, or where do they stand, *vis-à-vis* other systems of theoretical economics? These are stupendously large and difficult questions, to which only a fragmentary answer can be given in this book. But a fragmentary answer is better than no answer ... even though it makes the concluding chapters also the unfinished chapters of this book.

2 Essential ingredients of a theory about economic theories (or a meta-economic theory)

Most systems of theoretical economics are associated, explicitly or implicitly, with some theory about economic theories, even if this theory is not fully worked out. To abbreviate repetitive, long-winded allusions to such theories about economic theories in what follows, they will be referred to as *meta-economic theories*. (The term is sometimes used in a very different sense, to refer to unified theories which deal with the subject-matter of economics and related disciplines, or to neo-classical statics and dynamics, or to behaviouristic economic theories. The usage proposed here has nothing to do with the use of the term in the contexts just mentioned. However, there is *some* analogy between the sense in which the term meta-economics is used here and the well-known use of the term meta-mathematics to refer to the language that is *about* mathematics (Nagel and Newman, 1968, chapter 3, p. 28).)

Examples of meta-economic theories in our sense will be found in the *magna opera* of Adam Smith, Leon Walras, Alfred Marshall, John Maynard Keynes, Joseph Schumpeter, the modern exponents of linear programming theory of economics (specially in the writings of Samuelson), and, of course, Karl Marx.

These theories about economic theories contain, explicitly, or implicitly, some or all of the following ingredients:

1 A classification of alternative economic theories on the basis of some principle of classification (or taxonomy).

2 A gradation or ordering of these theories on the basis of some criterion.

3 An interpretation of economic theories as a reflection of or responses to changes in the environment in which economic phenomena occur.

3 The incomplete nature of most meta-economic theories

Of course, in all meta-economic theories there is a very unbalanced representation of ingredients 1–3.

Most of them are limited to tracing the geneses of concepts or tools of analysis used as building-blocks in the system of theoretical economics with which they are associated. This usually incorporates highly selective fragments of ingredients 1 and 2 in the meta-economic theories.

As a matter of fact, as regards 2, the dominant tendency is for a meta-economic theorist to pretend, as it turns out, unsuccessfully, that the economic theory with which his meta-economic theory is associated is like classical or modern physics, i.e. it is *the* system of theoretical economics which discards the errors of rival systems, absorbs all the useful insights they had, or reduces error-free rival systems into special cases or complementary systems.

But the proof of the pudding is in the eating. Unlike physics, which has survived attacks on its monolithic character because of an enthusiastic (or grudging) acceptance of Bohr's principle of complementarity (Bohr, 1958, pp. 67–74; Heisenberg, 1959, chapter 8, pp. 114–28), rival systems of theoretical economics have at best enjoyed brief spells of unchallenged sway.

Thus, umpteen attempts at writing *finis* to Marxian political economy has not destroyed it – the last serious attempt was made by Samuelson in 1957 (1957, section 7, pp. 911–12). On the other hand, Marx's 1873 *pronunciamento* about the European revolutions of 1830 having 'sounded the knell of scientific bourgeois economy' proved premature (as the evidence considered in Part One of this book seems to suggest).

Hence, the pretence that there is a single, monolithic economic theory, like physics, being *non*-enforceable in practice, has sometimes given rise to tendencies which usually find expression in proselytizing religions.

However, there are exceptions to this general rule. Schumpeter, an inspired Walrasian, but respectful towards the Austrians, and both respectful and knowledgeable about Marx's economics, made a genuine attempt at establishing a synthesized economic theology. But this was rather like the non-proselytizing synthesizing religions, and no more successful in containing or displacing the proselytizing economic theories.

A point-by-point critique of Schumpeter's attempted synthesis, spread over his monumental writings (1954; 1955;

1956), is beyond the scope of this book. But some attention *must* be paid in a book such as this – and *is* paid in chapter 17, section 4 and in chapter 18, section 3 – to suggestions that a particular piece of synthesis, of Marxian theory and Marshallian demand–supply analysis, is valid.

The thinnest part of all meta-economic theories is ingredient 3, i.e. an interpretation of economic theories as a reflection of or responses to changes in the environment in which economic phenomena occur. Even Marx, who is probably the only writer who explicitly included ingredient 3 as a part of his meta-economic theory (which, in turn, was a part of the study of the dialectical interaction of the economic basis and the superstructure in his materialistic interpretation of history), devoted only one major *obiter dictum* to it, in his *Afterword* to the second German edition of *Capital*, volume one (Marx, 1958, pp. 12–16). Empirical data of a kind which is hard to come by is required for a serious discussion of ingredient 3. So nothing much will be said about it in chapters 17 and 18.

4 The next two chapters

Chapter 17 is devoted to a more detailed discussion of the Marxian meta-economic theory which, as already stated, has all three ingredients of such a theory, though they are unevenly spelt out. (Indeed, Marx seems to have established the only comprehensive framework available of a theory about economic theories, in which *all* economic theories can be fitted in. It supplies, more or less ready-made, the framework of a post-Marxian meta-economic theory whose fragments are presented in chapter 18.)

However, Marx's and later Marxian ordering of alternative economic theories (i.e. ingredient 3 of these meta-economic theories) leaves certain unsolved problems. A brief reference is made to these in chapter 17, section 4, and in chapter 18, section 3, where these problems are discussed from the vantage point of post-Marxian political economy.

17 A Marxian Theory About Economic Theories

1 Introduction

As indicated in section 4 in the previous chapter, the Marxian literature contains all three ingredients of a theory about economic theories, or a meta-economic theory (as defined in chapter 16, section 2).

However, certain problems are encountered when we try to piece together a systematic account of a Marxian meta-economic theory. First, ingredient 1, i.e. the classification of alternative economic theories, in a Marxian meta-economic theory seems to be the most comprehensive there is (in the sense that it contains every label that seems to have been used by *any* writer about *any* economic theory). But, since Marx seems to have used some of the labels interchangeably, at least in some places, there is some doubt as to how many distinctive labels there really are in the Marxian classification in section 3. Second, there is also some ambiguity about the *gradation* of the alternative economic theories, i.e. about ingredient 2, which has hardly been clarified by later Marxists, as we shall see in section 4. Third, as stated in chapter 16, section 3, ingredient 3 is mainly represented by an *obiter dictum*, instead of being supported by detailed empirical evidence that supports ingredient 1 in the Marxian literature. This makes ingredient 3 the weakest element in a Marxian meta-economic theory. Furthermore, it creates complications when it comes to grading alternative economic theories, i.e. with respect to ingredient 2 also, as we shall see in section 5 below.

2 A Marxian classification of alternative economic theories

In Marx's writings, there are references, mostly explicit, but mostly implicit with respect to ingredient 3 or Marxian political economy, to six types of economic theories:

1 Classical political economy;

2 The economics of 'surface economic relations' (Marx, 1958, p. 81);

3 Marxian political economy, or the economic theory of scientific socialism;

4 Syncretic economics (Marx, 1950, p. 15; 1971, p. 501), which tries to reconcile the principles of (bourgeois) classical political economy with the claims of the proletariat;

5 Vulgar socialism (Marx, 1971, pp. 467–8, 523–7), which advocates programmes which are not based on the scientific discoveries of classical political economy or Marxian political economy;

6 Economic 'apologetics' or special pleading in the interests of various classes or groups in capitalist society (Marx, 1968, pp. 119–20; 1971, pp. 61, 501–2).

It is certain that Marx regarded 4 as a 'falsification of science' (Marx, 1968, pp. 115–17, 120). He also generally expressed a very poor opinion of the scientific acumen of Proudhon and the Saint-Simonians who were referred to as 'vulgar socialist' writers (Marx, 1971, pp. 467–8, 523). He also referred to 2 as a systematic (and comprehensive) account of 'surface phenomena' as they appear to 'an unscientific observer' or to one 'who is actually involved and interested in the process of bourgeois production' (Marx, 1968, p. 165).

3 Ambiguities in the Marxian classification of economic theories

The sixfold classification of economic theories given in the previous section is *not* unambiguously stated, or consistently adhered to, by Marx himself.

In the first place, according to Marx, 1 is never found in its pure form, but, as in Adam Smith, is found side by side with 2, intermingling with it, or being contradicted by it (Marx, 1968, pp. 165–6).

Secondly, the distinction between 2 and 4 (or even 5) is often blurred (Marx, 1971, pp. 501–2). Indeed, Marx used the generic term 'vulgar economy' also to refer to 2, 4 and 6, so that, on this reckoning, Marx had a fourfold classification of 'scientific bourgeois economy' (to refer, roughly to much of 1, Marxian political economy, 'vulgar economy' and 'vulgar socialism').

What could be the rationale of such a fourfold classification? It is based on the Marxian doctrine of 'mystification' of economic relations under capitalism, to which reference has been made in chapter 2, section 2.

Thus, 'scientific (political) economy' – whether 'bourgeois' or 'proletarian' (Marxian) – refers to contributions to economic literature which penetrates the haze of 'mystification' and 'exposes the economic contradictions between the classes – as shown by the intrinsic relations ... and consequently ... discovers the root of the historical struggle and development' (Marx, 1968, p. 166, with reference to Ricardo).

'Vulgar economy', on the other hand, refers to a contribution which 'takes the external phenomena of life as they seem and appear' (in contrast to scientific political economy which fathoms the inner connections, the 'physiology, so to speak, of the bourgeois system') and merely describes, catalogues, recounts and arranges them under formal definitions', and does this 'superficially, but quite systematically' (Marx, 1968, p. 165).

In other words, on the basis of his doctrine of 'mystification' of economic relations under capitalism, Marx makes his study of alternative economic theories an exercise in ontology, i.e. an investigation into the existence of different kinds of 'real' or 'mystified' relations of production and distribution under capitalism.

How far such a Marxian classification of alternative

economic theories can 'account for', as it were, all the major systems of theoretical economics known before or after Marx, including all those which have been referred to in Part One of this book, is a question which will be further considered in chapter 18, section 2.

4 The Marxian gradation of alternative economic theories

In a sense, there is no ambiguity in the Marxian ordering or gradation of alternative economic theories. Implicitly with Marx, and explicitly with Engels and later Marxian writers, Marxian political economy is at the top of the grade as the most scientific, which successfully 'de-mystifies' economic relations under capitalism, and 'bourgeois apologetics', which deliberately 'falsifies science' in the service of the capitalists, is at the bottom as the worst.

However, there *is* some ambiguity about the exact status of the 'economics of surface economic relations' in the Marxian classification of theories.

In his *Capital*, volume three (Marx, 1959, p. 186) Marx seemed confident that demand-and-supply analysis (which is the core of modern neo-classical versions of the economic of 'surface economic relations') cannot be used to prove the existence of competitive equilibrium. On the other hand, in his *Theories of Surplus Value*, part 2 (Marx, 1968, p. 165), he seems to express the view that a systematic and comprehensive survey of the observable 'surface economic phenomena', more or less achieved by Adam Smith, was necessary for the development of scientific political economy, though it also resulted in the possibility of a complete separation of an account of 'surface economic phenomena' as a special branch of economics (Marx, 1971, p. 501).

Later Marxian writers have conceded that 'competitive supply-and-demand theory of price determination is . . . not only not inconsistent with the labour theory (of Marx); rather it forms an integral part of the labour theory . . .' (Sweezy, 1949, p. 47). It has been reaffirmed by Marxist writers recently that Marshallian supply–demand analysis and Marxist price theory etc. 'are perfectly compatible'

(Sherman, 1970, p. 291; Hunt and Sherman, 1972, p. 41). (It has also been said that a Marshallian supply–demand analysis ought to be incorporated in a (post-) Marxian economic theory which uses Sraffa's commodity-production model, which has been used in Part One of this book (Hunt and Sherman, 1972, p. 41). Some attention will be paid to this argument in chapter 18, section 3 below.)

5 The Marxian interpretation of alternative economic theories as responses to the environment in which economic phenomena occur

As already stated in chapter 16, section 3, there is very little except one major *obiter dictum* in Marx's writings about alternative economic theories identified as responses to changes in the environment in which economic phenomena occur (see 'Afterword' to the second German edition of *Capital*, volume one, in Marx, 1958, pp. 12–16). (Less well-known is the passage in *The Theories of Surplus Value* (Marx, 1971, pp. 500–502) which goes over more or less the same ground.)

In these passages, the analysis of the 'dynamics' by which economic theories change in response to changes in the environment is in terms of a process of dialectical inter-action. The process involves (a) the 'de-mystification' of capitalist relations through advances made by scientific political economy, (b) the resulting growth of counteracting 'syncretic' economic theory, and (c) the final emergence of 'bourgeois economic apologetics' (represented by 'hired prize-fighters') in response to a growth of capitalist production relations, and the increased revolutionary consciousness of the proletariat.

Unfortunately, the hypothesis just sketched was left as a skeletal hypothesis by Marx, in sharp contrast to the voluminous (though unpublished) work left by him to fill in his classificatory scheme of alternative economic theories. Nor has much progress been made (except in some recent monographs) by Marxian writers or others in the past hundred years in testing the hypothesis with empirical evidence.

This has several consequences. In the next chapter, we shall be able to discuss the fragments of a post-Marxian classification of alternative economic theories (including neoclassical Walrasian and Marshallian theories to which no reference is found in the writings of Marx and Engels or Lenin). We shall also say something about a post-Marxian gradation of alternative economic theories. But very little will be said about the untested Marxian hypothesis mentioned in this section.

18 Fragments of a Post-Marxian Meta-Economic Theory

1 Introduction

To write a *post*-Marxian theory about economic theory, or meta-economic theory, is an undertaking of truly colossal dimensions. It cannot be attempted in this introduction to post-Marxian political economy for several reasons.

First, there is the reason that such a theory would have to include *all* the ingredients of a meta-economic theory listed in chapter 16, section 2. Thus, ingredient 1, or a classification of alternative economic theories will have to be included, if only because, as already stated, all major economic theories are, implicitly or explicitly, underpinned by such a classification. Ingredient 2, or a grading or ordering of alternative economic theories placed in the classificatory scheme would also have to be included, again because all major theoretical systems in economics have such a grading, or at least a partial grading. (This is pretty explicitly spelt out, usually to put the economic theory in question at the top of the hierarchical classificatory scheme with which it is associated.) Nor can ingredient 3, which has reference to the interaction between economic events and economic theories, be excluded. As we have tried to demonstrate in Part One, no post-Marxian theory *of* economics or *about* economics can afford to start with a pre-conception that an (empirically) untested Marxian hypothesis can be ignored.

The second reason is that there has been an enormous growth of relevant theoretical–empirical literature, specially in the past twenty years or so, with respect to ingredients 1 and 2, and modern methods and facilities for research may multiply, rapidly, the number of monographs available as ingredient 3.

In particular, a post-Marxian meta-economic theory must try to incorporate in its classification and ordering of alternative economic theories, (a) entirely new branches of theoretical economics which have emerged in recent years (and some of which have, as we have seen in Part One, made notable contributions to clearing up controversies about key propositions in Marxian political economy, and towards the construction of post-Marxian political economy), and (b) the vastly increased literature now available for the first time about the neo-classical (Walrasian and Marshallian) economic theories which were ignored by Marx, as well as by Engels and Lenin.

The third reason is that a modern, post-Marxian meta-economic theory cannot rely on anecdotal material (which is about all that seems to be available, as we shall see in section 4) for empirical substantiation of its ingredient 3. (As indicated in chapter 1, section 4, in a modern post-Marxian theoretical approach, we do *not* worship uncritically modern methods of empirical research. But equally, we do not make a virtue of reliance on anecdotal material as a substitute for empirical data.)

However, all that has been said in this introductory section notwithstanding, this book on Marxian and post-Marxian political economy cannot possibly conclude without some fragments of a post-Marxian meta-economic theory (about economic theories) being presented to the reader. One of the attractive features of Marxian political economy was its partly substantiated hypotheses which add up to a verifiable meta-economic theory. An introduction to a *post*-Marxian political economy cannot afford to be completely silent about the implicit meta-economic theory which is associated with it.

So, in this concluding chapter of the book, we first discuss a possible post-Marxian classification of economic theory (i.e. ingredient 1 of a meta-economic theory). This is done in section 2. In section 3 we concentrate on a proposal for a 'synthesis' between Marshallian supply–demand analysis and a post-Marxian political economy which uses modern commodity-production models (to which reference has been made in chapter 17, section 4). In section 4, we discuss, briefly, from the vantage point of post-Marxian political economy, the selective survey of controversies with respect to Marxian political economy (in Part One), and some modern anecdotal empirical data – the Marxian hypothesis (referred to in chapter 17, section 5) about the interaction between scientific political economy, 'syncretic economics' and the development of capitalist production relations, culminating in the rise of 'bourgeois economic apologetics'.

2 A post-Marxian classification of alternative economic theories

There is no reason why in a post-Marxian meta-economic theory, we should not adopt the sixfold Marxian classificatory scheme (of chapter 17, section 2) rather than the fourfold one (of chapter 17, section 3).

But we must add to the list one more type of economic theory (type 7: 'socialist apologetics'), and introduce an amendment regarding the description of type 2 – the 'economics of surface phenomena' – and a clarification regarding type 4 – 'syncretic economics' as it appears in its modern garb.

We have seen in chapter 3, section 3, that Marx disapproved of, and ultimately denounced, the Ricardian-socialist tenet that 'labour is the only source of value', which remains the basic tenet of orthodox, modern interpretations of Marxian political economy. Marx himself traced Proudhon's 'vulgar socialist' ideas – which owed very little, directly, to rigorous Ricardian principles and methods – to the Ricardian socialists of England (Marx, 1956, ch. 1, p. 77). But the modern exponents of the Ricardian-socialist tenet that labour is the only source of value, are far more sophisticated in their exposition of this idea, which Marx ultimately denounced, as we have seen, as a 'bourgeois idea'. They should therefore be classified separately from Marx's 'vulgar socialists', who generally lacked theoretical sophistication, and who (e.g. Proudhon and the Saint-Simonians) have very little influence now. It is therefore best to classify them as exponents of 'socialist apologetics'. (On the other hand, a modern writer (e.g. Gottheil, 1960, p. 718), who may choose to ignore the results of modern analysis which explicitly exclude (as we saw in chapter 7, section 2), the possibility of a simultaneous long-run decline in *both* profits and wages, are making an error which puts them perilously near the borderline of 'vulgar socialism'.)

As regards type 2, i.e. the economic theory which gives a systematic account of the (observable) external phenomena of economic life from the viewpoint of the capitalist producer (as identified by Marx, 1968, p. 165), there is no doubt that the core of modern Walrasian and Marshallian economic theory belongs to this category, and should be included as such in a post-Marxian classification of economic theories.

However, there are two points on which assessment and content of this category of theories in a modern, post-Marxian reckoning may differ from the nineteenth-century Marxian one.

First, Marx took Say as the leading representative of this category of theorists, and said their systematization of surface economic phenomena represented a 'superficial' systematization from the viewpoint of '. . . an unscientific observer' (Marx, 1968, p. 165). This is strictly true *ex definitione*, if science in economics is defined strictly, and *solely*, in terms of the main object of economic investigation from a Marxian, or a post-Marxian viewpoint, viz. the de-mystification of capitalist economic relations (which was discussed in chapter 2, section 3). But, as will be noted again in section 4, the rigorous scientific method of analysis used in modern extensions of Walrasian theory is qualitatively superior to the methods of analysis employed by Say. Although *both* are undoubtedly preoccupied with surface economic phenomena, the latter *is* superficial (it contains no proof of the existence of equilibrium, for instance), but the former is *not*. Both cannot be bracketed as systematization from the viewpoint of an 'unscientific observer'.

Second, in a post-Marxian classification, the category of theory dealing with surface phenomena must explicitly include the work of the modern behaviourist school on the theory of the capitalist firm (e.g. Marris, 1964; Simon, 1959) or the socialist enterprise (Ames, 1965, pp. 50–65) or of economic systems (see reference in Kornai, 1971; Part 2, pp. 35–217, Part 3, pp. 221–343). (It is possible, though unlikely, that these behaviouristic theories which professedly deal with what Marx classified as a systematic account of 'economic relations as they appear' to an (involved) observer, will some day remain as the *sole* representatives of the economics of surface economic phenomena, having extinguished all rival theories. In any case, they must be included in a modern, post-Marxian classification of economic theories.)

Like the modern type 2 theories just discussed, modern type 4 theories (of 'syncretic economics') are also a vast improvement on Marx's prototype for this type of theory, viz. the theory of John Stuart Mill. They are represented by the Walras–Lange–Lerner theory of capitalist exploitation under competitive conditions (see chapter 3, section 2), the modern neo-Marxian theories of capitalist exploitation under competitive capitalism (chapter 3, section 4) and the Pigovian theories of exploitation under monopolistic capitalism (discussed in chapter 3, section 5). As theories they are superior to nineteenth-century syncretic economics because (a) they explicitly rely on value judgements which are grafted on to the type 2 kind of analysis to reach conclusions which are critical of capitalism, and/or (b) they are backed by exact mathematical proofs of 'existence' of equilibrium which the nineteenth-century versions of this type of theory did not have.

3 Can Marshallian supply–demand analysis be incorporated in a post-Marxian political economy which uses the tools of modern commodity-production theory?

We now turn to an interesting proposal which was noticed in section 4 of chapter 17, but discussion was postponed to this section. This is the proposal recently made by a group of Marxist writers that Marshallian supply–demand analysis can be incorporated into a post-Marxian political economy using the tools of modern commodity-production theory originating in the work of Sraffa (Hunt and Sherman, 1972, p. 41).

The proposal looks plausible for at least two reasons. First, the Marshallian supply–demand analysis does *not* require the use of an apologetic notion of aggregate capital-quantities whose value is uniquely determined without reference to the profit-rate and prices, which, as we saw in chapter 3, section 4, has been the butt of modern neo-Marxian (and neo-Keynesian) attacks. It is compatible with a heterogeneous capital-goods model. In line with what has just been said, there is a second feature of these models which makes the Hunt–Sherman proposal look plausible. As (rightly) claimed by them, Marshall had a separate 'apologetic' theory of profit as a reward for capitalists' 'waiting', which can be excised from the main corpus of supply–demand analysis, and still leave supply–demand analysis intact.

Nevertheless, the proposal must be rejected completely on strictly formal grounds (for reasons, see chapter 6, section 2). There is no place for demand functions in a post-Marxian theory which uses a modern commodity-production model of competitive equilibrium (or, for that matter, in a collective choice theory model of the type used in the Appendix to chapter 6, where a 'pre-ordering'[1] postulate is all that is needed). The 'incorporation' of demand (and supply) functions, as proposed, would overdetermine the models.

There is the related question as to whether Marshallian supply–demand analysis dealing with 'existential' surface economic phenomena can usefully coexist with (and complement) a post-Marxian theory which unravels 'de-mystified' capitalist relations.

The answer to this question, too, seems to be: No. The general reason is that *Marshallian* supply–demand analysis does *not* seem to be an operational theory of surface phenomena of economic life, but a drastically simplified conceptual

1. 'If an individual acts consistently in his choices and has habitually no difficulty in choosing between alternatives, he can be assumed to have a preference pre-ordering' (Sen, 1967b, p. 15).

model. This is well brought out in a recently-published comprehensive assessment of *empirically usable* techniques of supply–demand analysis in the light of British empirical experience (Turvey, 1971). Some of the findings are: (a) Marshallian demand curves (relating the price of a commodity to the quantity of it demanded, *ceteris paribus*) are of hardly any practical use; more comprehensive demand functions do *not* improve upon common-sense (Turvey, 1971, ch. 1, sec. 1.2); (b) with respect to the Marshallian classification of firms and industries which are, and those which are not, subject to economies of scale: '... historically speaking, technical progress and the realization of scale economies are often one phenomenon, not two ...' (p. 51), and no generalization *at all* is possible with regard to economies of scale in whole businesses (p. 53); (c) with respect to the Marshallian long-run cost curves, the divergence of the accountant's and the economist's estimates, each of which is correct from a separate point of view, makes it impossible to settle for any one cost curve in a particular context, even if full information is available (pp. 56–61); (d) demand and supply are often, but *not always*, mediated by price as the most important factor; but non-price factors matter, and cannot be fitted easily into Marshallian demand–supply analysis (p. 89).

Thus, we are left with the conclusion that there is hardly a case for a general 'division of labour' between Marshallian supply–demand analysis, used for systematic investigation between surface economic phenomena, and post-Marxian commodity-production analysis, used for investigating de-mystified capitalist relations. Of course, the 'forces of supply and demand' matter, and cannot be ignored in *any* theory of economic phenomena. As suggested in chapters 9–11, they matter even if we are using post-Marxian tools of analysis to investigate revolutionary or non-revolutionary institutional change under capitalism or socialism. An investigation of the dimensions of the forces of supply and demand in quantitative terms has to be undertaken to reach economic policy conclusions in *any* society, whatever the tools of economic analysis used. The methods of investigation employed in practice in such cases (as reported by Turvey, 1971) are perfectly compatible with a post-Marxian political economy which uses modern commodity-production models, and dispenses with Marshallian demand curves.

4 Post-Marxian *obiter dicta* on the Marxian hypothesis of alternative economic theories as responses to changes in the environment in which economic phenomena occur

As already stated in chapter 17, section 5, Marx had a hypothesis, which has remained empirically untested for a century, about the triangular interaction between (a) the advances of 'de-mystifying' scientific political economy, (b) the growth of vulgar economy (which is 'nourished' by scientific political economy, and, parasitically, 'does not produce anything by itself'), and (c) the growth of (contradictory) capitalist relations – whose end product is that 'vulgar economy deliberately becomes increasingly *apologetic*, and makes strenuous attempts to talk out of existence the ideas which contain the contradictions . . .' (Marx, 1971, p. 501).

In the absence of empirical testing, only a few *obiter dicta* can be recorded about this Marxian hypothesis, delivered from a post-Marxian viewpoint.

First, a cursory glance back at chapter 3, section 2, which discusses the Walras–Lange–Lerner theory of capitalist exploitation under ideal, competitive conditions, will show that point (b) in the Marxian hypothesis summarized above, seems to be confirmed by developments over the past hundred years, if we interpret 'vulgar economy' in this context to refer to the John Stuart Mill type of syncretic economics, to which the Walras–Lange–Lerner theory belongs. (It is even true that this modern syncretic economics 'does not produce anything by itself', as Marx foretold. However, it borrowed its building-blocks, wholesale, from the economics of surface phenomena, in its modern Walrasian or Marshallian garb, and *not* from bourgeois or Marxian scientific political economy.)

Secondly, there *is* some basis for claiming, by referring back to the short account of its genesis (chapter 6 and Appendix to chapter 6), that modern post-Marxian political economy owes nothing either to modern syncretic economics, or to the modern economics of surface phenomena (and certainly not to modern socialist apologetics, as defined in section 2). It seems to pick up the thread where Ricardo and Marx left scientific political economy (and, in the case of the choice-theory version of modern post-Marxian political economy, where eighteenth-century French writers left political voting theory). (Arrow, 1970, ch. 8, p. 94). Nevertheless such an interpretation is somewhat forced.

In contrast to pure syncretic economic theory of the Mill–Lange type, the economics of surface phenomena in its modern Walrasian version *did* use advanced mathematical methods to 'produce' a great deal of theory in its own right. As indicated in chapter 5, section 5, the problem of proving the 'existence' of competitive capitalist equilibrium was first formulated by Ricardo and Marx. Its solution by Sraffa (discussed in chapter 6) owed nothing to the Walrasians (except indirectly via von Bortkiewicz, who borrowed from Walras). But the fact remains that the first mathematically valid solutions of the problem of existence of competitive (capitalist) equilibrium was *published* by Austro-Walrasian neo-classical theorists who owed nothing (as far as is known and recorded), directly or indirectly, to Marx or the Marxians.[2]

Furthermore, the rigorous mathematical methods of the modern neo-classicals have also been used to confirm (as already noted in chapter 7, section 2), the inverse wage–profit relation (on certain assumptions as regards technology), which plays a key role in modern commodity-production theory. (The mathematical methods of modern neo-classical economic theory have also been used, albeit belatedly, and after much prodding by anti neo-classical critics, to confirm the non-existence of 'capital quantities' which are determined

2. Hicks (1967, pp. 79–81); Dorfman, Samuelson and Solow (1958, ch. 13, sec. 13–4, pp. 366–75). The Austro-Walrasian Wald published his proof in 1935, Sraffa, the founder of modern commodity-production theory, published his in 1960. But Sraffa had worked out the core of his theory as early as 1928 (Sraffa, 1960, p. vi).

independently of prices and the profit-rate, and usable as quantities of a single factor of production (Samuelson, 1966, pp. 568–83).

Thirdly, and finally, due to lack of empirical evidence, judgement must be suspended on Marx's prediction that the triangular interaction between advances in scientific political economy, the growth of vulgar economy (of the syncretic type), and the development of the capitalist mode of production, would make vulgar political economy *increasingly* apologetic.[3] There is no doubt, of course, that in standard academic usage, the economics of surface phenomena in its Walrasian (or Marshallian) version in capitalist societies has served as capitalist apologetics. It has done this by propagating the ideology that an economic theory of capitalism is adequate to explain *all* types of economic phenomena, in socialist as well as in capitalist societies, and that a socialist system works better, the more it resembles or 'converges' towards the Walrasian (or Marshallian) model of capitalism. However this is a species of capitalist apologetics which was non-existent in Marx's day and was ignored by him. But it cannot be ignored in a post-Marxian meta-economic theory.

3. But it is worth noting that the long-sustained Marxist onslaught on self-conscious (motivated) 'bourgeois apologetics' has at last found a definite target, on the basis of a piece of anecdotal evidence. In a recent survey of the literature on the Marxian theory of exploitation and the 'transformation' of Marxian 'values' into competitive prices (Samuelson, 1971, Part 3, sec. 12, p. 423), attention has been drawn to the testimony of the economist J. M. Clark in 1951, that his father, J. B. Clark (chief exponent of the 'capital quantity' concept in modern neo-classical economics) deliberately gave the marginal productivity theory of distribution an apologetic interpretation because he wanted to defend the competitive (capitalist) system from the challenge offered by Marxian notions of (capitalist) exploitation.

References

AMES, E. (1965), *Soviet Economic Processes*, Irwin, reprinted as
'The economic theory of output-maximizing enterprises', in
G. C. Archibald (ed.), *The Theory of the Firm*, Penguin, 1971,
pp. 270–86.

ARROW, K. J. (1970), *Social Choice and Individual Values*, Yale
University Press; first published in 1951.

BARAN, P. (1969), *The Longer View*, Monthly Review Press, New
York.

BARAN, P., and SWEEZY, P. (1970), *Monopoly Capital*, Penguin.

BARONE, E. (1908), *The Ministry of Production in a Collectivist
State*; reprinted in F. Hayek (ed.), *Collectivist Economic Planning*,
Routledge & Kegan Paul, 1935.

BATOR, F. (1958), 'The anatomy of market failure', *Q. J. Econ.*,
August, pp. 351–79; reprinted in W. Breit and H. Hochman (eds.),
Readings in Microeconomics, Holt, Rinehart & Winston, 1968,
pp. 457–76.

BATRA, R. (1972), 'Monopoly theory in general equilibrium and the
two-sector model of economic growth', *J. econ. Theory*, June,
pp. 355–71.

BECKETT, S. (1956), *Waiting for Godot*, Faber.

BHADURI, A. (1969), 'On the significance of recent controversies in
capital theory: a Marxian view', *Econ. J.*, September, pp. 532–9.

BHAGWATI, J. (1967), 'The tying of aid', *UNCTAD Secretariat*,
TD/7/Supp. 4, United Nations; reprinted in J. Bhagwati and
R. S. Eckaus (eds.), *Foreign Aid*, Penguin, 1970, pp. 235–93.

BHAGWATI, J. (1970), Introduction to J. Bhagwati and
R. S. Eckaus (eds.), *Foreign Aid*, Penguin, pp. 7–18.

BLISS, C. J. (1972), 'Prices, markets and planning', *Econ. J.*, March,
pp. 87–100.

BOHR, N. (1958), *Atomic Physics and Human Knowledge*, Wiley.

BODMER, W. F. (1972), 'Race and IQ: the genetic background', in
K. Richardson and D. Spears (eds.), *Race, Culture and Intelligence*,
Penguin, 1972, pp. 83–113.

BORDA, J. C. DE (1784), *Mémoire sur les élections au scrutin*.

BOSE, A. (1964a), 'The "labour approach" and the "commodity
approach" in Mr Sraffa's price theory', *Econ. J.*, September,
pp. 723–6.

BOSE, A. (1964b), 'Production of commodities – a further note', *Econ. J.*, September, p. 728.

BOSE, A. (1965), 'Consumers' demand, distributive shares and prices', *Econ. J.*, December, pp. 771–86.

BOSE, A. (1971), 'Marx on value, capital and exploitation', *Hist. polit. Econ.*, vol. 3, no. 2, pp. 298–334.

BOSE, A. (1972), 'Modern capitalist apologetics and Marxian economics', *Science and Society*, vol. 36, no. 2, pp. 217–20.

BRAITHWAITE, R. B. (1955), *The Theory of Games as a Tool for the Moral Philosopher*, Cambridge University Press.

BRECHT, B.´(1963), *The Caucasian Chalk Circle*, Methuen.

BRODY, A. (1965), 'Three types of price systems', *Econ. Planning*, vol. 5, no. 3, pp. 58–68.

BRONFENBRENNER, M. (1965), '*Das Kapital* for the modern man', *Science and Society*, vol. 29, reprinted in D. Horowitz (ed.), *Marx and Modern Economics*, MacGibbon & Kee, 1968.

BRUTON, J. (1969), 'The two gap approach to aid and development', *Amer. econ. Rev.*, June, pp. 439–46.

BURMEISTER, E. (1968), 'On a theorem of Sraffa', *Economica*, February, pp. 83–7.

CHAKRAVARTY, S. (1969), *An Essay on the Marxian Theory of Value*, unpublished.

CHAMPERNOWNE, D. (1945–6), 'A note on J. V. Neumann's article on "A model of general economic equilibrium" ', *Rev. econ. Stud.*, pp. 10–18; reprinted in P. Newman (ed.), *Readings in Mathematical Economics*, John Hopkins Press, 1968.

CHENERY, H. B. (1969), 'The two gap approach to aid and development, a reply to Bruton', *Amer. econ. Rev.*, June, pp. 446–9.

CONDORCET, MARQUIS DE (1785), *Essai sur l'application de l'analyse à la probabilité des dècisions rendue à la pluralité de voix*.

CRAIG, R. P., and STEPHENSON, M. A. (1970), 'A note on Marxian alienation', *Oxf. Econ. Pap.*, November, pp. 438–42.

DAHL, R. A. (1956), *A Preface to Democratic Theory*, University of Chicago Press.

DEBREU, G. (1959), *Theory of Value*, Wiley.

DEBREU, G., and HERSTEIN, I. N. (1953), 'Non-negative square matrices', *Econometrica*, pp. 597–607.

DICKINSON, H. D. (1969), 'Von Thünen's economics', *Econ. J.*, December, pp. 894–902.

DIMITRIEV, V. K. (1968), *Essais Économique*, Editions du Centre National de la Rècherche Scientifique, Paris.

DOBB, M. (1937), *Political Economy and Capitalism*, Routledge & Kegan Paul, ch. 3; reprinted as 'Classical political economy', in D. Horowitz (ed.), *Marx and Modern Economics*, MacGibbon & Kee, 1968.

DOBB, M. (1967), Introduction to an Italian edition of *Capital*, the English translation printed in M. Dobb, *Capitalism, Development and Planning*, Allied Publishers, Delhi, 1967.

DOBB, M. (1970a), *Introduction to Karl Marx, A Contribution to the Critique of Political Economy*, Progress Publishers, Moscow.

DOBB, M. (1970b), 'The Sraffa system and the critique of the neo-classical theory of distribution', *De Economist*, vol. 118, pp. 347–62; reprinted in E. K. Hunt and J. G. Schwartz, *A Critique of Economic Theory*, Penguin, 1972, pp. 205–21.

DORFMAN, R., SAMUELSON, P. A., and SOLOW, R. M. (1958), *Linear Programming and Economic Analysis*, McGraw-Hill.

ECKAUS, R. S. (1970), 'Economic criteria for foreign aid for economic development', in J. Bhagwati and R. S. Eckaus (eds.), *Foreign Aid*, Penguin.

ELLMAN, M. (1971), *Soviet Planning Today: Proposals for an Optimally Functioning Economic System*, Cambridge University Press.

ENGELS, F. (1956), Preface to K. Marx, *Poverty of Philosophy*, Foreign Languages Publishing House, Moscow.

ENGELS, F. (1938), 'Letter to Schmidt, 12 March 1895', in K. Marx and F. Engels, *Selected Correspondence*, Lawrence & Wishart.

ENGELS, F. (1947), *Anti-Duhring*, Foreign Languages Publishing House, Moscow.

ENGELS, F. (1949), 'Ludwig Feuerbach and the end of classical German philosophy', in K. Marx and F. Engels, *Selected Works*, vol. 2, Foreign Languages Publishing House, Moscow.

ENGELS, F. (1950), Introduction to 'Wage Labour and Capital' in K. Marx and F. Engels, *Selected Works*, Foreign Languages Publishing House, Moscow.

ENGELS, F. (1957), Preface to K. Marx *Capital*, vol. 2, Foreign Languages Publishing House, Moscow.

ENOS, J. L., and GRIFFIN, K. B. (1971), 'Foreign assistance: objectives and consequences, a reply to our critics', *Economic Development and Cultural Change*, vol. 20, no. 1, pp. 155–8.

FAN-HUNG (1939), 'Keynes and Marx on the theory of capital accumulation, money and interest', *Rev. econ. Stud.*, October pp. 28–41; reprinted in D. Horowitz (ed.), *Marx and Modern Economics*, MacGibbon & Kee, 1968, pp. 117–37.

FARQUARSON, R. (1970), *Theory of Voting*, Blackwell.

FEINSTEIN, C. H. (ed.) (1967), *Socialism, Capitalism and Economic Growth*, Cambridge University Press.

FISHER, F. M. (1972), 'On price adjustment without an auctioneer', *Rev. econ. Stud.*, vol. 39(1), no. 117, pp. 1–15.

FRANCE, A. (1931), *Penguin Island*, Watts.

GANTMACHER, F. R. (1959), *Application of Theory of Matrices*, Interscience.

GAREGNANI, P. (1970), 'Heterogeneous capital and production function and the theory of distribution', *Rev. econ. Stud.*, vol. 37, pp. 407–36.

GEORGESCU-ROEGEN, N. (1966), *Analytical Economics: Issues and Problems*, Harvard University Press.

GEORGESCU-ROEGEN, N. (1971), *The Entropy Law and the Economic Process*, Harvard University Press.

GOTTHEIL, F. M. (1960), 'Marxian economic models: comment', *Amer. econ. Rev.*, September, pp. 715–19.

GOVERNMENT OF INDIA PLANNING COMMISSION (1973), *Approach to the Fifth Plan*, New Delhi.

HAHN, F. H., and BRECHLING, F. P. R. (eds.) (1965), *Theory of Interest Rates*, Macmillan.

HARE, R. M. (1964), *The Language of Morals*, Oxford University Press.

HARROD, R. F. (1968), 'What is a model?', in J. N. Wolfe (ed.), *Value, Capital and Growth*, Edinburgh University Press.

HAMBLEY, J. (1972), in 'Diversity: a development perspective', in K. Richardson and D. Spears (eds.) *Race, Culture and Intelligence*, Penguin.

HARSANYI, J. C. (1955), 'Cardinal welfare, individualistic ethics and inter-personal comparisons of utility', *J. polit. Econ.*, August, pp. 309–21.

HAYTER, T. (1971), *Aid as Imperialism*, Penguin.

HEISENBERG, W. (1959), *Physics and Philosophy: Revolution in Modern Science*, Allen & Unwin.

HICKS, J. R. (1946), *Value and Capital*, Oxford University Press.

HICKS, J. R. (1967), 'Linear theory', in *Surveys of Economic Theory*, vol. 3, 'Resource Allocation', Macmillan, for American Economic Society and Royal Economic Society, pp. 75–113.

HICKS, J. R. (1970), 'Neo-Austrian growth theory', *Econ. J.*, June, pp. 257–81.

HINICH, M. J., LEDYARD, J. O., and ORDESHOOK, P. C. (1972), 'Non-voting and the existence of equilibrium under majority rule', *J. econ. Theory*, vol. 4, pp. 144–53.

HODGSKIN, T. (1825), *Labour Defended Against the Claims of Capital*, reprinted with foreword by G. D. H. Cole, 1922, reprinted 1963, Kelley, New York.

HOROWITZ, D. (1968), *Marx and Modern Economics*, MacGibbon & Kee.

HUNT, E. K., and SHERMAN, H. (1972), 'Value, alienation and distribution', *Science and Society*, Spring, pp. 29–46.

HUNT, E. K., and SCHWARTZ, J. G. (eds.) (1972), *A Critique of Economic Theory*, Penguin.

INADA, I. K. I. (1964), 'On the economic welfare function', *Econometrica*, October, pp. 525–30.

IONESCO, E. (1960), 'The Bald Prima Donna', in *Plays*, vol. 1,

Calder & Boyars.

IONESCO, E. (1961), 'Rhinoceros', in *Plays*, vol. 4, Calder & Boyars.

JOHANSEN, L. (1961), 'A note on "aggregation in Leontief matrices and the labour theory of value"', *Econometrica*, April, pp. 21–2.

KAFKA, F. (1970), *The Castle*, Penguin.

KAUL, J. M. (1973), 'Through Mao's eyes', *Economic and Political Weekly*, Bombay, 6 October, quoting E. Snow, *The Long Revolution*, Hutchinson, 1973.

KEYNES, J. M. (1936), *A General Theory of Employment, Interest and Money*, Macmillan.

KOLAKOWSKI, L. (1972), *Positivist Philosophy*, Penguin.

KOOPMANS, T. C. (1951), *Activity Analysis of Production and Allocation*, Wiley.

KORNAI, J. (1971), *Anti-Equilibrium: On Economic Systems Theory, and the Task of Research*, North-Holland.

KORNAI, J., and LIPTAK, T. (1965), 'Two-level planning', *Econometrica*, pp. 141–69.

KRAMER, G. (1969), *On a class of equilibrium conditions for majority rule*, Cowles Foundation Discussion Paper number 284, Yale Station, New Haven.

KYN, O., SEKERKA, B., and HEIJL, L. (1967), 'A model for the planning of prices', in C. H. Feinstein (ed.), *Socialism, Capitalism and Economic Growth*, Cambridge University Press, pp. 101–24.

LANGE, O. (1935), 'Marxian economics and modern economic theory', *Rev. econ. Stud.*, vol. 2; reprinted in D. Horowitz (ed.), *Marx and Modern Economics*, MacGibbon & Kee, 1968.

LANGE, O. (1936, 1937), 'On the economic theory of socialism', *Rev. econ. Stud.*, vol. 3; reprinted in B. E. Lippincott (ed.), *On the Economic Theory of Socialism*, University of Minnesota Press, 1956, and in A. Nove and D. M. Nuti (eds.), *Socialist Economics*, Penguin, pp. 92–110.

LANGE, O. (1963), *Political Economy*, vol. 1, Pergamon.

LANGE, O. (1967), 'The computer and the market', in C. H. Feinstein (ed.), *Socialism, Capitalism and Economic Growth*, Cambridge University Press; reprinted in A. Nove and D. M. Nuti (eds.) (1972), *Socialist Economics*, Penguin, 1972.

LANGE, O., and TAYLOR, F. (1956), *On the Economic Theory of Socialism*, McGraw-Hill.

LERNER, A. P. (1939), 'From vulgar political economy to vulgar Marxism', *J. polit. Econ.*, pp. 557–67.

LERNER, A. P. (1940), 'A further note', *J. polit. Econ.*, pp. 258–60.

LERNER, A. P. (1972), 'A note on "understanding the Marxian notion of exploitation"', *J. econ. Lit.*, March, pp. 50–51.

LENIN, V. I. (1947), 'State and revolution', in *Selected Works*, vol. 2, Foreign Languages Publishing House, Moscow.

LENIN, V. I. (1963), 'A characteristic of economic romanticism', in

Collected Works, vol. 2, pp. 140–50, Progress Publishers, Moscow.

LENIN, V. I. (1964a), 'Imperialism, the highest stage of capitalism', in *Collected Works*, vol. 22, Progress Publishers, Moscow.

LENIN, V. I. (1964b), 'The impending catastrophe and how to combat it', in *Collected Works*, vol. 25, pp. 309–65, Progress Publishers, Moscow.

LENIN, V. I. (1964c), 'Political report of the Central Committee, 7 March 1918', in *Collected Works*, vol. 27, pp. 89–90. Progress Publishers, Moscow.

LENIN, V. I. (1964d), ' "Left-wing" childishness and petty-bourgeois mentality', in *Collected Works*, vol. 27, pp. 323–54, Progress Publishers, Moscow.

LENIN, V. I. (1964e), 'The immediate tasks of the Soviet Government, March–April 1918', in *Collected Works*, vol. 27, pp. 237–77, Progress Publishers, Moscow.

LENIN, V. I. (1965), *Collected Works*, vol. 9, Progress Publishers, Moscow.

LEONTIEF, W. W. (1938), *The Significance of Marxian Economics for Present-Day Economic Theory*; reprinted in *Essays in Economics*, Oxford University Press, New York, 1967.

LIBERMAN, E. G. (1962), 'The plan profits and bonuses', Pravda, 9 September 1962; reprinted in A. Nove and D. M. Nuti, *Socialist Economics*, Penguin, 1972.

LUCE, D., and RAIFFA, H. (1957), *Games and Decisions*, Wiley.

LUTZ, F. A., and HAGUE, D. C. (1963), *Theory of Capital*, Macmillan.

McLELLAN, D. (1971), *Marx's Grundrisse*, Macmillan; reprinted with additions, Paladin, 1973.

MANDEL, E. (1968), *Marxist Economic Theory*, vol. 2, Merlin Press.

MANDEVILLE, B. (1970), *The Fable of the Bees* (ed. P. Harth), Penguin.

MAO TSE-TUNG (1956), 'On coalition government' in *Selected Works*, vol. 4, People's Publishing House, Bombay.

MARGLIN, S. (1969), 'Information in price and command systems of planning', in J. Margolis and H. Guitton (eds.), *Public Economics*, Macmillan.

MARRIS, R. (1964), *The Economic Theory of 'Managerial' Capitalism*, Macmillan, pp. 1–40, revised and abridged in G. C. Archibald (ed.), *The Theory of the Firm*, Penguin, pp. 291–317.

MARX, K. (1904), *A Contribution to the Critique of Political Economy*, Kerr, Chicago.

MARX, K. (1909), *Capital*, vol. 3, Kerr, Chicago.

MARX, K. (1938a), 'Letter to L. Kugelmann, 11 July 1868', in K. Marx and F. Engels, *Selected Correspondence*, Lawrence & Wishart.

MARX, K. (1938b), 'Letter to Engels, 2 August 1862', in K. Marx and F. Engels, *Selected Correspondence*, Lawrence & Wishart.

MARX, K. (1949a), 'Critique of the Gotha programme', in K. Marx and F. Engels, *Selected Works*, vol. 2, Foreign Languages Publishing House, Moscow.

MARX, K. (1949b), 'Eleventh thesis on Feuerbach', in K. Marx and F. Engels, *Selected Works*, vol. 2, p. 367, Foreign Languages House, Moscow.

MARX, K. (1950a), 'Wage labour and capital', in K. Marx and F. Engels, *Selected Works*, vol. 1, p. 82, Foreign Languages Publishing House, Moscow.

MARX, K. (1950b), 'Wages, prices and profit', in K. Marx and F. Engels, *Selected Works*, vol. 1, pp. 378–9, Foreign Languages Publishing House, Moscow.

MARX, K. (1954), *Capital*, vol. 1, Foreign Languages Publishing House, Moscow.

MARX, K. (1956), *Poverty of Philosophy*, English translation from the French edition of 1847, with corrections made by Marx in 1876 and by Engels in 1885 and 1892, Foreign Languages Publishing House, Moscow.

MARX, K. (1957), *Capital*, vol. 2, Foreign Languages Publishing House, Moscow.

MARX, K. (1958), *Capital*, vol. 1, Foreign Languages Publishing House, Moscow.

MARX, K. (1959), *Capital*, vol. 3, Foreign Languages Publishing House, Moscow.

MARX, K. (1961), *The Economic and Philosophical Manuscripts of 1844*, Foreign Languages Publishing House, Moscow.

MARX, K. (1963), *Oeuvres*, vol. 1 (ed. M. Rubel), Paris.

MARX, K. (1964), *Theories of Surplus Value*, Part 1, Foreign Languages Publishing House, Moscow.

MARX, K. (1968), *Theories of Surplus Value*, Part 2, Progress Publishers, Moscow.

MARX, K. (1970), *A Contribution to the Critique of Political Economy* (with Introduction by M. Dobb, pp. 1–16), Progress Publishers, Moscow.

MARX, K. (1971), *Theories of Surplus Value*, Part 3, Progress Publishers, Moscow.

MARX, K., and ENGELS, F. (1950), 'Communist Manifesto', in *Selected Works*, Foreign Languages Publishing House, Moscow.

MASSEY, G. (1965), 'Professor Samuelson on theory and realism: comment', *Amer. econ. Rev.*, vol. 55, pp. 1155–63.

MAY, K. (1948), 'Value and price of production: a note on Winternitz's solution', *Econ. J.*, December, pp. 596–9.

MEDIO, A. (1972), 'Profits and surplus value: appearance and reality in capitalist production', in E. K. Hunt and J. G. Schwartz, *A Critique of Economic Theory*, Penguin, 1972, pp. 143–57.

MEEK, R. L. (1961), 'Sraffa's rehabilitation of classical economics', *Science and Society*, vol. 35, pp. 139–56; reprinted in *Economics and Ideology*, Chapman Hall, 1967.

MEEK, R. L. (1967), *Economics and Ideology*, Chapman Hall.

MORGENSTERN, O. (1950), *On the Accuracy of Economic Observations*, Oxford University Press.

MORISHIMA, M. (1958a), 'A dynamic analysis of structural change in a Leontief model', *Economica*, May, pp. 119–25.

MORISHIMA, M. (1958b), 'Prices, interest and profits in a dynamic Leontief system', *Econometrica*, July, pp. 358–80.

MORISHIMA, M. (1964), *Equilibrium, Stability and Growth*, Oxford University Press.

MORISHIMA, M. (1966), 'Refutation of the nonswitching theorem', *Q.J. Econ.*, pp. 520–25.

MORISHIMA, M. (1973), *Marx's Economics: A Dual Theory of Value and Growth*, Cambridge University Press.

MORISHIMA, M., and MURATA, Y. (1968), 'An input–output system involving non-transferable goods', *Econometrica*, January, pp. 71–92.

MORISHIMA, M., and SETON, F. (1961), 'Aggregation of Leontief matrices and the labour theory of value', *Econometrica*, April, pp. 203–20.

MORRIS, W. (1946), *Stories in Prose, Stories in Verse, Shorter Poems, Lectures and Essays* (ed. G. D. H. Cole), Nonesuch Press.

NAGEL, E., and NEWMAN, J. R. (1971), *Godel's Proof*, Routledge & Kegan Paul.

NASH, J. F. (1950), 'The bargaining problem', *Econometrica*, April, pp. 520–25.

NELL, E. J. (1970), 'A note on Cambridge controversies in capital theory', *J. econ. Lit.*, March, pp. 41–5.

NELL, E. J. (1972), 'The revival of political economy', *Social Research*, Spring, pp. 32–52.

NELL, E. J., and NELL, O. (1972), 'On justice under socialism', *Dissent*, Summer, pp. 483–91.

NEWMAN, J. R. (1965), 'Godel's proof', in *International Encyclopedia of Science*, vol. 2, pp. 52–3, Nelson.

NEWMAN, P. (1962), 'Production of commodities by means of commodities', *Schweizerische zeitschrift fur volkvirschaft und statistik*, vol. 98, no. 1, pp. 58–75.

NEWMAN, P. (1969), *Readings in Mathematical Economics*, vol. 1, *Value Theory*, vol. 2, *Capital and Growth*, John Hopkins Press.

NORTHROP, F. S. C. (1959), Introduction to W. Heisenberg, *Physics and Philosophy: Revolution in Modern Science*, Allen & Unwin.

NOVE, A., and NUTI, D. M. (eds.) (1972), *Socialist Economics*, Penguin, especially the Introduction, pp. 9–16.

NOWELL-SMITH, P. H. (1954), *Ethics*, Penguin.

NUTI, D. M. (1970), ' "Vulgar Economy" in the theory of

distribution', *De Economist*, vol. 118, pp. 363–9; reprinted in
E. K. Hunt and J. G. Schwartz (eds.), *A Critique of Economic Theory*, Penguin, 1972.

OLLMAN, B. (1971), *Alienation: Marx's Concept of Man in a Capitalist Society*, Cambridge University Press.

PARKINSON, C. N. (1958), *Parkinson's Law or The Pursuit of Progress*, Murray.

PASINETTI, L. (1960), 'A mathematical formulation of the Ricardian system', *Rev. econ. Stud.*, vol. 27, pp. 78–98; reprinted in P. Newman (ed.), *Readings in Mathematical Economics*, vol. 2, John Hopkins Press, 1969.

PASINETTI, L. (1966), 'Change in the rate of profits and switches of techniques', *Q. J. Econ.*, November, pp. 503–17.

PATTANAIK, P. (1966), *A Sufficient Condition for Stability in Voting*, mimeograph for private circulation, Delhi School of Economics.

PATTANAIK, P. (1971), *Voting and Collective Choice*, Cambridge University Press.

PATTANAIK, P. (1974), 'On the stability of sincere voting conditions', *J. econ. Theory*, forthcoming.

PHELPS BROWN, E. H. (1972), 'The underdevelopment of economics', *Econ. J.*, March, pp. 1–10.

PINCUS, J. A. (1963), 'The cost of foreign aid', *Rev. econ. Stat.*, vol. 45, no. 4, pp. 360–67; reprinted in J. Bhagwati and R. S. Eckaus (eds.), *Foreign Aid*, Penguin, 1970.

PREOBRAZHENSKY, E. (1965), *The New Economics*, Clarendon Press; excerpt reprinted in A. Nove and D. M. Nuti (eds.), *Socialist Economics*, Penguin, pp. 130–48.

RAWLS, J. (1972), *Theory of Justice*, Clarendon Press.

REDER, M. W. (1961), 'P. Sraffa, production of commodities by means of commodities', *Amer. econ. Rev.*, September, pp. 688–95.

RICARDO, D. (1951), *Works and Correspondence* (eds. P. Sraffa and M. Dobb), vol. 1, Cambridge University Press.

RICHARDSON, K., and SPEARS, D. (eds.) (1972), *Race, Culture and Intelligence*, Penguin.

ROBBINS, L. (1932), *An Essay on the Nature and Significance of Economic Science*, Macmillan.

ROBINSON, J. (1950), Review of P. Sweezy (ed.), *E. Bohm-Bawerk's Karl Marx and the Close of his System*, *Econ. J.*, June, pp. 358–63.

ROBINSON, J. (1964), *Economic Philosophy*, Penguin.

ROBINSON, J. (1965), 'A reconsideration of the theory of value', reprinted in *Collected Economic Papers*, vol. 3, Macmillan.

ROBINSON, J. (1967), *An Essay on Marxian Economics*, Macmillan.

ROBINSON, J. (1969), *The Economics of Imperfect Competition*, second edition, Macmillan.

ROBINSON, J. (1968), *The Cultural Revolution in China*, Penguin.

SAMUELSON, P. A. (1957), 'Wages and interest: a modern dissection

310 References

of Marxian economic models', *Amer. econ. Rev.*, vol. 47, pp. 884–92; reprinted in J. E. Stiglitz (ed.), *Collected Scientific Works of Paul A. Samuelson*, vol. 1, pp. 341–69, Massachusetts Institute of Technology Press, 1966.

SAMUELSON, P. A. (1959), 'A modern treatment of the Ricardian economy: the pricing of goods and of labour and land services, *Q.J. Econ.*, February, pp. 1–35; reprinted in J. E. Stiglitz (ed.), *Collected Scientific Works of Paul A. Samuelson*, vol. 1, pp. 373–407, Massachusetts Institute of Technology Press, 1966.

SAMUELSON, P. A. (1960), 'Wages and interest: a modern dissection of Marxian economic models: a reply', *Amer. econ. Rev.*, September, pp. 719–21; reprinted in J. E. Stiglitz (ed.), *Collected Scientific Works of Paul A. Samuelson*, vol. 1, pp. 370–72, Massachusetts Institute of Technology Press, 1966.

SAMUELSON, P. A. (1961), 'A new theorem on nonsubstitution', in H. Hegeland (ed.), *Money, Growth and Methodology*, Lund Humpheries; reprinted in J. E. Stiglitz (ed.), *Collected Scientific Works of Paul A. Samuelson*, vol. 1, pp. 520–36, Massachusetts Institute of Technology Press, 1966.

SAMUELSON, P. (1965), 'Professor Samuelson on theory and realism: reply', *Amer. econ. Rev.*, vol. 55, pp. 1164–72.

SAMUELSON, P. (1966), 'A summing up,' *Q.J. Econ.*, November, pp. 568–83.

SAMUELSON, P. A. (1970), *Economics*, eighth edition, McGraw-Hill.

SAMUELSON, P. A. (1971), 'Understanding the Marxian notion of exploitation: a summary of the so-called transformation problem between Marxian values and competitive prices', *J. econ. Lit.*, June, pp. 399–431.

SAMUELSON, P. A. (1972), 'The economics of Marx; an ecumenical reply', *J. econ. Lit.*, June, pp. 51–7.

SCHULTZ, T. W. (1960), 'Value of US farm surpluses to underdeveloped countries', *J. Farm Econ.*, vol. 42, pp. 1019–30; reprinted in J. Bhagwati and R. S. Eckaus (eds.), *Foreign Aid*, Penguin, 1970, pp. 305–19.

SCHUMPETER, J. A. (1949), 'Science and ideology', *Amer. econ. Rev.*, March, pp. 345–59.

SCHUMPETER, J. A. (1954), *Economic Doctrine and Method*, Allen & Unwin.

SCHUMPETER, J. A. (1955), *History of Economic Analysis*, Allen & Unwin.

SCHUMPETER, J. A. (1956), *Ten Great Economists*, Allen & Unwin.

SCHWARTZ, J. T. (1961), *Lectures on the Mathematical Method in Analytical Economics*, Gordon & Breach, New York.

SEN, A. K. (1961), 'On optimising the rate of saving', *Econ. J.*, September, pp. 479–96.

SEN, A. K. (1962), *Choice of Techniques*, second edition, Oxford University Press, Bombay; Blackwell, 1968.

SEN, A. K. (1966a), 'A possibility theorem on majority decisions', *Econometrica*, April, pp. 491–9.

SEN, A. K. (1966), 'Labour allocation in the cooperative enterprises', *Rev. econ. Stud.*, October, pp. 361–71.

SEN, A. K. (1967b), 'Isolation, assurance and the social rate of discount', *Q.J. Econ.*, February, pp. 112–24.

SEN, A. K. (1967a), *Use Value, Welfare and Marxian Economics*, mimeograph, private circulation.

SEN, A. K. (1969a), 'A game-theoretic analysis of theories of collectivism in allocation', in T. Majumdar, *Growth and Choice: Essays in Honour of U.N. Ghoshal*, Oxford University Press, Bombay.

SEN, A. K. (1969b), 'Planners' preferences: optimality, distribution and social welfare', in J. Margolis and H. Guitton (eds.), *Public Economics*, Macmillan.

SEN, A. K. (1970), *Collective Choice and Social Welfare*, Oliver & Boyd.

SEN, A. K. (1973), *On Economic Inequality*, Oxford University Press.

SHERMAN, H. J. (1971), 'Marxist models of cyclical growth', *Hist. polit. Econ.*, vol. 3, pp. 28–55.

SIMON, H. A. (1959), 'Theories of decision-making in economics and behavioural science', *Amer. econ. Rev.*, vol. 49, pp. 253–83; reprinted in G. P. E. Clarkson (ed.), *Managerial Economics*, Penguin, 1968.

SPULBER, N. (ed.) (1964), *Foundations of the Soviet Strategy for Economic Growth*, Indiana University Press.

SRAFFA, P. (1951), Introduction to *Works and Correspondence of David Ricardo*, vol. 1, pp. 13–23, Cambridge University Press.

SRAFFA, P. (1960), *Production of Commodities by Means of Commodities*, Cambridge University Press.

SRAFFA, P. (1962), 'Production of commodities: a comment', *Econ. J.*, June, pp. 477–9.

SRAFFA, P. (1963), in F. A. Lutz and D. C. Hague (eds), *Theory of Capital*, Macmillan, pp. 305–6, 325.

STALIN, J. (1947), *Problems of Leninism*, Foreign Languages Publishing House, Moscow.

STIGLITZ, J. E. (1970), 'Non-substitution theorem with durable capital goods', *Rev. econ. Stud.*, October, pp. 343–5.

SUPPES, P. (1969), *An Introduction to Logic*, Van Nostrand Reinhold.

SWEEZY, P. (1949), *The Theory of Capitalist Development*, Dobson.

THOMPSON, W. (1824), *An Inquiry into the Principle of Distribution of Wealth*; reprinted 1963, Kelly, New York.

TUGAN-BARANOWSKY, M. (1905), *Theoritische Grundlagen des Marxismus*, Dunker und Humboldt, Leipzig.

TSURU, S. (1955), 'Keynes and Marx: The methodology of aggregates', in K. Kurihara (ed.), *Post-Keynesian Economics*, Allen & Unwin; reprinted in D. Horowitz, *Marx and Modern Economics*, MacGibbon & Kee, 1968.

VEBLEN, T. (1906), 'The socialist economics of Karl Marx and his followers', *Q. J. Econ.*, vol. 20, pp. 575–95.

VON BORTKIEWICZ, L. (1907), *Value and Price in the Marxian System*; reprinted in *International Economic Papers No. 2*, Macmillan, pp. 5–60.

VON HAYEK, F. A. (1935), *Collectivist Economic Planning*, Allen & Unwin.

VON NEUMANN, J. (1945–6), 'A model of general economic equilibrium', *Rev. econ. Stud.*, vol. 13, pp. 1–9; reprinted in P. Newman (ed.), *Readings in Mathematical Economics*, vol. 2, John Hopkins Press.

VON THÜNEN, J. H. (1863), *Der Isolierte Staat*, Part II.

VON WEISZACKER, C. (1972), *Modern Capital Theory and the Concept of Exploitation*, Working Papers, no. 2, Institute of Mathematical Economics, Bielefeld University; reprinted in *Kyklos*, vol. 26, no. 2, 1973.

WALRAS, L. (1954), *Elements of Pure Economics*, (ed. W. Jaffa), Allen & Unwin.

WEITZMAN, M. (1970), 'Iterative multilevel planning with production targets', *Econometrica*, January, pp. 50–65.

WEST, E. G. (1969), 'The political economy of alienation', *Oxf. Econ. Pap.*, March, pp. 1–23.

WHEELWRIGHT, E. L., and MCFARLANE, B. (1973), *The Chinese Road to Socialism*, Penguin.

WILCZYNSKI, J. (1972), *Socialist Economic Development and Reforms*, Macmillan.

WINTERNITZ, J. (1948), 'Values and prices: a solution of the so-called transformation problem', *Econ. J.*, June, pp. 163–84.

WORSWICK, G. D. N. (1972), 'Is progress in economic science possible?', *Econ. J.*, March, pp. 73–86.

Index

More about Penguins and Pelicans

Penguinews, which appears every month, contains details of all the new books issued by Penguins as they are published. From time to time it is supplemented by *Penguins in Print*, which is a complete list of all titles available. (There are some five thousand of these.)

A specimen copy of *Penguinews* will be sent to you free on request. For a year's issues (including the complete lists) please send 50p if you live in the British Isles, or 75p if you live elsewhere. Just write to Dept EP, Penguin Books Ltd, Harmondsworth, Middlesex, enclosing a cheque or postal order, and your name will be added to the mailing list.

In the U.S.A.: For a complete list of books available from Penguin in the United States write to Dept CS, Penguin Books Inc., 7110 Ambassador Road, Baltimore, Maryland 21207.

In Canada: For a complete list of books available from Penguin in Canada write to Penguin Books Canada Ltd, 41 Steelcase Road West, Markham, Ontario.

David McLellan

Marx before Marxism

'The book can be thoroughly recommended as an introduction to a fascinating subject' – *Economist*

Taking us up to Marx's twenty-seventh year *Marx before Marxism* gives a detailed account of the evolution of Marx's thought during the formative years. Amongst the questions carefully studied by David McLellan are the controversies Marx engaged in as a young man, the gradual development of some of his key ideas, the conversion to, and reaction from, Hegelianism, and his exile in Paris and the famous Paris manuscripts. There is also an assessment of the importance of this early phase for the later and greater works.

'Dr McLellan's work on the young Marx has been an outstanding contribution in recent years . . . His calm explication makes an effective foil to Marx's turbulent dialectic' – *Times Educational Supplement*

'Dr McLellan is a rising light among younger Marx scholars. He writes with sobriety and authority' – *Sunday Times*

Marx on Economics

Edited by Robert Freedman

It is all too easy to agree or disagree with the theories of Karl Marx without having read them. It is not so easy to read them. His great work, *Capital*, and his other writings (which include the famous *Communist Manifesto*, published in 1848) are – to quote Professor Freedman's preface – 'forbidding in volume and turgid in prose'.

This condensed version enables the ordinary reader, for the first time, to make an impartial and intelligent study of Marx's economic theories and his critique of capitalism. It is a systematic compilation of extracts which are drawn from all his publications and presented in a logical order with brief summaries of the argument.

These extracts throw into sharp relief those economic truths with which Marx and Engels showed a pioneering insight: and they also reveal the major shortcomings of Marxian doctrine – in particular its failure to foresee the extent to which capitalism was capable of reform and also its vague Utopianism when viewed as a political programme.

Marx in his own Words

Edited by Ernst Fischer

This is a brief and lucid guide to what Marx really said, compiled by one of the great figures of modern Marxism. The body of the book is a discussion of the central themes of Marxism, expressed mainly in Marx's own words, but Ernst Fischer and Franz Marek have also included a chronology of his life and longer passages from three of his major works: the Prefaces to *A Contribution to the Critique of Political Economy* and *Capital*, and an extract from *The Eighteenth Brumaire of Louis Bonaparte*.

'The comments set Marx very much in a contemporary perspective, showing the absurdity of the verdict of obsolescence passed by modern social commentators . . . Fischer is well placed to emphasize the young Karl, heady on Schiller's aesthetics and an erotic creed maintained in our own day by such libidinalist radicals as Herbert Marcuse and Norman O. Brown . . . He shows that Marx foresaw problems not only of public consumption, but industrial over-consumption of materials, an area emphasized recently by Buckminster Fuller and conservationist thinkers . . . I don't know a better introduction to Marx' – Martin Day in *The Times Educational Supplement*

C. Wright Mills

The Marxists

For the past hundred years the Marxists have posed the chief political alternative to capitalist society. They have been successful revolutionaries in Russia, China, and Yugoslavia. They are now the technicians and philosophers whose appeals to the under-developed nations of Asia, Africa, and Latin America may be decisive.

In this Pelican book they speak for themselves – in documents by the leading theorists and rulers from Marx, by way of Lenin, Trotsky, and Stalin, to Khrushchev, Mao Tse-tung, and even 'Che' Guevara of Cuba.

As a guide through these theories C. Wright Mills, the controversial and outspoken author of *The Power Elite* and other sociological studies, maps out the essential ideas of Marxism and examines them critically. He sketches their historical development – the divisions and revisions, the successes and failures – and points to their implications for the present and the future.